Pain and Passion

Lives and Times of Frederick Funston and Eda Blankhart

Pain and Passion

The Lives and Times of Frederick Funston and Eda Blankhart

Richard Taylor

WordTaylors Productions

> Cover photograph of Brigadier General Frederick Funston
> Courtesy of National Archives

Copyright © 2015 by Richard Taylor

All rights reserved. In accordance with the U.S. Copyright Act of 1976 the scanning, uploading, and electronic sharing of any part of this book without permission of the publisher constitutes unlawful piracy and theft of the author's intellectual property. For permission, contact the author through Amazon or CreateSpace.

Copyright © 2015 Richard Taylor
All rights reserved.
ISBN-13: 978-1516802708
ISBN-10: 1516802705

I have made for you a song,
And it may be right or wrong,
But only you can tell me if it's true;
I have tried for to explain
Both your pleasure and your pain,
And, Thomas, here's my best respects to you!

> Rudyard Kipling's Dedication to
> Barracks Room Ballads

As life is action and passion, it is required of a man
that he should share the passion and action of his time
at peril of being judged not to have lived.

> Oliver Wendell Holmes

ONE

If an accounting of romance in war was made, there may be no more uncommon story of pain and passion than that of Frederick Funston and Eda Blankhart. This unlikely couple—one, a reckless adventurer, an intrepid mercenary, and a dauntless soldier; the other, a beautiful debutant, a gifted musician, a woman of refined tastes with unbounded loyalty—shared lives that sway imagination.

§

Fred Funston was an unlikely hero. Although physically rugged with stocky trunk, thick neck, and a fighter's jaw, well developed shoulders and chest, he was short with a small bone structure and lacking athletic abilities. Despite his size his posture was erect, steps lively, arm gestures wide, with twinkling grey eyes. His face radiated when he laughed, conveying confidence, vigor, and the heartiness of a Kansas farm boy—healthy with a strong constitution. His hair was sandy, eyes dark brown and searching, sparkling mischievously—attending a sharp intelligence despite a poor showing in classrooms. Fred Funston was eager and anxious and dismissed doubt he would reach pinnacles others never dreamed of.

He dropped from college and struck out with an engineering crew surveying the Atchison, Topeka, and Santa Fe Railroad, and then was hired as a ticket collector. Railroad conductors were mostly elderly, but for him the job was more than collecting tickets from old ladies, ranch hands, farmers, white-collar merchants and politicians crossing western states.

A drunken, heavy set cowboy, with bulging muscles, sprawled in the aisle on his back blasting holes in the roof with his .44 revolver. The twenty-three-year-old, one hundred pound, ticket collector, burst into the cabin to punch the cowboy's ticket. He kicked the pistol from the two hundred-pounder's hand and dragged him through the cars to dump him on the rear dais. When the train stopped, he rolled him onto the platform. The angry wrangler threw a rock, breaking a window. Fred chased him down the tracks for a mile, delaying the train for an hour until he returned winded, only to find another cowhand with no ticket and another large revolver and pointed at him. "I'm ride'n on this," he declared.

"That's good, that's good," said Fred as he backed away. Then he returned with a long rifle aimed at the cowboy and cocked it. "I came back to punch that ticket," he said. The cowboy paid his fare in cash.

§

While Fred Funston was making adventure of the mundane, a seemingly unrelated event occurred in another Midwest state. Otto Blankhart and Theresa Kohler had emigrated from Germany to the small town of Quincy, Illinois, near the Mississippi River just north of St. Louis. Otto was German, Theresa a French Huguenot exiled in Germany. Both were talented musicians. Otto had studied violin in Mannheim and played second violin with the Jean Becker Quartette before relocating to the United States, where he met and married Theresa in 1870. The next year, their first born girl, Elizabeth, was born. In 1874, they welcomed another beautiful baby, Eda, into the world, just in time to move west when she only a few weeks old. Moving was imprinted on Eda's future in ways she could never envision.

Otto and Theresa had become frustrated serenading farmers in Illinois and with insufficient opportunities in St. Louis, so decided to move again with Elizabeth and little Eda, this time to San Francisco, where musical interests were more refined and appreciated by polite society and earning prospects were improved. At an early age, Eda and her sisters learned the violin and piano from their parents, preparing for musical futures. But Otto, the German musician, was annoyed Americans didn't appreciate the finer arts, especially music, as Europeans did, especially his Germans. Then in 1879, a third girl, Magdalena, or "Mattie," rounded out the family.

Eda Blankhart was born lovely with her searching eyes wide open, but she was certainly unable to foresee how her life would later unfold with so much unexpected pleasure, passion, and pain.

§

After railroading, Fred convinced the editor of the *Kansas City Journal*, where his old friend Billy White was working as a reporter, to hire him without experience. Fred shared a room with two double beds between four others; it worked, since two or three were always on the news hunt. Fred drew the police beat and roamed the city with Billy White like two "sheep-killing dogs," looking for stories and excitement. They made friends with policemen, dope dealers and users, male and female toughs prowling the red-light district long after midnight. When they'd absorbed enough local color, the two friends strolled to their room, too impatient for the slow-running trolley, bellowing "Blow the Man Down" and other salty songs.

Later, while working at the *Fort Smith Tribune* in Arkansas, Fred made friends with the famous federal "hanging judge," Isaac Parker. He observed criminal trials and reported on them, and met with the judge in chambers to discuss the cases, characters, and crimes. But Judge Parker considered his reporting strongly-opinionated and advised him to leave Fort Smith quickly for his own safety—he was marked for reprisals. The handwriting was on the wall just as Fred discovered the real power of the written word.

He stayed on, but exerted the power of the pen before departing on his terms. He was already at odds with the liberal newspaper, and while his boss was away on the eve of an important local election, Fred was left in charge of publication. He took advantage, censoring left-wing articles and editorials and replacing them with right-wing pieces and scathing letters critical of Democrats. Displeased locals were roiled and threatened to burn down the *Tribune* office. Fred created a small army of employees to fight for freedom of speech and save the paper. They grabbed weapons to defend the building, grounds, and presses, but the publisher received an urgent telegram from a patron, advising him of all this. He rushed back in the nick of time, intending to fire Fred—but he'd already heard threats of "tar and feathers" and skipped town on a fast train.

"I was tired of the rotten politics," he said, "and tired of the rotten town, and tired of the rotten sheet, and ready to go anyway, so I thought I might as well wake the place up and let 'em know I was alive before I left."

Whenever trouble overlooked Fred Funston, he found it on his own accord.

TWO

Frederick Funston was born in Midwest America in 1865 as General Sherman tore through the South in the traumatic Civil War. When General Lee finally surrendered to General Grant, Lieutenant Edward Funston could go home to Ohio to plant seeds of war and high adventures with his young son. Fred thrived on hard times and excitement and when normalcy threatened, he struck out for higher adventures, dangerous explorations, natural catastrophes, unnatural wars—and along the way found love. Love enhanced his life, but even that never changed him.

Edward Funston was born of hearty Scot-Irish stock in 1836 near New Carlyle, Ohio. He learned to read and write in one-room rural schoolhouses and at Linden Hill Academy before Ohio's Marietta College part-time. Edward taught school before working as a traveling salesman for a nursery company. This son of a farmer assumed his first son, Fred, would also follow the plow.

When Civil War erupted, Edward enlisted in the 16th Ohio Artillery under Captain Anderson Mitchell. Just before marching off to fight, he married eighteen-year old Ann Eliza Mitchell, cousin of his battery commander and great grandniece of Daniel Boone. Ann was petite, attractive, and sensitive—traits passed to her first son with her appreciation for music, beauty, and culture; his father contributed brashness, strong determination, and facility with written and spoken words, plus rugged individuality, forcefulness, and gameness for a full life.

When Fred was two, Edward left Ohio on a train, stagecoach, and horseback to stake a homestead on the Kansas plains. Ann followed with Fred and a second son, Burt, the following year. Edward settled on a small prairie farm north of Iola in Allen County, the geographic center of the country. Fertile rolling hills were well suited for wheat and corn and the two boys grew until they were able to plow. Burt guided the plow, while Fred rode "old Nellie," entertaining them both with stories—some he read, others he invented. Over the years, the one hundred sixty acre farm expanded to two hundred forty, enough to raise cattle and hogs. But the crown jewel of the prospering farm was a comfortable, middle class home with outbuildings for hired hands and livestock.

In the evenings, Ann played melodies on an enormous rosewood piano accompanied by family singing from a Civil War songbook brought home by Edward. She furnished their home with fancy heirlooms handed down—marble-top tables, a Jenny Lind bed, rosewood dresser, swinging mirror, and the region's first bathtub—in contrast to rough hand-hewn furniture of neighbors. She used Edward's experience in horticulture to enhance the property's appeal as he and the boys developed original landscape designs with a wide variety of trees for shade and beauty and a thousand fruit trees. Fred studied flora and could name them all. A white picket fence, colorful roses and other flowering plants, vines, and shrubs adorned their inviting oasis on the plains, and visitors were often invited to the Funston homestead.

Edward's library of over six hundred volumes was the largest in Allen County, but his affinity was speaking with a bombastic delivery. Oratorical skills earned him election twice to represent the 47th District in the state legislature in Topeka, rising to speaker of the house—and a nickname of "Foghorn Funston." According to his daughter, Ella, "his prayers in church would bring the Lord closer.... His voice so deep and full of reverence that I always felt it had gone straight to heaven." He later represented the 17th District of Kansas as a Republican in Congress from 1884 to 1894—a staunch member of the Grand Army of the Republic, local Republican Party leader, and chairman of the influential Agricultural Committee. Friends called him "Farmer Funston."

Edward Funston arrived in Kansas with only his physical, mental, and moral strength and a young family. With those he provided well for his family, defended the union, and brought pride to his state. Legendary Edward Funston instilled those same characteristics into his diminutive elder son—imprinted with that independent streak, conservative political views, yearning for adventure, and love of literature; his small size, attractive features, and cultural appreciation gifts from his lovely mother.

Edward Funston was so politically engaged their farmhouse often swelled with colleagues trouping from the railhead in Carlyle Township, displacing family for political meetings. Fred rose at four a.m. to study after rowdy crowds had gone, then rode a horse ten miles to school, whistling camp tunes all the way. His horse was a vicious little buckskin bronco, captured on the Texas plains, that no one else would ride. He mounted it in the stable yard and let it cavort until it gave up trying to shake him off, then raced all the way to school—the return trip, another race.

Fred was overshadowed by his father's prominence, his bullhorn voice, and dominating size at six feet two and two hundred pounds. He strived to escape his father's shadow with independence, courage, and determination, and one area of heated conflict. Edward was a teetotaler but kept liquor on hand for guests. Fred, however, early discovered the pleasure of drink, driving a wedge between them, increasing his determination to venture out.

Fred was a bit reclusive at five feet, five inches and just over one hundred ten pounds. By the age of two he knew all the letters of the alphabet, and soon spent hours alone reading from his father's library, taking books everywhere, even fishing or plowing. His reading tastes varied widely but he was drawn to tales of exploration and larger-than-life heroes—Cromwell, Napoleon, and the voyages of Captain James Cook—and listened spell-bound to Edward's tales from the war. When Edward locked his library to prevent him becoming a bookworm, he borrowed from neighbors.

Ella remembered her brother's appreciation for beauty, especially the poetry of Shelly, Burns, Cowper, Campbell, and Moore, but later the rugged and poetic tales of Rudyard Kipling. He also appreciated birds and flowers, calling out species to his sister. When she was about to pluck a tulip he stopped her. "Don't," he warned, "for you take its life and it dies."

As an outdoorsman, he caught more catfish from Deer Creek than anyone, yanking them from the water so hard they snagged in trees overhead. When not reading, fishing, hunting, or plowing, he raided a neighbor's melon field. And while he wasn't a skilled marksman, he collected more old, rusty, or broken revolvers than any other boy in Allen County.

Prairie life was formative for Fred, but he needed to break constraints, so he studied American history, practiced shooting and swordsmanship, and then took the competitive examination for the U. S. Military Academy. His father would have gladly appointed him but he was rejected due to mediocre grades, poor performance on the entrance examination, and his size, so Charles Crawford went instead. Fred despaired over rejection, but finished North Maple Grove and Iola High School, graduating in 1886. He loved learning, but found school boring; an inveterate reader that his father complained was filling his head with useless trivia. But when Edward made his first run for Congress in 1884, he had no staff, so he depended on Fred to help. He woke him one night to ask about British tariffs on their former crown colonies. Fred supplied the facts, as well as books and page numbers to back it up. And when Edward was campaigning to a hostile audience he was being "torn to shreds" by some who disagreed with him. Sixteen-year old Fred mounted the stage and quieted them with personal stories about his father, turning them in his favor.

Fred established his reputation early among friends, as fearsome and fearless. "He's not afraid of anything that walks," said his good friend, William Allen White. Fred and friends haunted the thickest woods, hunting for raccoons with long rifles. Older boys learned of one of their hunting trips and decided to frighten them by howling like a panther. The youngsters ran for their lives—all but Fred. He took a stance, aimed, and fired just over their heads. They never tried that again if Fred was around.

After schooling, he taught for a while at the remote rural schoolhouse. When a large bully decided to take on the new little teacher with a loaded pistol, Fred attacked with fists flailing and taught a lesson not in the curriculum. After the fight, he looked for the other students, but the entire class had climbed out open windows.

Fred was restless and unsettled before starting college at the University of Kansas, sometimes wandering aimlessly and alone. Once he ended up in Mexico, where he gained an appreciation for people south of the border while improving his Spanish language skills—early manifestations of a compelling urge to roam which was never cured.

Formative years in the rugged west of the 1870s and 1880s marked Fred with the natural environment and activity—prairie schooners with settlers hacking out a living in former Indian Territory, the grasshopper plague of 1874 and devastating power of nature, northern plains Indians streaming past on a "trail of tears." Indian threats were common on the farm so emergency plans had Ann rushing the boys into a shrub-covered cave on a nearby hillside. All this filled him with restlessness and determination to leap headlong into anything.

§

Fred had little patience for formal schooling, but needed higher education, still disappointed by rejection by West Point. He enrolled at the University of Kansas, looking for a niche in chemistry, botany, or economics even as he preferred classical literature—no future there. Classrooms were stifling; he favored independent study in the library—or in the woods, streams, or nearby saloons his father damned.

Like normal college men, he was attracted to college women—but encountered a string of rejections. Coeds considered him too short for a life mate, and his personality swung radically between too jovial, too sullen, or too quick to anger—not proper for sorority women. He disliked the exclusiveness of fraternities, but friends enticed him into Phi Delta Theta. He couldn't foresee that the fraternity connection would eventually lead him to the woman of his dreams.

Fred was always short on cash and Edward insisted he finance part of his expenses to appreciate the value of education. He took part-time jobs which exhausted time and energy while contributing to his short attention span. Dr. James Canfield, a liberal professor of history and economics, knew he was the son of "Foghorn Funston," who stood on opposite sides of most issues. Yet, Canfield enjoyed engaging Fred in debates as he brought levity to the classroom with his quick wit and eagerness to engage. Canfield saw rare self-confidence, maturity, frankness, easy friendship— despite a quick temper. They became confidants and stayed in contact for many years. While Fred didn't excel in any of his classes, he was always one of Canfield's favored students.

Fred stayed in character during college— falling in and out of love, fighting, and drinking—drinking led to fighting, and he drank often. His friend, Billy White, who later won a Pulitzer Prize, said, "If Fred even smelled a rotten apple, he began tearing up the sidewalks." But he was affectionate and sensitive, meticulous with personal grooming, and fond of expensive clothes he couldn't afford. He was always ripe for romance, invariably falling head over heels. His innocent, but sincere, amour was always directed to the most desirable young ladies, only to face repeated rejections. The cycle recurred every few months, ending in heartbreak. His most serious affair involved a beautiful Spanish girl from a wealthy family. This was so serious he learned Spanish and escorted her to Iola to meet the family. But when her studies ended, she too, disappeared, breaking his heart again.

Fred tired of the university and decided to leave. He sought out Canfield to break the news. Canfield didn't discourage him when Fred told him, "I want an active role in something, not just loitering in a desert of theories and dreams." His eyes drifted to the mottos Canfield hung on his walls. He had already memorized them.

1. All at it, and all the time at it; that is what wins.
2. What you can do, or dream you can do, begin it. Boldness hath genius, power, and magic in it.
3. The public business of America is the private business of every citizen.

Fred Funston didn't take much from college when he hit the dusty road, except the valuable guide posts from Canfield's three mottos for life. Although he left without a degree he set his cap for excitement, his course for adventure. He used the steel of his spine and courage of his heart to make conquests he could only read about before.

Years later, at a formal dinner with Vice President Theodore Roosevelt, Canfield listened as others spoke of Funston and he recalled when he left college. "I think others regretted more than me the fact that Funston didn't graduate. I came to believe his nature might be cramped, or warped, by methods and restrictions of a university course."

Fred Funston needed to set his own sails and Canfield was one who could see the future in the restless young man, "as though the life of great future was stirring within him." Both realized he could never satisfy an unquenchable thirst for adventure—but he must strike out in search of it.

THREE

For Fred Funston, trains offered mobility, excitement, and a small paycheck—but they were stuck on rails going in one direction or back. His head was in the clouds, his mind on freedom of the woods and wilderness and he spent as much time there as possible. A favored pastime of Fred and his friends, Billy White and Vernon Kellogg, was camping and tramping around Table Mountain in the Estes Park area of Colorado. Despite warning by an old stage driver, Funston, Kellogg, and White determined to follow a stream into the high peaks to find its source. They began on foot with three days supplies and rented a burro to carry the load to a campsite at the timberline entrance to the gorge. Early on the second day, Funston and Kellogg left White and the burro at the camp to explore the canyon with only a lunch and their rifles. The higher they climbed, the deeper the snow. At eleven thousand feet, they took to the sides of Table Mountain believing the crust of frozen snow made better footing.

During a lunch break, a late season storm assailed them with whipping winds, cracking thunder, dark clouds, and plunging temperatures. They raced the blizzard to get below the timberline to shelter. They had no survival gear and found the snow too deep in the valley to make good time, so chose the higher elevation to circle the gorge with firmer footing. Weather beat them to the punch. Sailing sheets of snow blinded eyes, battered hands and faces, and burned exposed skin.

Kellogg shielded behind a large rock until Funston caught up. He said, "Old boy, this is the worst we were ever in. I guess we're at the end of our rope!" But neither was ready to lie down and die. Funston later wrote of their trial, "There was no complaining, no whining, only a sort of mad desperation which made us resolve to keep moving to the last."

As the storm's fury strengthened, they weakened. Ice-crusted snow blocked their path down to the timberline, a steep and slippery snowfield along a dead drop of hundreds of feet. Kellogg used his rifle as an ice pick to traverse the steep slope. Behind him, Fred slipped and slid fast down the incline until he dug the barrel of his Winchester deep enough to anchor him in place. Kellogg started for him but Fred waved him off. He painstakingly fumbled for his pocket knife to cut handholds, clawing twenty feet back up the slope until he reached Kellogg's outstretched hand. They resumed their trek without comment on their close encounter with death. Funston later recalled, "It was severe treatment to give valuable guns, but they had to suffer in the best interests of their owners."

They eventually reached solid granite just as night was falling. Looking back, Funston wrote, "It was a grand picture—such as only those who have the hardihood to climb the highest mountains can hope to look upon. Any attempt of art to imitate them can be but mere mockery." And when they looked in the other direction, the direction of safety, he said, "We saw, far below, the world we had almost given up forever; and as we stood there it looked to us grander than any picture of sun-burnished clouds and snow-covered peaks."

Back in camp, they swore to be more careful. Of course, Fred Funston would never keep that pledge.

§

Edward Funston worried about his errant son—it was bad enough that he had no interest in farming, but intermittent newspapering, railroading, hunting, camping, wandering, and dropping out of college were pathways to nowhere. And drinking and singing and fighting were sure to land him in jail. They argued. The Congressman didn't like using his influence with the Agriculture Committee for personal gain, but he finally reached out to Frederick Coville at the Department of Agriculture. Coville had an opportunity for a young man to collect botany samples in the Dakotas and Montana during the summer of 1890. This interested Fred and he eagerly worked with a team of scientists collecting and studying specimens of native grasses. For once, he was non-combative and thrived on the challenges. The team was satisfied with his work and Coville invited him to join another, longer expedition—this time into Death Valley in Lower California and Nevada. Funston wrote to his friend Charles Scott in Iola, "I expected to find the terror of the place exaggerated … it was not."

Seventy of seventy-two "Forty-Niners" had died crossing Death Valley in 1850. Discovery of silver and gold in the 1860's and twenty-mule teams of borax mining added to the lore, but the Army Mapping Service had produced only generalized maps by 1871. The field team consisted of eight field scientists, eight hired hands as teamsters and packers, and one Chinese cook. Fred was promoted as assistant to the chief botanist. For eight months they collected and recorded various floras from extreme conditions for plants, beasts, and men in temperatures reaching one hundred forty degrees Fahrenheit. Over two-thousand species were cataloged including one hundred fifty previously undocumented. They rode out terrible storms and shortages of food and water and survived for two weeks on gophers, blackbirds, badgers, and chuck-wallies. But Funston, more than anyone, was in his element.

Fred and his team leader crossed one hundred seventy-eight miles of incredibly harsh terrain to pick up and deliver mail in Ash Meadows, Nevada. During the return trek, a storm struck while in they were at the most difficult part of the crossing. They released the burros and took to ground, crawling on hands and knees. When the storm abated, they found the burros following the crazy humans so they rode back into camp as if nothing had happened. In another instance, his horse stumbled and fell over a thousand foot drop, killing the horse. Fred clutched a shrub and clawed his way back up as he had in the snow storm in Colorado. Slavish labor and extreme danger was common in Death Valley but this trial only served as an appetizer for his craving for adventure.

§

Near death experiences heightened Fred Funston's thirst for more. Rejected by West Point, spurned by lovers, conflicts with his father—all in the past—now it was him against the worse the world could throw at him. He craved ever greater challenges. While waiting for the next one, he helped open a new trail in Yosemite Valley and lived for a time with Panamint Indians in California. Then, the Department of Agriculture sent a telegram. He was needed again—this time in the frozen Yukon.

From 1891 to 1894, he made two lone botanical expeditions into Alaska Territory under remote supervision. The first for only a summer around

Yakutat Bay and along the coast near Mount McKinley, using a coastal survey steamer as a base and doing much of his work in an Indian canoe, pushing into inlets and going ashore to collect samples. This was so successful Coville assigned him a more daunting mission.

On the second excursion he crossed the mountains and followed the Yukon River to its confluence with the Porcupine flowing out of the Arctic Circle, collecting and labeling botany samples along the way. He would winter over in 1893-1894 above the Arctic Circle and in the spring retrace his route to the Yukon and Porcupine Rivers, and out to the Bearing Sea to hitch a ride home on a Coast Guard cutter. No one accompanied him.

He started on an ocean liner through the Inland Passage in southeastern Alaska, past Juneau and the sleepy capital at Sitka, admiring the great glaciers, stunning fiords, semi-wild Indians and resplendent totems. But beyond the majestic white range of mountains lay another, far different land, the valley of the Yukon, a vast and desolate stretch where Canadian winter is sovereign for nine months of the year. The only inhabitants were savages, gold miners, and bears. He would cross the British Northwest Territory, over the coastal range from Dyea Inlet, to reach a chain of lakes surrounded by high mountains. There the source of a small stream eventually becomes the mighty Yukon River flowing northwest, fed by numerous tributaries and the melting snows of summer. At its mouth, the Yukon opens to three miles wide, thirty feet deep and runs with a current of five miles-per-hour where it empties into the Bearing Sea.

Three men with similar destinations linked up at Dyea Inlet on April 10, 1893, a hundred miles north of Juneau—McConnell, a grizzly older Canadian; Thompson, a miner from Idaho; and Mattern, a good-natured German seeking gold. They were bound for the interior gold-mining camp at Forty-Mile Creek where new discoveries increased the population of miners to three hundred, with another seven hundred Indians and other supporters at the camp. Funston would collect botanical samples, take weather observations, and gather other scientific information.

Four men started out with two eight-foot hand-sleds with steel runners, two small tents, blankets, guns and ammunition; plus six-weeks provisions of flour, bacon, and coffee, a whip saw, axes, and other tools for boat building. Funston carried material for collecting samples, a camera, and in his bags were Kipling's *Soldiers Three* and *Barracks Room Ballads*, both recently published. Their load weighed out at over a thousand pounds.

They would use the established miners' route to the Yukon by crossing the Chilkoot Pass, descending to the frozen lakes on the other side of the range, dragging hand-sleds across the chain of frozen lakes to the source of the river. Where the trees were sufficiently large, they would set up a lumber mill and construct a boat to reach the camp at Forty-Mile Creek.

They dragged sleds up the valley of the Dyea River to the foot of Chilkoot Pass and hired local Indians to help portage the load up the steep incline, thousands of feet nearly straight up. When they began, the snow was soft and deep, getting firmer as they climbed. A hundred-foot rawhide safety line circled their waists at ten feet intervals. The first climber carried a hatchet to cut hand and footholds in the ice and hard-packed snow for a steep and slippery zigzag climb. When that became too difficult, Indians dropped half their loads to return for it from the top.

When all the gear was at the top, the Indians returned home. The four men re-packed all the goods on their two sleds and started down at breakneck speed without brakes. One sled struck a rough spot and flipped, scattering blankets, bacon, and mining tools. They reloaded and continued to a flat bottom where they struck out again, pulling sleds for days on end, with little sleep or food, until they reached the first of six lakes, then six miles across Lake Linderman to Lake Bennett before resting. Lake Bennett was twenty-six miles long, so they constructed a V-shaped mast and strung a tent fly over it for a sail. Using wind power, they sailed across frozen lakes until the snow was too mushy and they found trees to build a boat. The experienced men brought saws and first built a saw-mill to rip flat boards for boats. A dozen more men, also enroute to Forty Mile Creek miner's camp, caught up with them at the saw mill and began their boats as well.

Sixteen men spent two weeks building boats. Funston's team assembled a flat-bottomed skiff with two sets of oars and a mast for a sail, the seams sealed with pitch. They dragged it to the water and slid it over the rocks and christened it with a bucket of river water—*Nancy Hanks*—after a race horse named for Abraham Lincoln's mother.

The other teams also completed their six boats so the little fleet started out together from the banks of Lake Marsh which was still frozen so boats were loaded on sleds and dragged to the Yukon River, still a stream at this point. Funston's team tried using their sail to cross the frozen lake, but it made the boat top-heavy and it tipped over, strewing a thousand pounds of contents. Boat and sail were damaged and one sled wrecked, requiring jury-rigged repairs and reloading. This time they pulled their load twenty-two miles over the lake—a typical day on the tundra.

The next leg was a fifty-five-mile stretch of river between Lake Marsh and Lake Lebarge, the last and largest of the chain of frozen lakes. But between them lay the two most dangerous obstacles of the entire Yukon system—Miles Canyon and White Horse rapids.

The stream widened to a three hundred foot river, between two and six feet deep, and running swift. Ice flows on shallow bars piled up along the banks. Ice and boulders made navigation of the rapid river stimulating, demanding full attention. Soon they rounded a bend near Miles Canyon where a tall rocky ridge narrowed to thirty feet. The mighty river roared as it forced water through the narrow gap. They frantically pulled ashore before being forced through the steep perpendicular canyon walls.

There were two ways to the other side—float through the gap over the rapids in a few harrowing minutes, or man-handle everything over the hill for three miles over four days. Others waited there, considering risk and consequence. One Wisconsin lumberman decided to run the river alone, and steered to the center where his small boat was swept ahead, bobbing and tossing into the gap, then out of sight. After a few minutes a rifle shot rang out, signaling he'd made it. Then two young men from Colorado went; others started dragging their boats over the bluffs.

Without a word Fred's team walked to the *Nancy Hanks* without Thompson, who'd joined a team of miners. McConnell took the front, Mattern amidships, Fred in the stern. Oars were stowed and smaller canoe paddles used to push clear of the rocks. Fred later wrote, "I must confess that I have never felt sicker in my life than as we shoved away from shore and steered for the entrance." It was over in two terrifying minutes when they found a safe place to dock, thoroughly soaked and the boat swamped.

The worst was over, but rough rapids lay ahead even as the river widened to three hundred feet, shallow but swirling. A chain of white water rapids ran for half a mile and into another narrow chute. McConnell ran ahead and when the boat passed through Funston tossed him a line to secure it to the bank. They rested and next day drifted leisurely for twenty-five miles northwest. Ice and snow increased while caribou, moose, and savages watched them pass.

They had covered only two hundred of the seven hundred miles of river from the source to Forty-Mile Creek but the rest was easy. For Fred alone, another one thousand nine hundred miles remained to reach the mouth of the Yukon. The river became larger as it was joined by tributaries, reaching three-quarters of a mile wide, very deep and swift, with thousand-foot cliffs on each side. Finally, they rounded a bend and saw the cabins of Forty-Mile Creek, the loneliest mining camp on earth, where midnight lasts all winter and daylight all summer and mail came but once a year. Three hundred white miners clustered to hear news from the civilized world.

After their forty-two day journey, McConnell and Mattern went prospecting for gold, leaving Fred alone. He steered the *Nancy Hanks* alone northwest down the Yukon toward the Mackenzie River and the Arctic Ocean. When it became too icy to float, he left the boat with a friendly missionary and continued north with Indians on snow shoes, trekking two hundred miles to deliver supplies to another missionary at the most northern camp. He wintered over in this far north arctic region at Rampart House, a deserted Hudson Bay Company outpost, with a missionary called "Totty", his rifle, his botany specimens, and Kipling for company. By the end of winter, he'd memorized Kipling.

He hunted pelts to trade for ammunition, tea, and tobacco, learned Arctic survival from Indians, and trekked with them on snowshoes across the continental divide with sled dogs pulling cargo. They set out in November, 1893, with the thermometer reading forty degrees below zero, wearing heavy caribou coats and pants, hooded parkas, thick moose-skin moccasins and fur-lined mittens. But dried caribou meat and deer fallow soon ran out and they were forced to kill and eat one of the dogs. After resting at an isolated outpost, Le Pierre house, they continued over the Rockies.

The most northern reach was Peel River camp, or Fort McPherson on Fred's map. This camp was occupied by a Hudson Bay Company Scotsman named John Firth. Fred and Firth talked while Indians traded before returning to Rampart house where he learned from the Indians of a whaling fleet stuck in ice flows. Indians saw a favorable trading opportunity with stranded sailors. Fred struck out with them on another one hundred seventy-five mile trek to the Arctic Ocean out of curiosity. When they reached the ships, the captains were surprised to find an American among Indians and welcomed him into their warm cabins to trade tall tales over a bottle of spirits. As spirits ran high, they concocted a tall story to fool the crews of the seven vessels—the United States was at war with Russia and Great Britain. According to their version, Funston was sent to inform three hundred ice-bound American whalers that San Francisco was under siege and they must steam even further north to avoid capture.

Fred played his role for two days, embellishing the story with concocted details of other battles for Chicago, New York, and California. When sailors were resigned to a life on ice, he confessed, since he was returning with the Indians to camp. For the final leg of his excursion, he traveled alone on foot and rowboat more than three thousand five hundred miles before exchanging the *Nancy Hanks* with the missionary for a canoe.

Alaska proved rugged enough as he completed the three thousand miles to the Arctic Ocean on snowshoe and dogsled, a record for a white man. He had made his way from Yakutat Bay, over Chilkoot Pass and points above the Arctic Circle, paddled a canoe alone one thousand five hundred miles down the Yukon River to the sea, while hostile Indians shot arrows at him from the banks of the Klondike. He endured harsh winters of 1893 and 1894 with temperatures reaching sixty-two degrees below zero. His friend, Billie White, helped published his adventures in the *Iola Register*, earning a reputation as an excellent story-teller as well as an ardent adventurer.

§

Fred sold his accounts of the Yukon and Death Valley adventures around Kansas in lectures and printed articles for badly needed cash. He'd had enough extreme weather for a while and found some land in southern Mexico, intending to develop a coffee plantation with help from investors and friends, and perhaps find another beautiful *senorita* to settle down with. But Kansas, like Fred Funston, was long on wheat, corn, and sunflowers, short on funds. His federal stipend depleted, he needed fast cash to close the land deal and open a business. New York City and Wall Street beckoned, where cash was available for entrepreneurs. But living was expensive there, and he was quickly broke again.

He took a job as deputy comptroller with the Atchison, Topeka & Santa Fe Railroad, which was coming out of bankruptcy and issuing new securities. He had only to sign his name witnessing new stock and bond certificates. Three months of this bored him; he had fallen in love again—this time with exploration, adventure, and danger. When he heard Civil War General Daniel Sickles, a fiery supporter of Cuban insurgents fighting a real revolution against Spain, was making speeches, his heart skipped a beat and he went to find out more.

§

While Fred tried to satisfy his quest for adventure and travel, and cure his unrequited need for companionship, the Blankhart family prepared to move from the Midwest to the San Francisco Bay area of California. About the time of Mattie's birth they shifted again to Oakland, just across the bay from San Francisco. Otto and Theresa established a musical instrument shop and began giving private lessons to students while overseeing their girls practicing the scales on the family piano and violins. Soon, both music professors at California College were participating in musical reviews and private recitals and earned frequent mention in the Oakland and California papers.

Three young girls in puberty also took increasing notice of the masculine form but remained under strict supervision of their European parents. Recitals and chaperoned parties were good starts, but the middle girl, even more than the others, grew restless to break free of restraints. That opportunity would come soon enough.

FOUR

Lining up credit for a farm was difficult in New York and his shortage of cash led him to a friend and fellow Kansan, Charles Gleed, who arranged a temporary accounting position with the Atchison, Topeka, & Santa Fe Railroad, to pay for room and board. *The New York Times* was chock with news of the Cuban insurrection and that old stirring seized him. Using his experience as a reporter in Kansas City and Fort Smith, articles published in *Harper's Weekly, Scribner's, St Nicholas Magazine,* and the *Iola Register* recounting adventures in Colorado, Death Valley, and the frozen Yukon, he presented himself as a war correspondent to the managing editor of the *New York Sun.* He rejected his application—another rejection. Not giving up, he stormed the recruiting office of the 9th New York Infantry. He again failed minimum physical standards—yet another rejection.

Fred wandered past the Cuban Fair at Madison Square Garden and found Civil War Major General Daniel Sickles beginning a fiery speech supporting the Cubans. He listened and made a decision he explained to his friend, Charles Scott, "I am the only person in the world who can thoroughly understand the motives that influence me and it seems the motives in this case are sufficient." Later he wrote, "Since the outbreak of the insurrection I had taken considerable interest in its progress, and had indulged myself in a vague idea that I'd like to take part in it, I fear as much from a love of adventure and a desire to see some fighting as from any more worthy motive. Of course, I shared the prevailing sympathy with the Cubans, and believed their cause worthy. Whatever doubts I may have had on the expediency of mixing up in the rows of other people vanished after hearing General Sickle's speech and I returned to my room that evening with my mind made up and spent a sleepless night, as befits one who has just determined on going to his first war." War it would be.

Next morning he appeared unannounced at the office of the Cuban Junta on 56th Street and requested to see Mr. Palma. Thomas Estrada Palma was the revolutionary leader who eventually became the first president of the Cuban Republic. Instead of Palma, he met Mr. Zayas, an attaché, who insisted they were not sending Americans to Cuba. Fred didn't believe this, but realized his error of a direct approach since Cubans worried about American agents trying to stop illegal filibustering. He arranged to meet with General Sickles, with clear connections to the junta. They enjoyed a pleasant conversation at the general's residence and he left with Sickles' personal note of introduction to Palma.

Fred returned straight away to the junta offices and this time was escorted to Palma, who asked whether he had any military experience. He confessed he did not, but argued he was well read on military texts. Palma explained they couldn't send people directly into the fray since it violated neutrality laws, but he'd be free to join an illegal filibuster. In Cuba he could then offer his services to any insurgent chief he might find in the field.

Fred returned to Zayas who told him, "Plans are completely secret and can't be revealed in advance. Be patient and be prepared to react on short notice. Write down your address in my notebook and check back weekly for changes or new information." During another visit, Zayas said, "Our fighters suffer from failures in the field with artillery. You might learn as much as possible about gunnery before you go. That would be valuable to a fighting army." Fred knew of his father's artillery experience in the Civil War and was intrigued.

Now associated with the junta, he convinced the editor of *Harper's Weekly* to cast him as their reporter for Cuban forces. He didn't expect much pay from the Cubans but counted on income from reporting to cover expenses. He set up a stipend to be paid to his bank account for articles he got back to New York and stuffed a large camera in his bag to take pictures to illustrate them. Now ready, he waited for orders to go. All he needed to do now was find out something about artillery.

Zayas gave him a note introducing him to the firm of Hartley & Graham, the Cuban's arms dealer. At their warehouse, he saw a Hotchkiss breech-loading rifle that fired a twelve-pound shell, and was allowed to familiarize with the workings of the gun. Using the manual, he taught himself to disassemble and re-assemble it and studied tables of velocity, ranges, charges, and mechanics until he had committed large portions to memory, as he had Kipling's verses in Alaska.

Zayas was pleased with Fred's interest in weapons and asked, "Would you be willing to train some young Cubans?" So in the middle of New York City, in a small room over a saloon on Third Avenue, Fred plunged into the Cuban insurrection by violating a host of laws designed to stop him. That night, a crated weapon was delivered above the saloon. He drew the shades and turned lights low but noises of manhandling the Hotchkiss couldn't be muffled, even above noises in the bar. Fifteen chain-smoking Cuban boys, college age and inexperienced, were drilled by their novice instructor in broken Spanish. They set up the gun, disassembled it, and started all over again, repeating the process dozens of times. They practiced lifting the pieces high enough to load on make-believe burros, and sometimes dropped heavy components on the floor.

He was invited with others of the junta to the Long Island coast for a demonstration of a new invention, the Sims-Dudley dynamite gun, resembling a telescope more than a cannon. It was fired out to sea and the nitro gelatin-loaded shells erupted, throwing water a hundred feet in the air and scattering excursion boats. He would fire it in combat.

Summer wore on and he waited, studied artillery mechanics, memorized firing tables, and continued his boring job signing railroad stock certificates. Then, one afternoon in August, a telegram arrived—*Be at Cortland Street Ferry at 7 p.m., ready to leave the city*. He quickly packed a trunk with belongings to leave behind and crammed a few necessities into a small valise, "and with some sinking of the heart, I made my way to the ferry…." Zayas met him there and introduced him to Mr. Pagluchi, a well-dressed Italian smuggler and marine engineer, who kept steamers in service ferrying arms and reinforcements to Cuba. He had nerves of steel.

Fred met other westerners there—Charles Huntington, a handsome Canadian with soldierly bearing from the Northwest Mounted Police; Walinski, an Englishman of Polish descent; Welsford, a young man from New Jersey; and Arthur Potter, a former British marine.

Aboard the ferry-boat crossing the sound, five new companions speculated about next moves, but Pagluchi was stoic. They were going to Cuba, but how was secret because the operation violated American and Spanish laws—humans and weapons smuggled between countries for a revolution. Seventy-one such expeditions departed bases from the United States to

Cuba between 1895 and 1898. Spaniards intercepted only five, although they used sixty-seven vessels and two hundred thousand soldiers attempting to shut them down. Meanwhile, the United States used the navy, coast guard and revenue ships at sea, as well as justice and treasury undercover agents on shore to stop thirty-three expeditions before they reached Cuba.

At Jersey City, they were assigned sleeping berths on the *SS Pennsylvania* to bypass Washington, D.C. going south to Charleston, South Carolina. At Charleston they shifted to a hotel where thirty well-dressed Cubans were standing in clusters, whispering. Fred recognized General Emilio Nunez from the junta offices in New York, the eventual Governor of Havana Province after hostilities ended. Nunez remembered him and introduced General Rafael Cabrera, an older veteran of the Ten Years War, now in exile but returning to continue the struggle for a free Cuba. He would die without seeing it. The hotel had twenty other well-groomed strangers—operatives of Pinkerton Detective Agency, hired by the Spanish minister in Washington to keep track of them. Interspersed were U. S. Secret Service agents, intent to seize the renegade ship and arrest them.

Two G-men plied Fred for information with a mint julep. He refused, "I'm from Kansas. I don't like that sissy drink."

"How about an ice cream soda?" the agent asked.

Huntington, the ex-Royal Mounted Policeman, realized what they were doing. "Leave my friend and me alone," he said, glaring them into a corner. "Else I'll thrash both of you together." G-men kept their distance. They couldn't learn much anyway, because no one there knew the plan.

The *Commodore*, a well-known filibuster—a ship carrying soldiers and supplies without legal authority—was anchored in Charleston harbor being watched by an American revenue cutter waiting to make a move. The arrival of these men prompted more scrutiny too, because of its reputation as a smuggler. The *Commodore* was a diversion, and when it sailed away to Hampton Roads, the revenue cutter followed.

Next afternoon, Cubans departed the hotel in small groups with hand baggage, each trailed by one or more sleuths. Pagluchi rounded up his westerners and led them to the Plant Line railroad station where they boarded a passenger train and prepared to depart. Pagluchi's men sat in the last car with the Cubans and when detectives tried to board they were turned away as that coach was reserved by a Jacksonville businessman. Agents found seats one car ahead, facing the rear. The train left the station and rolled on through the night, stopping in the dark at an obscure station in a wooded area in the middle of nowhere. A second locomotive backed up to the last car and quietly uncoupled it from the original train. The passenger train pulled from the station and proceeded out of sight while the shorter train of one engine and one coach reversed course and sped away in a different direction. The secret plan worked to perfection.

At sunrise, the short train stopped at a small station in the piney woods of Woodbine, Georgia, near the southeast Atlantic coast. A large tugboat, the *Dauntless*, was moored in the Satilla River. The junta had purchased the three-year old *Dauntless* at Brunswick, Georgia, for $30,000 to make runs with a cargo of sixty-six tons, operating under the ownership of a building contractor, a front organization, based in Jacksonville, Florida. Parked on a siding were three freight cars with cargo marked "saw mill machinery," actually arms and ammunition, including the Hotchkiss. When passengers disembarked, the engineer shouted as he rolled away, "Good-by and good luck, don't let them Spanions git you!"

Following a breakfast of strong coffee and hard bread everyone transferred cargo from freight cars to the tug, five hours under hot sun and high humidity. The cargo included the Hotchkiss twelve-pounder, several hundred riding saddles and lots of pack saddles and other gear, eight hundred shells, one thousand three hundred Mauser and Remington rifles, one hundred revolvers, one thousand cavalry machetes, eight hundred pounds of dynamite, half a ton of medical supplies, and four hundred sixty thousand rounds of small arms ammunition. Sickles' fund-raiser at Madison Square Garden had been that successful.

Tugboat Captain John "Dynamite" O'Brien, an old blockade-runner of some repute, manned the bridge as the *Dauntless* cast off. The tug sounded three defiant toots as they slipped down river toward the sea. "Dynamite" O'Brien's nickname came from the many revolutions he supplied in Latin America. He was an experienced seaman, resourceful and cool under fire—filibustering only for strong hearts. In future years O'Brien became the chief harbor pilot in Havana.

The *Commodore* had made its feint north, drawing the coast guard cutter away, while the *Dauntless* chugged to the Atlantic, keeping a sharp lookout, nevertheless. Passengers and crew faced four days of rolling and pitching on heavy swells, a trip normally made in two, but this time preserving fuel for the return voyage—or escape from the Spanish navy. Fred and the others huddled on wet blankets, sometimes rushing to the railing to give up a meal. On the afternoon of August 16th, the coast of Cuba appeared on the horizon, just as wind and rough seas moderated. The coast was routinely patrolled by gun-boats and armed launches—capture meant certain death. The five westerners had considered that possibility and Fred quoted Kipling:

> *Just roll to your rifle and blow out your brains,*
> *And go to your God like a soldier.*

They were determined to fight. The Hotchkiss twelve-pounder was unpacked on the deck and mounted with chocks beneath the wheels and ropes to secure it, muzzle pointed over the port bow. A tarpaulin covered it until a target sailed into firing range. The stationary cannon could only be aimed by maneuvering the tug. General Cabrera placed Fred in charge, the only one with knowledge of the gun, although he had never fired an artillery piece, only studied manuals in New York, on the train, and on the tug, committing them to memory. As they approached the coast, he selected two small books to keep and tossed the others overboard.

A low mangrove-covered coastline loomed in the distance with visible hills behind. Funston recalled, "We stood on deck with beating hearts and tense faces as the little steamer drew near the inlet known as Nuevas Grandes ... on the east coast of the Province of Puerto Principe or Camaguey.... Our teeth were chattering, and not from the cold...." Captain O'Brien and Generals Nunez and Cabrera were anxious and in private consultations on the bridge. A crewman took soundings in the dark, his voice and throbbing engines the only sounds on the water. Nervous westerners grouped around the gun, which was loaded with primer inserted.

The *Dauntless'* engines stopped a half mile from shore. Stacked on the deck were eight flat-bottomed skiffs, each with two pairs of oars and a steering rudder. Flat bottoms accommodated piles of cargo. One westerner was in charge of each of five skiffs, Cubans the other three. The crew brought the cargo up piece by piece, passing it over the side to the boats. Lights were extinguished except for one lantern hanging over the shore side for ship-to-shore navigation and return trips. Boats shuttled cargo from tug to shore in a circuit, jettisoning loads on the beach and returning for another run. On Fred's sixth such trip to the *Dauntless*, a white searchlight swept the horizon from the north. As the beam drew nearer, searching, tensions rose. Dynamite rang the tug's bell three times and a column of black smoke belched from the stacks. A race for life began, the *Dauntless* heading out to sea and the flat bottomed boats toward shore.

The searchlight caught the *Dauntless'* higher hull and Spanish guns boomed. The tug plunged ahead until out of sight in darkness. On the skiffs it was worse. According to Fred, "With heavy hearts we rowed ashore, and members of the expedition gathered about piles of cartridge boxes and bundles of rifles on the beach, shivered in their wet clothing, and in subdued tones discussed the situation." All men were present, but only three quarters of the cargo had been off loaded; that now scattered over the beach. With first light, Fred positioned the Hotchkiss in a gully behind a log. They prepared to take on a ship, but the muzzle wouldn't depress enough to stop a ground assault. The men had coffee and bacon over a fire along with hard bread before collecting scattered supplies to hide.

They scanned the coast constantly while working through the day, waiting for the Cuban army or navy. Then they spotted a ship plowing toward them. They readied the gun to fire, but she turned broadside—profiling the *Dauntless*. Runs were quickly organized to recover the remainder of arms, ammunition, and medical supplies. As the last boat shoved off, the *Dauntless* rendered a last salute with three defiant blasts from her whistle, and then steamed away, leaving them alone on an inhospitable beach.

Fred recalled, "As we watched her fade from sight we realized we had burned our bridges behind us and were in for the war."

FIVE

The *Dauntless* dumped Fred and thirty-five compatriots on the Cuban beach and steamed off for another run, leaving them with tons of arms, ammunition and supplies. When the tug departed, four Cubans ventured into the interior to contact rebels. An insurgent challenge echoed, "*Alto! Quien va?*" The reply, "*Cuba!*" The insurgent, a scout of General Maximo Gomez's command, was ragged, unwashed, armed with a machete and Remington rifle. Fred recalled he "was so glad to see us he insisted on bestowing on us the *abrazo*, a form of embrace much in vogue in Cuba. I took my medicine along with the rest...."

The scout was followed by six hundred men and numerous pack animals, all as raunchy as the first. The day was late, so they camped nearby and early next morning loaded every horse and man to the limit to journey into the interior. The ragtag band made thirty miles in one day and when they stopped, the new arrivals were exhausted. This camp was set in a pasture with a thousand of General Gomez's armed men. Four Americans had earlier joined—William Jones, a New Yorker who had lived in Cuba for ten years, and after the war was chief of the harbor police of Havana; Arthur Royal Joyce, of Massachusetts, who would soon be badly wounded; William Smith, second in command of Gomez's personal guard; and James Pennie, of Washington, D.C., who lost a leg in the war.

Fred's first job was dismantling and cleaning artillery pieces exposed to salt water and sand. Throughout the day trains of pack-animals arrived with more arms, ammunition, and supplies from the beach. The merged group of westerners sat around the campfire swapping experiences, the newest listening to those slightly more experienced. That evening Fred was notified he would be officially presented to Maximo Gomez. As he passed shabby rebels, he noticed they were ragged but well-armed, and nearly all were mounted. The majority were Caucasians from a predominantly white province, although some blacks were scattered among them.

Fred stood by as Gomez sat in his canvas hammock, strung between two trees, reading mail from the New York junta brought by the *Dauntless*, dictated replies to his secretary, and took a mid-day siesta. When he awoke, he publicly dressed down Major Miguel Tarafa—staff officer, interpreter—a banker in peacetime—for a minor infraction. Fred watched from afar with misgivings. Then he was summoned.

But Gomez expressed appreciation for all the *expedicionarios* for leaving safety to cast in with insurgents fighting for freedom. He asked Fred point-blank, "What do you know knew about artillery?"

"Not very much," he said. "Only what I've read and practiced in New York."

"Well, you can't know less that other American who came down here and said he knew it all." Gomez put him in charge of the Hotchkiss and a smaller 1.65-inch caliber gun already on hand. "You'll be an officer with the same privileges as the others, but on probation until I see what you can do," he said. "Now, have you ever chewed sugar cane?" to which Fred replied he never had. "Well, you can't be a real rebel until you know how to eat sugar-cane." Gomez peeled the stalk with his knife to get at the sweet pulp, bit off a chunk and chewed. "Now you do it." They both laughed at Fred's clumsy attempts, but Gomez seemed swayed by his honesty, sincerity, and willingness to laugh at himself.

Fred considered Gomez a stern, hard man with a violent temper, yet kind. He was thin and wiry with a snow-white mustache and goatee and toasty Spanish complexion. Officers were generally planters, cattlemen, farmers, and professional or businessmen, usually a class above commoners. Many spoke English, educated in the United States, dressed neatly in white duck with appropriate insignia and mounted on sturdy horses. The lower ranks were workers from cattle ranches and plantations, clerks, mechanics, or hard laborers, who were ragged, some barefoot, armed with Remington rifles or Mausers, with heavy ammunition bandoliers draped around their bodies. Officers carried a long cavalry machete manufactured in Providence, Rhode Island, while enlisted carried one shorter and locally fabricated. Machetes were used to cut cane, chop wood, or dig—even to kill Spaniards. He noticed weapons were rusty, dirty, and not often cleaned after firing. These were the men of the Free Cuban Army, with whom they risked lives by joining.

President Cisneros, seventy-five years old and head of the insurgent Cuban Republic, rode on horseback to meet General Cabrera, accompanied by Arthur Royal Joyce, who had been with him four months. Joyce met the new men and asked, "There should be another. Is someone was missing?"

Huntington said, "Yes, there's a little fellow over there named Funston doing guard duty over the stores.... He'll swear he's the only one on the expedition who's done his share of guard duty since we left New York."

Gomez' army moved constantly. Reveille sounded at 0300 on the second morning after they arrived. Excess cargo was stowed under sheds, but large quantities of ammunition and medical stores were carried. They stumbled along a narrow, winding road going south. Soon daylight tinted rolling interior uplands and lush primeval forests, clearings planted with ripe corn, beans, sugar-cane, squash, sweet potatoes, yucca, manioc, and other vegetables interspersed with prairies of guinea grass and grazing herds of fat cattle, all sources of sustenance for a rebel army on the move. Usually, the small army marched in a wavering column of twos, meandering aimlessly about the interior. Not now—they were going to fight!

Fred allowed volunteers to carry some of his personal belongings on the march, despite warnings against it. Too late he discovered most of his gear disappeared, including the camera to take pictures for *Harper's Weekly* articles. But he was most upset his large rubber blanket that sheltered him through his Arctic trek was gone. He was left with only a Spanish phrase book, his hunting jacket, and scratchy corduroy trousers.

New York clothing was inappropriate and prickly in the back country, identifying greenhorns. At noon, the column stopped and scattered into woods. Riders unsaddled and picketed horses to graze, while others swung hammocks and struck cooking fires. One black Cuban, assigned to them as cook, plundered for food. Soon kettles of vegetables and beef stewed over cooking fires for the first meal of the day, delicious and nourishing to starved westerners. But that meal was soon deemed "everlasting stew" since the menu never varied. Looking back, Fred considered those sad days as better than those ahead. "Luckily for our peace of mind, we couldn't look into the future and see days when the whole country was desolated by war, when cattle were gone and we lived almost exclusively on fruits and vegetables, and mighty few of those."

After a meal—siesta—after that the camp came alive with visiting, cards, and singing. Outdated newspapers from New York passed between hands until frail pages were tattered and frayed. After dark, the second and final meal was served, exactly like the first. Campfire chatter continued until "tattoo" then "taps" signaled quiet time until "reveille," again 0300. Marching days for the next two years were all the same. But on this day they passed from lush countryside untouched by war into devastation along the *Camino Real* where houses were burned, barbed-wire fences cut and hanging in tangled meshes, cattle and crops scarce from clashes for seventy miles from Puerto Principe to Guaimaro. This was the battle zone!

At La Yaya, an abandoned cattle ranch, Funston, Huntington, Potter, and Welsford were placed with a Cuban family while Gomez went on an undisclosed mission. Walinski left with General Cabrera and wasn't seen again by them. They were measured and outfitted in duck suits, heavy shoes, leggings, and Panama hats—suitably dressed as rebels.

When Gomez returned he sent for Funston and delivered a surprising report. "We will attack the garrison in Cascorra, but will likely fail! The Spanish commander of the 4th Battalion of Tarragona has excellent skills and courage and his soldiers are strong fighters."

Fred let that soak in and said, "Our artillery might damage structures but is useless against troops because the shells are only explosives with no shrapnel."

Then Gomez's exploded with Spanish curses. "How can the junta be so stupid? They send me shells that cannot kill?"

After several days to rest and plan, the march resumed, stopping outside the town of Guaimaro, a Spanish flag flying over the garrison. The insurgent battle flag was also visible to them but neither exchanged fire. Gomez sat erect on horseback atop a ridge within plain sight to observe the city, in deep thought about the future.

After they had moved away, Gomez asked Fred to test-fire his two artillery guns. They stopped at a pasture eight hundred yards from a large rock. He'd never fired live artillery, his marksmanship questionable—the first shot missed the rock but struck the ground with an ear-splitting burst and substantial smoke. Everyone was impressed with the noise and smoke.

In preparation for the assault on Cascorra, Gomez sent Funston and General Vega forward to select artillery firing positions. They crawled completely around the perimeter, using the entire day for a thorough reconnaissance. Funston wanted to set the guns on a low ridge with good visibility of town, at fifteen hundred meters distance. Vega recalled that inaccurate practice shot even at close range, and selected a position in high grass four hundred yards out, hoping he could just hit the town.

Cascorra's normal population was only two hundred, but most non-combatants left when it was occupied and fortified by a Spanish garrison of one hundred sixty infantrymen. They held three strong points—a brick tavern, reinforced by sand bags; a strong stone church reinforced with sand bags and surrounded by trenches; and a main earthen redoubt defended by half the troops, the command post, and reserves, also surrounded by trenches and barbed wire. The three outposts formed an equilateral triangle. Funston recalled from his reconnaissance, "It was plain, even to a layman in the art of war, that we had a big job cut out for us."

When they returned the camp came alive—leaders briefed, detailed planning and intense preparations. In the morning Gomez and eight hundred men marched to striking distance and took positions surrounding the garrison. During the night, engineers had constructed a parapet at the artillery position selected by Vega. Ammunition and infantry guards were protected behind the berm, but gunners were exposed while loading, aiming, and firing. All Funston had to do was hit the targets—something he had never before done.

Insurgents moved so quietly they weren't discovered. Only the Hotchkiss twelve-pounder would be employed initially, but when the sun rose a sizzling rain of small arms fire raked the town first. The decision to fire was Funston's and he told his crew, "Get ready!" Jones, Joyce, and Pennie hand-rolled and lit cigarettes while Welsford bit off a plug of tobacco. Potter opened the breech block, and Joyce passed a shell to Huntington, who slammed it into the breach. Pennie grabbed the lanyard. Funston squatted behind the gun and elevated the screws to visually aim at the tavern. Then he climbed on the parapet to observe, and yelled, "Fire!"

He didn't cover his ears and was nearly deafened by the blast. Flame and smoke erupted high on the tavern and bricks tumbled down. He jumped from the parapet and landed on a Cuban porter, putting him out of action—the first friendly casualty of the battle. They learned later from a partisan in the city that four soldiers were killed in that first-ever shot.

As smoke bellowed, eager Cubans shouted battle cries, *"Cuba Libre!"* *"Bravo!"* The crew rushed a second round and punctured a hole in the tavern. Suddenly, the air erupted with popping of small arms fire to silence another barrage. Leaves snapped off trees, erratic waves coursed through high grass, and bullets slammed the parapet like heavy rain. One rang against a gun wheel. The big gun fired on until the barrel became red hot. Firing then slowed, but the new gunners knew they were up to the job.

A Cuban providing security was hit in the thigh and crumpled, bleeding profusely as others carried him away. Funston was aiming another shot when a blow struck the sole of his foot, knocking him down. The bullet split the sole of his left shoe, slicing off the heel and leaving a black bruise. Still more wounded soldiers were hit and carried away. This was a battle of eighty Spanish riflemen against five cannon-cockers with a single gun.

The Hotchkiss overheated again and stopped firing, so Funston walked to Gomez's headquarters to confer. He suggested a new parapet oriented toward the church. When he returned to the gun, the breech-block had expanded and seized. He took it apart and oiled it, poured water to cool it, but the water was not cool enough so it needed more time to contract. When it could be fired again, they fired one round every half hour until dark. Gomez praised the work of the crew, but was undecided about the next step. Funston told him, "You'll never take the town without an infantry attack!" A presumptuous statement for someone in his first fight to another who'd had been under fire before he was born.

Gomez patiently explained, "My men have made plenty of attacks, but never against alert defenders in solid trenches with entanglements. If they are repulsed, it would demoralize my good fighters."

The second day was like the first and that night Fred appealed once more for a new parapet to hit the church, and for an infantry assault—even volunteering to lead it. "If they commit their reserve we could overwhelm those in town and take their main position. The battle would be won!" Rebel officers overheard and offered to lead their units in such an attack. Gomez contemplated, but ultimately declared them all insane and refused. He agreed to build a parapet closer to the trenches to reach their infantry.

General Avelino Rosa, a Columbian exile, was operational commander of infantry and cavalry troops. During the second day's battle he worked his infantrymen close to the trenches using natural defiles in the ground. From there, they exchanged close fire with the Spanish. He agreed they could also be moved closer and Gomez ordered him to do it, but several were killed building a parapet so near the enemy. The pit was short, with only eight feet of cover on each side of the gun portal, but with added overhead cover. The new main position was one hundred sixteen yards from the trenches; A secondary one two hundred yards to the left rear was for the smaller gun under Jones' control.

At first light Fred sent a twelve-pound shell into the sand bags protecting the trench, and the two-pounder followed. They pulled the larger gun backward with ropes, reloaded under cover, and pushed it back into position, firing repeatedly this way. Spanish rifles fired back intensely. Funston recalled later: "It has fallen to me to participate in a good many fights in Cuba and the Philippines, but never anywhere have I seen the equal of what was poured into us during the hour we held this position."

The air was alive, bullets ripped bark from trees, small bushes cut to ribbons, and the top of the parapet torn apart by blasts from the gun firing out. Gunners were exposed while aiming but the target was so close it was just point and shoot. Their trenches were blasted apart, but their fire never diminished. Funston aimed his fifteenth shot when a bullet hit the trunnion near his nose. He rolled over and away from the line of fire. Joyce checked aim and Pennie, smoking a cigarette, pulled the lanyard. General Rosa halted the gun's operation and ordered them to better cover. With the gun out of action, Spanish firing was redirected toward rebel infantry, resulting in more casualties. The two-pounder, further away, kept firing while they hauled the twelve-pounder away with ropes.

Two Cuban non-combatants escaped from Cascorra and told what they knew of the situation inside. The Spanish garrison was badly worn down but well supplied with ammunition and food. Defenses were restored each night, anticipating a ground attack. Twenty Spanish casualties had resulted from shell fire. That news cheered the gun crews.

Early on the fourth day, General Vega and Funston scouted new artillery positions to fire on the redoubt and the church. This time Fred's original choice was selected on the low ridge. Any rounds overshooting the redoubt would impact near the tavern. The smaller Hotchkiss was left in the original position to attack from two directions. The first shot fell in the center of the works and continued slowly with ammunition running low. Cuban infantry still held the low ground in the ravine and exchanged fire with the Spanish, useless without a ground attack.

On the fifth day, Gomez visited the gun in action and thought he could do better. He lowered the muzzle, but the round hit only three hundred yards away. Funston blamed faulty shells and Gomez' staff officers readily agreed. Funston's marksmanship was unquestioned after that.

Later Gomez returned to the gun emplacement with his entire staff. He dictated a letter to his secretary, and after it was copied, he signed it. A Puerto Rican major mounted his horse, accepted the letter, and holding a white flag aloft trotted toward the redoubt. Spaniards fired on the white flag and its bearer as if he were making a lone cavalry charge. He rode on despite the firing. Firing ceased when two Spanish officers met him and accepted the letter. The major was required to face away from Spanish lines and stay on his horse while the other two went for instructions. The major galloped straight back to deliver the reply. Gomez's letter praised the Spanish for a spirited fight and invited them to surrender. The reply assured him they would defend until the very last man. Firing resumed.

Informants had reported soldiers slept in the buildings, expecting no incoming fire at night. Gomez told Funston, "Sight the gun on the church before dark, keep a guard on it, and pull the lanyard at 2200 hours." Four men inside the church were killed or wounded as they slept—there was no more sleeping that night. But the siege was drawing down—artillery ammunition nearly depleted. Only thirty shells remained for the twelve-pounder and a hundred for the smaller gun. More were ordered but wouldn't arrive for days. Attacking trenches with artillery was useless and infantry was wasting bullets at entrenched soldiers, but the standoff lasted four more days.

Informants advised a sergeant had gone to Puerto Principe for relief and a column of soldiers was on the way. Rebel cavalry harassed them by striking, withdrawing, striking again, while Gomez reinforced the siege with more men, bringing them to fifteen hundred. He ordered all remaining artillery shells fired into Cascorra. Funston argued against this, wanting to reserve some for the reinforcements. He was overruled.

In the final flurry a bullet hit Joyce in the thigh and he was carried under fire to an aide station for treatment. Rain fell in torrents throughout the miserable night, but the small cannon pumped until the last round was gone. Then it fell silent. Gomez went to Funston with his most stern manner, but he extended his hand for the splendid use of the guns.

After the battle, Thomas White Steep, writing for Scripps-McRae, came to look for Fred. He found him in a clump of coconut trees, ragged, hungry and virtually unknown outside Kansas. His long uncombed hair poked through holes in his Panama hat, an unkempt beard covered his face. He wore a loose cotton shirt, and his trousers, in shreds and dangling below his knees. His shoes were now sandals and he had no socks. Steep asked him, "Where's this gun I've been hearing about?"

"We're out of shells," he said, "so we hid it." He looked at Streep's shoes, and asked, "I'm out of socks, too. Do you have a spare pair?"

Steep later wrote, "He never forgave me for having no spare socks." But he studied Fred's appearance and said, "You look yellow, Funston. Got a fever?"

"Nope," he replied. "Bathing in the river—mud just sticks to you. No towels. Drying in the sun gives you that brown powdery look. Try it."

Steep remembered Funston stooping over in the light of the fire, scooping food from a banana leaf with a stick. "He was an adventurous dreamer, but one who knew how to paddle his canoe when high tide came."

§

The siege ended but couriers raced into camp reporting progress of the Spanish reinforcements, twenty-five hundred men with ten guns and ammunition under General Castellanos. Rebel guns, without ammunition, were hidden, but gunners remained. The artillerymen asked to join the cavalry as volunteers and were issued carbines. The Spanish column clashed with Cuban cavalry at La Machuca. Gomez couldn't prevent relief of the garrison but was determined the Spanish would pay a price. Cavalry skirmishes continued for three hours until the column delivered supplies, ammunition, and reinforcements.

But when they left, rebel cavalry harassed them on their departure. At 0300 on October 7th 1896, an excited scout informed Gomez the relief column was trying to avoid another encounter by an early morning exit. Gomez decided to strike hard at them in the open. He ordered his command to move at once under drizzling rain and darkened skies. All fifteen hundred rebels drew up along both sides of the *Camino Real*, but the Spanish evaded their ambush by passing to their left side. Gomez reacted quickly, pursuing aggressively with cavalry moving on a parallel route. Two miles separated them. Gomez changed his orders to a direct attack.

The Spanish halted along the main road and Gomez allowed his men to rest and eat during the night. Shortly, faint whistling stirred men from their hammocks. Gomez prodded them, struggling through the dark to draw abreast of the expected Spanish route. Before dawn, Gomez ordered four hundred seventy-nine cavalrymen in the saddle near an estate called Desmayo. He set up a field aid station in the woods with one hundred infantrymen on guard and divided mounted cavalrymen into two ranks and took a position on the far left of the line. Funston was a simple cavalryman on the far right. As they got into position, he propped against a tree to wait for daylight and battle.

Gomez intended to ambush the column on the road and run them down in the confusion. At daybreak a heavy fog obscured the battlefield, limiting visibility to ten yards. Men around Funston were in a state of high anxiety. The Spanish commander anticipated the ambush and altered his route off the main road. In darkness, Fred listened to the rattle of two thousand Spanish soldiers approaching until, in the foggy morning, it became eerily quiet. He strained to see.

A slight breeze lifted fog off the ground and he saw what appeared to be a high fence four hundred yards in front. As visibility improved, it was clear this was no fence, but a massed wedge of Spanish infantry in two ranks—the front kneeling, the second standing. Bayonets were fixed, pointed across the road at the ragged line of Cubans. Behind Spanish infantry, two field artillery pieces stood ready to let fly. Gomez could order a retreat to allow them to leave, or attack into the teeth of their defenses.

A rebel bugle ended speculation—"Charge!" The double line of cavalry trotted forward, first at a gallop, shouting and waving carbines, met by artillery canister and rifle fire. Funston found himself in a classic cavalry charge. Dash and audacity of cavalry slammed against strength of massed infantry. Fortunately for the cavalry, marksmanship of nervous Spanish soldiers was poor—too high or too low for a merciless slaughter. But, it was good enough to drop horses and men in numbers—two hundred rebels killed or wounded. Half the cavalrymen were cut down.

Just when the cavalry could have prevailed, they faltered. Instead of breaking straight through the infantry line, sacrificing horses to bayonets, they drew up short at forty yards and engaged in direct, close rifle fire. Cavalrymen simply rode up and down the line, like Indians against a wagon train, firing from their saddles. Funston saw their artillery withdraw, anticipating a breakthrough. Yet their infantry held fast. One side had to break off or everyone would die at Desmayo.

At that critical moment, a heavy fusillade of fire struck the Spanish right flank. Gomez had committed a reserve force of three hundred Cuban infantry to roll up the Spanish flank. Within minutes, enfilading fire did what the cavalry charge failed to do. Spanish formations were forced back, pivoting to face the new threat, but disciplined soldiers maintained tight control, never panicked, leaving no opportunity for cavalry to reorganize and re-engage. The Spanish lost two hundred men in the battle, and the bloody battle of Desmayo ended in another stalemate. Had Gomez foreseen how the Spanish commander would array for battle, he would have been better served to attack with infantry and use his cavalry in the reserve on the flanking attack. Battle seldom progresses as planned.

The next morning Cuban cavalry threw another savage attack at the Spanish rear guard as they marched away, although they suffered another three killed and sixteen wounded. Among the seriously wounded was Potter, with both legs shattered he was confined for a year in a Cuban field hospital. He never left Cuba, but remained after the war as a citizen of Puerto Principe, where he lived until his natural death. Spanish soldiers reached the railroad line under constant harassment and left the scene of battle in troop cars. After the battle of Desmayo, insurgents under General Gomez joined forces with those of General Calixto Garcia. The combined force was sufficient to make up the losses from Desmayo and Cascorra.

For the next five months, between November 1896 and March 1897, Funston served with Calixto Garcia as a roving guerilla infantryman or cavalryman instead of an artillery officer. Ammunition was needed before the guns could be employed. They marched through Oriente and Camaguey provinces at will and engaged the Spanish in ambushes of supply convoys, hit and run raids on Spanish posts, and small-scale sieges of isolated garrisons. Spanish-led Cuban auxiliaries attacked rebel hospitals and slaughtered sick and wounded men. Funston joined in the cavalry attacks as payback. By now he was a war-hardened veteran, skilled in artillery, infantry, and cavalry tactics, knowledgeable of insurgency and counterinsurgency, still in good health, still not wounded.

§

Fred developed strong bonds with his comrades and they held him in high regard. Close relations among fellow foreigners was essential and they enjoyed hearing of his adventures as a fledgling newspaperman, botanist in Death Valley and the Yukon. Often they sat around campfires singing. This was the best part of a soldiers' life and he relished it. Arthur Royal Joyce found him a great admirer of Kipling's verses, needing little encouragement to pounce into impromptu recitations. Joyce believed, "Our two years' experience in the Cuban army produced many unpleasant experiences, but as the years roll on, a kindly memory clouds these over and leaves only the remembrance of many pleasant ones and the loyal friends we made."

Eventually Spanish pressure wore Garcia and Funston down. Insurgents moved continuously, hard scrabbling for food during the winter. Ammunition ran low and horses grew weak, too undernourished to pull the artillery. Despite these hardships, Funston enjoyed soldiering and believed he lived a charmed life. Two horses had already died beneath him in Cuba, yet he had never been hit. But, the Cuban cause had begun to lose some of its luster.

Fred had dispatched two articles to *Harper's Weekly* by courier, but they were never received. He soon gave up the pretense of serving as war correspondent and soldier since it was too difficult to get material out. Lack of shelter or even a blanket to sleep under, plus inadequate food, took a toll on his health. His body was undernourished—complexion yellow from malnutrition, and waking at night dreaming of bacon and fresh bread. He spent many nights in the throes of chills and fevers from malaria. Discomfort made the war seem endless. Meanwhile, he learned from belated letters his friend Charles Scott sent via the New York junta that many of his old friends had married—he was remorseful he had no such prospects. Even among battle buddies he began to think more of home, becoming morose and isolated. Garcia pressed him to stay on. Funston despaired and admitted to Scott he'd shed a few tears of homesickness and loss for the first time since the long winter at Rampart House in the frozen Yukon. But other occasions approached to shake him hard from despair, back to the pain of hard reality.

SIX

Fred Funston was now battle-tested but while Cubans had been fighting the Spanish for freedom continuously for years—more lay ahead. Results of the siege and battles at Cascorra and Desmayo were not impressive. Although rebels acquitted themselves with bravery, both had failed. A ground infantry assault advocated by Funston might have produced better results, or not. Running cavalry clashes against reinforcements were more effective, yet didn't stop the Spanish from bucking up the garrison, making it a more formidable target.

Gomez's army was reduced by casualties and by detachments sent on other missions. His remaining forces numbered one thousand—infantry, cavalry, and two artillery pieces. After Desmayo they turned south and camped with Calixto Garcia's two thousand men, combining forces. Garcia, subordinate to Gomez, had artillery and those weapons were consolidated.

Funston and his crew set out to find Garcia's *expedicionarios* and make introductions—Major Winchester Dana Osgood, a renowned football player from Cornell and the University of Pennsylvania, was the senior artillery officer, therefore in charge of the combined artillery group; Captain William Cox from Philadelphia; Lieutenants Stuart S. Janney and Osmun Latrobe, Jr., both of Baltimore; and James Devine of Texas and Dr. Harry Danforth of Milwaukee, Wisconsin, rounded out the group—all artillerymen except Dr. Danforth, who was a medical officer.

Fred believed artillery was over-officered, with all firing operators being officers. This was an inherent cultural weakness of the rebel force—too many officers in proportion to fighters.

He found Garcia striking at over six feet tall, heavyset, hair and mustache snow-white. His most prominent feature was a hole in the center of his forehead which drained continuously and was generally stuffed with a cotton wad—like the one stuck in Gomez' neck. In 1874, Garcia, a veteran of the Ten Year's War, was about to be captured and attempted suicide rather than a Spanish firing squad. He fired his revolver up through his jaw, but the bullet passed through his mouth and sinuses, exiting through his forehead. He was still captured, but while in prison, a skilled Spanish surgeon guarded his life for four years until the end of that phase of the war. Garcia was profoundly courageous, yet a courteous gentleman, dignified, approachable, but seldom smiled—his entire life was of war and prison but he bore it with distinction.

His staff included a dozen young men from well-placed Cuban families who spoke English, educated in the United States. The Chief of Staff, Colonel Mario Menocal, was a civil engineer and graduate of Cornell, who had risen through the ranks and marched with Garcia to Havana during the Ten Years War. His staff included his son, Colonel Carlos Garcia, the "go to" problem-solver for the *expedicionarios*. Carlos Garcia eventually became the Cuban ambassador to the United States.

Gomez's force was primarily from white provinces of Cuba, but Garcia's was from the black side of the island. Two of his commanders were Rabi and Cebreco, capable black guerilla fighters. The social line between blacks and whites was distinct, but white officers often served under black commanders or on their staff.

On October 16th, after a few days' rest, the combined force of three thousand marched toward Guiamaro, sixteen miles from Cascorra. Fearing battle, most Cuban civilians departed, leaving only Spanish shopkeepers and their families, and three hundred soldiers commanded by an experienced major.

Defenses included eleven positions, primarily two-story blockhouses called *fortines*. Strongest points were a brick church with a stone tower on the south side, and barracks to the south-west, each reinforced with earth piled to the lower portholes, barbed wire entanglements and fighting trenches. Key terrain for the rebels was *Fortin* Gonfu, an isolated blockhouse on a low-lying hill several hundred yards from the circle of *fortines* surrounding the town center. The nearest supporting site was *Fortin* Isabella. If Gonfu was taken, they would hold the dominant position over all the others within easy artillery range. Since Gonfu was isolated and not so strong, it appeared to be easy picking.

After a night of singing, reveille sounded at 0300, as usual. Rebels made no effort to conceal their presence. Funston recalled fifteen years later, "...I have certainly heard reveille several thousand times since that occasion; it invariably to this day brings to mind that depressing, chilly morning that ushered in the siege of Guiamaro...."

The Spanish garrison sounded bugles in response to the rebel challenge. Those inside were cut off from the outside world between supply convoys, but welcomed a fight. They had heard cannons and gunfire from the battle of Cascorra only a few miles distant and knew it hadn't been taken.

Only one gun was used against the Gonfu blockhouse, Garcia's twelve-pounder. Cubans had constructed a short parapet four hundred yards west of the target and dragged if into position before daylight. Osgood took personal command with Funston and Pennie relegated as spectators. The first shot was low, but ricocheted off the ground and pierced the blockhouse without exploding. Sixteen Spaniards inside returned fire, but after several shots connected they repositioned to trenches outside.

Osgood shifted fire from blockhouse to trenches, but the trajectory was so low he couldn't drop one in, most skipping overhead and exploding ineffectively. Problems developed with ammunition carried through rain for weeks—wet and frequently malfunctioned. Funston and Pennie sprinted to the gun, to be closer to the action, in time to see the twelve-pounder recoil hard, striking down a Cuban behind it. Brake ropes were tightened after every shot but heavy charges in light-weight guns generated a dangerous blowback.

Spanish small-arms fire struck the parapet hard and low, requiring the gun crew to work under arduous conditions. Osgood decided the gun had done all it could by driving the enemy into trenches. The situation again called for an infantry attack to dislodge Spanish infantry from protected positions. A staff officer appeared, as if on cue, and announced a ground attack was planned. He directed the artillery crew to keep a sharp lookout for them as they approached the objective and cease firing when they were endangered.

A bugle and shouted commands initiated the attack. Cheers, and a rattle of shots, rose from both sides. Colonel Menocal, Garcia's chief of staff, led the charge—not usually a mission for a staff leader, but error here was not acceptable. The slope was steep and the attack commenced at a slow walk, in a single line, characterized by more firing and shouting than running.

Pennie shouted, "This is for me!" He joined the skirmish line headed for the blockhouse. Funston, Janney, Latrobe, and others joined them rushing from the gun position with revolvers drawn. The blockhouse was quickly taken as defenders ran towards *Fortin* Isabella. Menocal quickly consolidated the position, but they were within sight of the other Spanish positions and came under intense fire. Although the incoming rifle fire was heavy, Pennie ignored the danger and chased a cackling hen. No shots hit either Pennie or the hen and he finally killed it with his machete.

Garcia's staff arrived and pointed out the Spanish flag still flying overhead, nailed to the top of the flag staff. Lieutenant Luis Rodolfo Miranda, started climbing to the roof of the blockhouse then shimmied up the eighteen-foot pole. He was the primary target for every enemy rifle within sight and every one tried to take him down. Bullets beat a tattoo against the blockhouse, some striking the wooden pole, but none hit him. He reached the flag, cut it away with a pocket knife, and slid down with it.

When that show ended, Funston approached Osgood in the blockhouse, still under continuous fire, to discuss getting a gun inside. As they talked, Devine took off, chasing a horse running free but the horse was hit by gunfire. Then Devine was also struck and fell face down. Osgood and Funston both raced for him but Janney beat them and dragged Devine to a sheltered trench. He was wounded in his hip and couldn't walk. He never fully recovered from the wound, although he did return to duty after two months, walking with a severe limp.

Garcia approached the blockhouse to examine the position, but one of his staff officers was killed upon arrival. Garcia decided to pull one of the guns there during the night and add infantrymen for security. To get the gun inside, a hole was knocked in the wall on the side away from enemy fire. Once in, a smaller one was punched through the opposite wall to fire through. By daylight, ammunition arrived and the piece was ready to shoot.

Osgood planted the first round on *Fortin* Isabella. Two hours of shelling drove Spaniards back into trenches. But the slight elevation from Gonfu increased the chances of dropping a round into a trench. Funston moved forty feet outside the blockhouse to call the shots as a forward observer.

Small-arms fire at the blockhouse slackened from the previous day, but those coming in were well placed. Accurate shots zinged inside through the firing port. The sniper, a well-trained Spanish officer, had a sniper rifle and scope. Funston ran inside to confer with Osgood and a shot narrowly missed. Osgood stooped over the gun to make a sight correction then said, "I think that will do it." At that moment, a bullet struck him in the head—a dull, sickening thud. He slumped over the contrails of the gun. Comrades carried him to the aid station but he never regained consciousness and died there. A year and a half later the sad duty of describing the circumstances of the incident to Major Osgood's father, Brigadier General Henry Brown Osgood, fell to Funston.

This tragic loss hit the small group hard. Funston said, "The little group of aliens, fighting in a strange land for a cause not their own, was sorely stricken. It was the first time one of our own had been killed. ... For a time we did nothing but sit in the blockhouse, well back from the fatal porthole, and gaze in awe at the spatter of blood on the gun trail...."

Either Captain Funston or Captain Cox would command after Major Osgood's death. Garcia preferred Cox, who had served under Osgood, but Gomez overruled him and appointed Funston artillery commander of the *Departamento del Oriente*. Cox was a good soldier and acceded, cooperating completely. But the sharpshooter was still in the church tower, threatening to take out another. Funston and the entire crew were obsessed. The gun was untouched after Osgood set the sights to fire, so Funston ordered the lanyard pulled as aimed. The shot penetrated the blockhouse, but did not get the sniper.

The highlight of the afternoon was an unsuccessful infantry attack against the badly battered Isabella blockhouse. For some reason, the battalion charged over four hundred yards of open terrain instead of using cover of nearby woods. Ranks broke under withering fire, leaving dead and wounded behind. Gomez witnessed the fiasco firsthand, court-martialed the officer in charge, and sentenced him to death. But the penalty was quickly commuted; the officer reduced to common soldier, and carried a rifle in the battalion he had commanded.

During the night a two-pounder Hotchkiss was brought up to supplement the twelve-pounder and another firing port cut to accommodate it. The smaller projectiles didn't pack much punch, but were more accurate. When the sniper next fired from the church tower, the small gun drove him away with pin-point fire. For the rest of the day, artillery fired alternately between the larger gun and the smaller one.

By the fourth day, artillery ammunition again ran low. A misfire added to the trouble when a shell jammed in the barrel and required a Cuban mechanic working carefully to remove it. Ammunition resupply was slow so shells were spread between ten targets instead of one single target.

Logistics were a persistent constraint. Sanitary condition of the camp was inadequate, requiring frequent moves to avoid spoiled ground. For food, large herds of cattle were driven in for meat, but vegetables were scarce. One night, Huntington made a lone foray through Spanish lines and returned with a turkey! Colonel Carlos Garcia's black servant knew the town and made another food raid. He got in, found the general store, and in the dark filled a sugar sack with heavy cans. For five hours he dragged the sack back through the lines and opened it to inventory his stock—eighteen cans of paint! Years later, Funston and Garcia, the Cuban minister to the United States, shared a laugh about that over dinner at Fort Leavenworth.

During final days of the siege, a Cuban inhabitant of Guaimaro was captured with a letter to General Castellanos in Puerto Principe, requesting reinforcements. He also had money in advance for delivering the letter. He was tried by military tribunal and hanged.

On the eleventh day, an ammunition pack train finally arrived. Garcia directed a heavy bombardment the following day, then another infantry attack. All operable guns were brought to bear. Funston placed Cox in charge of the Gonfu position; he took the two-pounder near the church along with Huntington, Pennie, and some Cuban soldiers. At daybreak, Funston placed the first shot through the church wall and continued all day.

At dark guns fell silent as usual. Garcia directed a gun at Gonfu aimed at the church before dark and fired at 2100 hours as a signal for the night ground assault. Final hours weighed heavily, tensions high as the attack hour neared. The gun was fired on time and Colonel Menocal again led the assault in coordination with Gomez and Garcia via runners. Everything was planned in detail, objectives assigned, and each commander understood bungling meant executions. Before the echo of the gun died, five hundred men stepped off without shouting or firing, advancing silently in a single line. Funston allowed Huntington and Pennie to join the infantry, since artillery was out of action. When they neared the objective, popping began. Cubans yelled, running the last one hundred yards. Within minutes, a detail began leading prisoners out of the captured blockhouse.

Funston refused to stay by a gun out of the action so joined his fellows at the front lines. In darkness and confusion of an infantry attack, all action was local, a series of detached fights. Hot lead was flying, confusion rampant, friendly and enemy fires equally dangerous.

Cubans hauled fifty pounds of dynamite to fill the trench adjacent to the church stronghold. Spaniards inside anticipated the end and asked to surrender, and were led out. By midnight, all positions were under Cuban control except the main barracks—the most heavily fortified and defended position. Cubans celebrated and looted.

Colonel Menocal and Funston reconnoitered their final objective, finding the one-story brick structure almost impregnable. A gun was needed and a two-pounder was brought to a building adjacent to the barracks. They broke through the walls and removed enough bricks to shove the muzzle only a few yards from the target. Ammunition was brought up and infantry waited with the artillerymen for sunrise. A Spanish hospital was next to the barracks, making the target difficult to hit without damaging the hospital and endangering those inside. The Spanish surgeon he said it was impossible to move the wounded out.

Menocal raised a white flag and walked to the middle of the street while Funston loaded the gun and aimed it. Huntington held the lanyard ready to pull. A Spanish captain met Menocal and said he was in charge after the commandant was seriously wounded by shell fire. Menocal demanded surrender of the barracks, but the captain replied they would fight to the last man. Menocal pointed to the barrel of the Hotchkiss only a few feet away. Cubans gathered to watch—surrender, or blast to smithereens.

As the two men considered, a lean pig dashed across the street and a dozen Cubans chased it. They caught the squealer near the wire and hearty cheers rose from Spaniards watching from the barracks. This entertaining act ended resistance. The barracks door flew open, a white flag unfurled from a window, followed by packs of cigarettes. Spanish soldiers held their Mausers until assured they would be treated well. Then they dropped their weapons and walked casually into the street, mingling freely with the Cubans—those they had tried to kill. Everyone was tired of fighting.

Gomez penned a letter to General Castellanos, the Spanish commander of Oriente, for delivery by a mounted courier. He wrote he had taken Guaimaro after a thirteen-day siege and every man not killed in the battle was a prisoner. He assured he would not follow the Spanish tradition of executing them and asked for an unarmed convoy of ambulances under the Red Cross flag to transport wounded soldiers to El Platano.

The worst of the rainy season plagued them on their march to the rendezvous at El Platano. As ambulances approached they were shadowed by Cuban cavalry, but the handover was executed with full military courtesy. Healthy prisoners were also released when logistics was too strained to support them. The army of four thousand returned to camp near La Yaya, where Gomez commissioned Funston a major in the Cuban army, replacing Osgood as the senior artilleryman in the department.

The fall of Guaimaro was an ominous warning for the small garrison still holding at Cascorra. General Castellanos sent a relief force of four thousand to evacuate the town the rebels couldn't take by force. Gomez and Garcia fought the relief column for a week in a continuous battle. Garcia lost his horse in the fighting, but the Spanish extricated the garrison. Gomez then marched west for other campaigns, and Huntington accompanied him; he was killed in fighting at Santa Clara. Garcia kept all the artillery and officers with him.

§

After the battle at Guaimaro, Fred wrote to his friend Charles Scott, editor of the *Iola Register* in his hometown, using a scrap of paper he picked up from one of the captured forts. "The mail facilities in this war-wasted island are so bad that there is almost no use in writing letters at all." But he pressed on, relating how his horse was shot out from under him at San Miguel and that with his promotion he now was allocated two servants, one to tend his horse and another to cook. But he admitted he missed the "Kansas ozone" and his mother's home-made pie. He continued, "It is a great thing to have read Kipling before one mixes it up in some real fighting and sees the bullets 'kicking up dust spots on the green' as they do in the ballad Gunga Din...."

Scott published excerpts of Funston's letters and they were picked up by larger state newspapers, including the *Kansas City Star*. A reporter traveled to "Foghorn" Funston's farm to gather additional insights. The big-city scribe was surprised to find the high-sounding name of Carlyle was an exaggeration of the little town, depressing even on a balmy day. When the train stopped, he watched a tall man with "sun-faded whiskers" lift a flabby mail sack and lug it towards one of four buildings in a flag-stop town dominated by a dazzlingly white church. The reporter chased him down, the only sign of life, to clear up a few logistics. His answers to various questions was always "no"—no carriage to ride him to the Funston farm, no place to have supper, no hotel to rest, no train to Iola until three in the morning, and "no, he didn't give a damn."

The reporter hired a horse to travel the dusty road to a white house set on two hundred forty acres of lush farmland. The bay window looked south toward a yard filled with "green things and bright blossoms"—a yellow yard "eloquent of summer flower beds and cacti" brought from Mexico by a once frequent traveler. He twisted the door bell ringer and was met by the starkest possible contrast to the puny postman in Carlyle—a young and jaunty-looking giant with a neatly cropped white mustache, wearing dark work clothes and cowhide boots rising high. Straw still clung to his shoulders. "I've been looking after the cows," explained Edward Funston.

A small woman hastened from the room with a small baby. A young cowboy, his horse hitched to the front gate, nodded a silent greeting. Edward Funston said, "Mother got a letter from him back in October; I don't reckon there is anything private in it." He thumbed through the family bible looking for it, but finally summoned his comely young daughter to find it, right where he had overlooked it before.

"Dear Mother—I shall only say that I am alive and well.... Don't worry about me, as I shall come out all right and be home next fall or winter." Funston checked the reporter; "Nothing very exciting about that, is there?" Then he went into some details on how his son ended up in Cuba and admitted he opposed his going, all the while gazing at a Civil War sword hanging over a bookcase near the blooming window sill.

The reporter asked how he felt about his son going to Cuba. "Oh, I don't allow myself to be worried. He'll come out all right...." Funston admitted he was more worried about Yellow Fever than bullets—"a little fighting and a good deal of running away; but that's the way to fight." Funston showed a few additional letters, mostly to Fred's mother, and spoke with pride of how his son had planted corn all day, whistling while he worked. Funston's sister, Ella, quiet at this meeting, later wrote that "no matter how far he traveled, Fred always wrote to this mother."

The reporter left the Funston farm to return to Iola, gathering more background from Charles Scott, "running one of the best newspapers in Kansas," though not a large one. They perused Funston's other letters and discussed earlier experiences, seeking reasons Frederick Funston behaved as he did.

§

The victory at Guaimaro was a significant morale boost for the Cubans. They had made their first successful assaults on infantry in trenches behind wire entanglements. They were honed for more bloody work in the next phases of the campaign. Although he didn't write home about that, those lessons were not lost on Fred Funston either.

SEVEN

For five months after victory at Guaimaro, Garcia's insurgent army roamed at will with ambushes and hit-and-run cavalry raids to harass and attack convoys carrying supplies to isolated garrisons over main roads of the interior. When not attacking, they followed and observed them with scouts. The Spanish recruited small bands of Cuban turncoats for raids against rebels and their sympathizers. Cuban-versus-Spanish clashes mostly adhered to civilized conduct in war, Cuban-versus-Cuban battles were unrestrained, brutal, even uncivilized.

An unplanned, horrific battle between Cubans ensued when Major Pablo Menocal with eighty rebel cavalry scouts surprised sixty Cuban mercenaries for the Spanish. Menocal hastened cavalrymen on line and launched a mounted charge, penning them against a barbed wire fence. The battle was fought entirely with long machetes on both sides and ended with every mercenary hacked to death—common for clashes between Cubans. Cuban mercenaries frequently hit soft targets—rebel hospitals—murdering helpless wounded in their beds. Revenge was exacting and bloody.

Food and clothing became increasingly scarce. Thousands of Cuban families who supported rebels could barely eke a living. Garcia's army swarmed like locusts, eating everything within ten miles, moving just to eat. Local women barely raised enough vegetables to survive, wearing gunny sacks for clothes, children naked, always in terror of mercenary raids. Rebels were also in tatters and many barefoot. They stayed hungry through the vegetable shortage as well, while beef herds were decimated.

After Guaimaro, Garcia refrained from attacks on Spanish garrisons in towns. But in March he ordered concentration near Jiguani. Insurgents confiscated sweet potatoes, corn, and bananas from families already struggling to subsist to prepare for an attack. Remnants of cattle herds were rounded up and driven east. The disparate insurgent army united in the dry season and by early March 1897, four thousand two hundred well-armed but hungry fighters assembled for battle.

Garcia's entire force marched to Jiguani and surrounded the town, wasting no time or sentiments. Funston recalled, "We had seen so much of death and misery that we were in a way hardened, and I believe had become the victims of a sort of fatalism, thinking that the war would last for years and that our chances of seeing home again were pretty small."

His crew received a gun they'd never used—a twelve-pounder Driggs-Schroeder naval landing gun—purchased with funds raised by Cubans in Key West. It resembled a field piece with a long barrel and fired with high velocity, but was too large to be broken down and packed on mules so it was drawn instead. Like the Hotchkiss, it used fixed ammunition but with a troublesome friction primer. When the lanyard was pulled, a bolt descended through the breech block to fire a cartridge, which in turn propelled the charge.

Jiguani was a commercial center and larger than either Guaimaro or Cascorra. The garrison was manned by eight hundred Spaniards, mostly infantry, but with artillery and a troop of Cuban mercenaries. Their artillery piece was one eight-centimeter Krupp gun. The commander of the garrison was the same officer who repulsed the siege on Cascorra, an indication of a stiff fight looming.

Key feature to fortifications was a two-story masonry fort known as *El Castillo*, the Castle, on the end of a ridge eighty feet above the city. An earthen redoubt, trenches and barbed wire, protected the Castle and the gun. A heliograph was on roof was to communicate with Bayamo for reinforcements and resupply. A dozen blockhouses surrounded the town, all protected by barbed-wire and trenches for defense in depth.

Fred commanded the main battery, with the Hotchkiss and naval gun, from a parapet on the same ridge as the Castle, eight hundred yards away. Another position on the south was in range of the smaller Hotchkiss, commanded by Cox and Janney. Jones, Latrobe, Joyce, and Pennie remained with the larger guns.

At dawn on March 13th, 1897, the day was clear and hot, visibility of the Castle and blockhouses unobstructed. Normal sounds of a community coming to life in town were heard—sentries being relieved, hungry dogs barking, a rooster calling the sun. On the ridge, guns were loaded, aimed, and awaiting orders. The naval gun unleashed the first round, crashing against the side of the fort with high velocity providing high accuracy. It should have quickly breached the walls, but fuses were too sensitive and shells exploded on impact without penetration. The heavy Hotchkiss loosed one round for a direct hit. From the other side, the smaller gun barked in unison.

Their Krupp answered with a rumble and the shell swished as it passed two feet overhead, tearing through trees and brush. Cuban infantry in the trees hurried to evacuate, but a second shell wounded some. Another artillery duel commenced with Fred trying to disabled the Krupp while avoiding being blown up. Then the heliograph flashed into action signaling Bayamo they were under attack. He switched targeting to the heliograph, and the first shot from the naval gun was a near miss, but the next hit the roof and smoke and dust obscured it. Rapidly, the sunlight signal was flashing again until the third shot swept the roof clean. Receivers at Bayamo already copied the report and scouts informed Garcia that General Linares was coming with a column of troops.

The Spanish Krupp returned fire by highly skilled gunners as fast as it could be loaded. Shells impacted the parapet, exploded, but didn't penetrate. Cuban big guns concentrated on the Castle, but were also unable to penetrate. Ammunition fuses for the naval gun were imbedded in the shells and couldn't be adjusted. Then the main Hotchkiss misfired, lodging a shell mid-way the barrel and putting it out of action for three months. The duel continued with only the fast-firing naval gun and the two-pounder opposing the Krupp, striving to put the other out of action first.

The Spanish Krupp fired rapid velocity shells but with less accuracy than the naval gun, but gunners were skilled and improving. The Spanish Krupp had to go. Funston's crew took careful aim on the small firing port, four feet in diameter. A naval shell struck the lower sill and obscured the target. The gun wasn't destroyed but the hole was enlarged. Another shell came back at Fred's crew, who ducked then returned another round in the same spot. This took the Krupp out of action for repairs. Most of the Krupp's original crew were killed or wounded. He then concentrated on demolishing the Castle.

Spanish infantry at the nearest blockhouse peppered the artillery parapet with small-arms fire. Funston used his elevation to place three shells in the trenches, sending survivors running to town. Finally, one corner of the Castle was shot away and abandoned. Attention turned to blockhouses. Garcia released a warning order to conduct a night attack. Funston argued to go then but Garcia believed darkness favored his infantry attack. Orders were already issued and a last minute change would cause confusion.

Fred and his crew waited for the attack, fighting off weariness that comes with failing health. Funston was sick and tired and rested in the shade of a tree—until he discovered it infested with ants. He danced, swiping at the stinging insects, just before a bullet smacked the tree. He returned to his gun, better tired than dead.

Cuban artillery wore away stone and earth structures of Spanish defenses, but the irritating Krupp still landed shells close to the valuable Hotchkiss. One came in slow and burst very near—a ragged shard smashed Fred's left arm. Field medics wrapped it in bandages and a sling, but his arm was immobile and painful. He ignored it and kept firing until ammunition was too low and they were forced to withdraw.

By late afternoon, the Spanish repaired the Krupp and manned it with a new crew. Their gunners changed firing positions to a protected earth work and the new crew seemed better than the original. Fred tried to hit it but their gun was loaded behind the parapet and shoved into position an instant before firing. Recoil rolled it back behind cover. The naval gun fired every time the Krupp was visible but the target was too fleeting. Garcia again ordered the naval gun to target ruins of the Castle, but hold fire until 2200, the signal for a night infantry attack.

The main attack included two thousand infantrymen. To the right of the artillery position, twelve hundred men under various commanders had distinct missions to capture various blockhouses and trenches on that side. The assault on the Castle ridge fell to General Enrique Collazo with eight hundred infantrymen in two units. Lieutenant Colonel Charles Hernandez would assault the Castle directly with only one hundred fifty men. But Spanish had returned to the ridge line at night and set up tight defenses in anticipation of a ground attack.

Funston broke silence by pulling the lanyard of the naval gun. The crash of the explosion was followed by more silence, disturbed only by men breaking through brush—then the roar of battle cries! The ridge sparkled with bright muzzle bursts from defenders. The wave of attackers, in a wavy line, pressed uphill. Then the ranks reached a stalemate—firing increased but the attack stalled, two hundred yards apart.

On the right, twelve hundred men of the largest group took those blockhouses. Hernandez rushed his hundred men up the ridge to within a grenade throw of the Castle. They clung tenuously to their small piece of ground for seven hours, refusing to give up an inch of the terrain they had paid for dearly. Some in the flanking attack gave ground against breech-loading, rapid-firing, magazine-fed rifles, making Hernandez' foothold more valuable—but more tenuous. Fighting raged in town with some houses bursting into flames. The outcome hung in the balance.

Then a scout watching Bayamo delivered grim news to Garcia—a large column of reinforcements was close and would arrive at daybreak. Garcia agonized—his troops were near victory, but scattered. A strong Spanish counterstroke would defeat his small formations piecemeal. He believed he had to order withdrawal under fire, a dreaded military maneuver. He sent messages to commanders to concentrate at an assembly point at daybreak. Two thousand men in reserve guarded routes into the objective and easily complied. Those in pitched fights in the town were more difficult to reach, their withdrawals difficult under fire. The first runner sent to warn Hernandez—still hugging his valuable ground under heavy fire—was killed before he arrived. Garcia received no acknowledgement and sent another, who got through at 0500. Hernandez painfully extracted survivors.

Funston described it best: "The sun rose over a sorrowful scene. Our wounded were everywhere, the few surgeons doing what they could to alleviate their sufferings. Our gray-haired and much-loved chieftain sat apart with bowed head, his grief made the more poignant by receipt of information that Linares's column was still miles away, guerillas scouting on his front in the darkness had been mistaken for the main body, so that his withdrawal was unnecessary."

Losses were heavy. Of Hernandez' one hundred fifty men, twenty-four were killed and many wounded, costing him thirty percent of his men. The main force of twelve hundred lost twenty percent, bringing total losses to four hundred. Defeat in battle is difficult to bear but when results hang in the balance for hours, then defeat is based on erroneous intelligence, it was especially bitter. Hernandez' troops, held terrain mere yards from their objective, under blistering fire and refusing to give an inch, a classic example of infantry courage under fire.

§

During warm and rainy weeks of spring and summer of 1887, the Cuban cause ebbed to a new low. Garcia waged low-level warfare, scrambling for food, followed by pin-prick attacks. Fred was permitted local leave time for recuperation of his left arm, severely wounded at Jiguani. Meanwhile, rebels met another resupply at the Bay of Banes, which brought arms, ammunition, and medical supplies. Food and medicine to treat malaria and yellow fever was still scarce, but a new weapon was welcomed, the newly invented Sims-Dudley dynamite gun. Fred saw it demonstrated in New York harbor before he deployed, a weapon never before fired in combat. Artillery was further beefed up with another large Hotchkiss, a Colt automatic gun, and ammunition. Other supplies included thirty-five hundred rifles, three million cartridges, dynamite, and machetes. Spanish tried unsuccessfully to intercept supplies delivered by the *Laurada* with an armed column and the gunboat *Jorge Juan*.

Arriving on the filibuster were also new men—Emory Fenn was chief of the mine department for General Mariano Torres. After the resupply at Bay of Banes, Garcia scattered his units to dispersed operating areas to avoid Spanish intercepts. Fenn met Funston prior to the next battle at Sama.

The march on Sama began early as usual on trails whacked through dense underbrush. Long trenches were dug during the night on a ridge overlooking the town. Funston initiated an artillery duel at dawn, sending a shell through the roof of a wooden fort. An immediate return volley from Spanish guns ensued and a round broke the carriage and axle of the larger Hotchkiss. The gun was dragged thirty miles to the nearest repair shop, taking it out of the fight. Infantry attacked for four days until driven back by a Spanish counterattack.

Garcia tried a siege at Sama, which also failed and depleted his force and supplies. He'd recalled Funston from his arm wound to prepare for the siege of Sama, and on June 20th, he was in a fight when a Mauser ball pierced both lungs and missed his heart by a fraction of an inch. The bullet passed completely through and killed a Cuban standing behind. He was carted in a hammock to a Cuban field hospital, which was poorly equipped and understaffed. Most hospitals had only one doctor with aides who had bandages, cotton, carbolic acid, and quinine, and short instructions—give first aid! Field hospitals were unsanitary and staff worried about Cuban mercenaries. Minor wounds often became serious, even deadly. Fred's wasn't a small wound. He remained in the field hospital for ten weeks in a hammock in critical condition, wheezing and coughing blood. Recovery was slowed by malnutrition. Even after he returned to Kansas, he coughed blood, but in August he returned to duty.

While stuck in a swaying hammock he wrote to his friend, Charles Scott, informing him of his promotion, complaining he was ready to go home, and detailing his many wounds and injuries—but warned him not to share that information lest the news reach his family.

§

In August, Garcia ordered an attack on Victoria de las Tunas. Tunas looked larger than any garrison they had hit before, but civilian towns were not normally constructed with military considerations. This one looked vulnerable on a level plain dominated by a low ridge within artillery range. The garrison inside had eight hundred infantry, two Krupp field pieces previously encountered at Jiguani, plus a guerilla troop of forty-seven Cuban mercenaries. Defenders were distributed among twenty-two defensive positions, nineteen blockhouses and a large brick cavalry barracks on the outer perimeter; inside a massive infantry barracks and a large L-shaped masonry building. A two-story heliograph fort was encircled by a five-foot brick wall surrounding an acre of ground. Buildings were defended with the typical firing ports, trenches, and barbed-wire entanglements.

Garcia mustered fifty-eight hundred insurgents for the mission, with two thousand at each approach to protect against counterattacks from Bayamo or Holguin. Each of them had contingency plans to reinforce the other, or the main attack, leaving eighteen hundred men for the main attack.

This was the baptism for the dynamite gun. Projectiles came in brass cases with a bursting charge of five pounds of nitro-gelatin. Smokeless powder propelled the explosive with compressed air to prevent an explosion inside the gun. Velocity of rounds was slow, causing the large dynamite charge to wobble in flight. With no shrapnel, it was useless against troops, but devastating to buildings.

Cubans tightened their noose around Tunas and Spaniards went on full alert, dispatching occasional shells from their Krupps gun. During the night, Cubans built artillery parapets on the low ridge. The new dynamite and naval guns, the two larger Hotchkiss guns, and most of the crew were under Funston's control in the main battery. The two smaller guns were set a half-mile to the right under Jones, along with Pennie and several Cubans. Four young Cuban lieutenants—Portuondo, Poey, Marti, and Sedano—had been assigned to the artillery command.

The dynamite gun fired first with a deceptively small blast of air and slight recoil. However, it smashed a hole as large as a truck in wall of the cavalry barracks. Other guns chimed in immediately, answered by a roar of Spanish small arms, then the Krupp guns. Incoming projectiles hit the sturdy parapet, showering Funston and his crew with fragments and dirt. One Krupp shell barely cleared their heads.

Funston ignored incoming and concentrated on defensive structures. The rifled breech-loaders created sizeable holes, but the destructive dynamite gun blew large quantities of brick and tile high into the air. Spanish troops fled the building. Barracks were quickly wrecked and trenches targeted. Higher elevation enabled dropping shells inside. Rebel artillery suppressed most Spanish small arms, but the Krupp guns were more fearsome pounding against parapets. Funston recalled, "...far from feeling any uneasiness we were as cool as cucumbers, and considered that we were having the time of our lives."

Weeds around the parapet obstructed observation of targets, so Janney dashed into the open and whacked weeds with a long machete, ignoring incoming bullets and shells. But the breech mechanism of one Hotchkiss malfunctioned and shut it down. Krupps blasted the parapet apart, endangering the dynamite gun and its highly explosive ammunition.

Funston shifted targeting from trenches and barracks to the two Krupp guns. As soon as the shells impacted nearby, both Krupp guns were hauled away behind sturdy buildings. Artillery then shifted to an occupied blockhouse. The dynamite gun lobbed a charge straight to the center where it penetrated and burst inside, killing sixteen Spanish soldiers.

Lieutenant Colonel Joseph Napoleon Chapleau, an American, was fighting with Cuban infantry. He led fifty Cubans through heavy fire to take the trenches around the destroyed blockhouse. There was too little room in the trenches for all his men, so he fought from the rim with his rifle. Quickly, a bullet struck his neck and severed an artery. He was rushed to an aid station, bleeding profusely. Nothing could be done and he promptly bled to death. Funston saw his courage and actions too surreal to be true, almost a melodrama. "The last sounds he heard were the booming of its guns and the crackle of the Mausers and the whistling of their bullets while the wisps of smoke blowing back from the battery gave a setting that could not be had on any stage."

Energized by Chapleau's death, Funston's crew poured heavy and continuous artillery fire on the blockhouse, overheating guns, parapet seriously damaged by Krupp fire. They huddled behind crumbling cover and contemplated Chapleau's eerie death scene while allowing the guns to cool. Spanish gunners took advantage to move their guns into position and fired on the chewed-up parapet again. The Cuban crew, under Portuondo, dropped a shell from the dynamite gun beneath one of the Krupps, killing the Spanish crew and wrecking the gun. Other gunners rushed their remaining gun to a pit near the telegraph fort. A direct shot from the rebel's naval gun took that one out, too.

Rebel artillery blasted the other blockhouses until a white flag unfurled on the roof of a building. Captain Cardenas mounted his horse and rode into town under a white flag to inquire about their flag of surrender. The Spanish were surprised to see a Chinese shopkeeper had hung a white flag with a black dragon, which he thought would spare him from becoming a target. But the black dragon had faded out. The Spanish commander removed the flag, but asked permission for women and children to leave.

Cardenas agreed and five hundred weeping women walked away from their men and all their possessions. During the exodus, the commander asked Cardenas about the dynamite gun—clearly unnerved by it.

Cardenas was debriefed by Colonel Menocal, who told Funston trenches around the cavalry barracks were the next objective for an infantry attack. Guns should fire in support until the last moment. The dynamite gun was set aside due to inaccuracy at that range, but Funston took the naval gun and Janney the big Hotchkiss. Colonel Carlos Garcia would lead the infantry assault with three hundred men.

Two lines rushed toward the front, yelling and firing. Artillery landed dangerously close and Funston kept saying, "Keep cool!" They fired three per minute from each gun, preventing defenders from returning fire. Fire suddenly hit the infantry flank, cutting down several officers; men bunched up and found cover—the attack wavered. Menocal and two others mounted horses and charged. Thirty yards from the trenches the horses were shot and Menocal's leg shattered in the fall. Colonel Garcia's infantrymen were inspired and attacked with machetes. Within minutes they hacked through the wire.

Funston waged another, personal, battle. While guns were out of action, he fell to waves of malarial attacks and collapsed to the ground. Every other day, burning fever and delirium hit him, followed by body-racking chills. Despite nearby battle noises, relief only came when unconscious. When he woke, all the guns were gone. Cubans informed him the town had been taken and guns were there. He rode to the town and found his crew after they turned back a counterattack. Now they were rolling up the other blockhouses, one by one, from inside the town.

The next objective was the massive infantry barracks in the center of town, but it was necessary to get a gun inside a captured building to strike at a right angle. A warehouse was selected one hundred fifty yards away at a thirty degree angle. The naval gun was low on ammunition, so the heavy Hotchkiss and dynamite guns were chosen, then disassembled to squeeze through the door, large holes battered through walls for firing ports. The first shot from the twelve-pounder glanced off the angle of the wall, the dynamite gun was no more effective, but drew heavy small arms fire in return, making the firing ports dangerous. During the day, the dynamite gun fired twenty-eight charges and the twelve-pounder another forty, to weaken the wall of the infantry barracks, the job so frustrating some artillerymen used Mausers to pick off defenders.

During the night, a Spanish soldier deserted and reported to Colonel Menocal he was sent by his fellow soldiers—not by their commander. He said their nerves were shot from dynamite bombs, and they were hungry, thirsty, and weary. Their commander was determined to fight to the finish, but they were ready to lay down arms at dawn. Funston, Janney, and a few Cuban officers tested that premise by walking out into the open. They were not fired on so rushed the gate and it swung open. Spanish soldiers simply dropped their weapons as leaders gawked in disbelief.

Those in the other blockhouses foresaw the inevitable end. Cuban mercenaries asked for quarter but were told, "The same that you have given the helpless wounded in our hospitals." They marched out anyway, and were brutally hacked to death by rebels with machetes. This act repulsed Funston and he protested strongly but to no avail. The brutality wasn't soon forgotten by him, and his objection to it was neither forgotten nor forgiven by his Cuban comrades.

The final military target was the telegraph fort. The Spanish surgeon's residence was adjacent to it and was easily taken. The wall was breached and the barrel of a large Hotchkiss poked through the hole sixty feet from the large infantry barracks. Cubans gathered to watch while Captain Barney Bueno sat at the surgeon's piano and played *Bayames,* then *Yankee Doodle*, and the *Washington Post March*. The Spanish commander realized it was finished, hauled down his flag and surrendered after fifty-one hours of continuous battle.

The rebel army enjoyed its greatest victory—they captured two Krupp guns and shells, fifteen hundred rifles and over a million cartridges, food, and seven hundred fifty pounds of valuable quinine. They couldn't feed all the Spanish prisoners and their authorities wouldn't accept parole, so they were marched to nearby garrisons and released, knowing they would soon be fighting against them.

§

General Garcia promoted all artillerymen one grade, making Funston a lieutenant colonel.

The revolution's end with American intervention was still a year away. But both sides were worn down. Rebels had effectively scouted the Spanish, striking where they were weakest and avoiding being surprised. And they kept meticulous records. After the war, a commission under Maximo Gomez revised army rolls and submitted a detailed report which determined 53,744 insurgents had served as officers and enlisted. By the American intervention, 35,000 were still under arms, 3,437 died of disease and 5,180 killed in actions or perished from wounds—a number higher than all Americans killed in the War of 1812, the Mexican War, Spanish-American War, and the Philippine insurgency combined. While there were no great and famous battles during the Cuban insurrection, the number of encounters was large and continuous. Maximo Gomez proved to be a capable leader, conducting swift marches of six hundred miles and fighting without letup. He employed cavalry raids, infantry attacks, artillery duels, and used logistical challenges to his advantage. However, Cubans failed to follow up successes, didn't maintain weapons, and wasted ammunition. They tended to react without plans, often in doubt about what would happen next.

Spanish soldiers were brave and patient but had little heart in the war. Diseases plagued both sides. Strategically, the Spanish erred by holding too many unimportant towns in the interior, rather than holding key ports and covering the country side with mobile troops. And their ponderous resupply columns to garrisons offered vulnerable targets for insurgent raids.

Fred Funston also learned important lessons about fighting, lessons that could never have been imparted at West Point.

§

In Funston's last cavalry charge in Cuba, his horse was hit and rolled over on him, pinning him against dirty splinters of a shattered tree stump. Large shards of wood dug deep into his hip, the larger pieces extracted by Cuban doctors, but surgery was needed to prevent infection that might kill him more painfully than the malaria that afflicted him, or another Spanish bullet. General Garcia reluctantly granted approval for him to return to the United States for medical care. Funston and Lieutenant James Penne, also ill, bid farewells and headed toward the northern coast, hoping to catch a filibustering steamer making a return trip to the United States. Funston and Penne carried with them safe-passage notes signed by Garcia in case insurgents stopped them—a death warrant if the Spanish found it.

First they were required to present themselves to the revolutionary republican government in Aguaro for permission to leave for health reasons, and to coordinate transit on a filibuster or scheduled steamer. Both were still officers commissioned in the Cuban army, and although Americans, they weren't permitted to leave at will. The Cuban Secretary of War denied permission, considering health insufficient reason—Cubans stayed until victory or death. They faced a serious dilemma—stay and die in a field hospital, or make a run for it. Garcia's pass might carry enough weight with a friendly ship's captain to allow them to board.

They chanced a run and headed out together on December 12th, 1897, riding toward the ocean on a dusty road along a raised railroad grade. Before them, the road veered sharply over the tracks. Funston spurred his horse and galloped ahead to scout the other side of the embankment, but when he crossed the tracks, he reined in abruptly. Directly in front were six Spanish soldiers with rifles aimed at him. He raised both hands high to warn Penne, who raced away. During animated protests, lies, and explanations, he opened his handkerchief to wipe his mouth. Garcia's pass was folded inside and he slipped it to his mouth, chewed and gulped. That note meant a certain firing squad.

Funston used his best Spanish to renounce all Cuban insurgents. He claimed to be tired, sick, and discouraged and trying to go home, which was actually true. His only protection was his verbal abilities of persuasion. He admitted he'd been with insurgents—too obvious to deny—but insisted he was sick of them and their methods, mentioned killing prisoners, and insisted he was deserting—technically all true. His story had enough validity to make them uncertain what to do, so he was bound hand and foot and taken to the Spanish headquarters at Puerto Principe. He told his story again to his enemy, General Castellanos, who convened a court martial. They could execute him, but the officers believed him and offered parole for an oath of non-aggression. He accepted and was transported by

Spanish ship to Havana where he sought the offices of the United States consul, Fitzhugh Lee, a former Confederate general.

Meanwhile, Lee had heard reports some Cubans intended to come to his office to assassinate him. Funston thoroughly surprised the old soldier when he appeared bedraggled, unshaved, and menacing. When Lee first saw Funston, he thought he was that assassin, grabbed his revolver to shoot in self-defense. Funston threw up his hands in surrender. "What do you want?" asked Lee.

Lee was surprised when Funston replied in English. "I have just come from General Gomez's camp suffering from a wound in the thigh," he said. "I want to leave Cuba. I want to go to the United States." When Lee asked him where he was from, he replied in his western drawl, "Kansas." Lee chuckled when he realized he was authentic, admitted he "had been a rebel once himself." But he knew he'd never looked as bad as this man did at that moment. Lee made arrangements for him to clean up and get into fresh clothes for a return trip to the United States, then helped him through a subterranean passage to the docks, where he boarded a steamship bound for New York.

Funston's war was winding down as disease and wounds drove him back to New York for medical care, then to his roots in Kansas to recuperate. His friend, Charles Gleed, had asked before he left for Cuba why he was joining their fight. Funston answered then, "For Free Cuba!" reciting the familiar battle cry. "Cuba must be cleaned up, and I am footloose and I may as well help as anyone else."

Twenty-three months later, Gleed was there to help retrieve him from a ship and gain admission into a hospital. Funston weighed only eighty pounds, still coughing blood. Gleed said he was "the most dilapidated young man in America, lame, and appeared to have suffered all the illnesses in the list."

From the hospital Funston penned a letter to Charles Scott in Kansas, confessing he had written several letters from Cuba but just discovered he never mailed them. He wrote again right after surgery, "A large rude surgeon ... has been stirring up my anatomy with a lot of stuff from a hardware store. I think he had knives, saws, monkey wrenches, crowbars and two or three other things...." And he complained many letters from friends were address to "Colonel ... I'd a whole lot rather be just plain Fred."

Fred Funston had risen from a naive civilian with no rank to lieutenant colonel in the Cuban army and chief of all eastern artillery. He had fought in twenty-two battles in the Cuban revolution before the United States even entered the Spanish-American War, had in fact, tried to stop him from going. Through all this, he was shot through the lungs, had one arm broken, contracted malaria, rolled under his horse bruising both legs and driving dirty splinters from a tree stump into a hip and thigh, and was nearly killed many other times. But he only needed time to recover—more feats lay ahead. Funston's spirit of high adventure was only heightened by his many close brushes with death.

EIGHT

On January 10, 1898, Fred Funston landed in New York wearing old tropical white ducking in a blinding snow storm with only six dollars in his pocket. He was in bad shape physically—wounds slow healing due to infection, racked with malaria and other ailments—eighty pounds and pale. He remained in a hospital for a month, paid by the Cuban junta in New York, where he rallied under sound care and strong medications. Despite his condition, he submitted to several newspaper interviews in those first days back. By April, he was anxious to disprove reports from those first interviews that he was physically wasted.

He returned to Kansas for rest and to regain his strength. His Cuban pay had been $220 per month and he collected the amount still owed, but that was nearly gone when he reached Kansas. He arrived broke, again, and without favorable prospects. He did receive offers from *Harper's Weekly* and *Cosmopolitan* for stories from Cuba, but needed time to process his thoughts and regain his health. Another alternative was paid lectures—faster than writing and more lucrative—at first, distasteful to him.

His weight was never over one hundred ten pounds, but he lost thirty in the bush with insurgents. In Iola, with family and Kansas friends, he enjoyed fresh vegetables, meat, and plenty of homemade pies. He always treasured his mother, and gave her the only souvenir he brought back from Cuba—the handkerchief that concealed his pass from Garcia, which he had swallowed. It remained a cherished keepsake to Ann.

Then the *USS Maine* exploded in Havana Bay! Politicians and yellow journalists alike stimulated passions for war with Spain to new heights. Fred believed American involvement could have been avoided, but now the course was set. His health improved quickly at home, but he had little hope for joining the war with Spain as an American soldier—twice rejected already—having failed to qualify for West Point or the New York National Guard.

William Allen White recalled when reporters and editors encouraged war in Cuba "without in the slightest affecting the reality of our lives...innocent of the fact that we were starting wars that would last far into the next century, threaten all that we loved and wreck much that we cherished. ... Our little immediate, intimate part of it came when Fred Funston sat around the big baseburner in our little parlor and told us about his adventures in Cuba. ... The story he told there at our fireside ... was a story that might have been told in the sixteenth or seventeenth century when an adventurer comes home from distant lands bringing the tales of his wonders to his admiring friends." He told his very personal story with "vast modesty ... debunking his own heroism."

He had become a sudden celebrity in Kansas and Billy White encouraged him to start that lecture tour locally to share the story he told in his parlor. University classmates set dates in their hometowns, beginning in Emporia at the First Presbyterian Church. Reporters said his two-hour lecture was "entirely devoid of any attempts at elocution and oratory," and he was "conversational, unstudied, unassuming, entertaining, and graceful." He arrived at Hamilton Hall, for the Elks Club in Topeka, in a carriage draped with a Cuban flag after meeting friends at the Copeland Hotel. He'd always enjoyed story-telling, but still coughed blood from his chest wound into a handkerchief.

Now seeing the lucrative potential of his lectures, he signed a contract with J.S. White of Kansas City to manage his tour for a percentage of billings. Paid lectures drew between $25 and $50, but he lectured free in churches to support mission funds, and in Odd Fellows Halls or Masonic Temples to help pay down their charitable debts.

The Populist Kansas Governor, John Leedy, heard one of the first lectures and thought it boring when Fred read from a prepared manuscript instead of speaking extemporaneously. Nevertheless, Leedy invited him to his office for a personal discussion and found him much more engaging in person. He was also testing his political aspirations considering "Foghorn Funston's" conservative views. In the end he decided he was a neutral warrior, not an ideological politician.

While he only engaged in a lecture tour to earn much-needed cash, it established him as a professional soldier and honorable war veteran, even without formal military education, training, or experience in the American army. He'd mastered combat arms and supporting services with actual experience, and familiarity with insurgents reinforced his natural distaste for pomp, pretentiousness, and position, unlike most Civil War veterans. He valued family and old friends, but was always open to make new friends. In the short run, he was biding time until that next call to action.

§

Kansas Governor Leedy came to power in an upswing for the Populist Party with an independent streak, sometimes creating fresh rules for governing. When Fred met with him after his lecture in Topeka and before declaration of war with Spain, Leedy was interested in sizing him up politically. When the President called for state volunteers—Kansas to provide three regiments of infantry, Leedy had doubts about the most logical candidate to command one. He'd read a complaint by a local woman who claimed she was treated rudely by Senator Harris of Kansas in Washington, but she'd thrown in gratuitous criticisms of the governor as well. Senator Harris' private secretary was William Sears, a brigadier general in the Kansas National Guard. Leedy blamed Sears for her criticism of him. So, he snubbed Sears and offered command of the first regiment to his secretary, Lieutenant Colonel Edward Little. But, Little was reluctant to command a regiment in combat, and declined, agreeing to command of a battalion instead. He suggested Funston for the regiment. The governor hesitated because of his father's politics, but Little argued keeping partisan politics out of the military selection process—a rule he had already violated in bypassing Sears.

Leedy sent a telegram to Funston's home requesting he come to Topeka, but Fred was lecturing at Fort Leavenworth. The telegram was forwarded there and he caught the next train to Topeka to meet with Leedy. The governor said he was bypassing National Guard organizations to build three new regiments from scratch. "I want you to command the first regiment," he said.

Fred realized the need for combat experience in units going to war, and he had that, but he knew his failings in basic military training, tactical drills, fundamentals, and formalities. Based on that, he disagreed with cutting out officers and men who already had military training. Sending raw recruits to be led by an untrained officer was a recipe for disaster. Leedy agreed to allow trained guardsmen to join the new organizations as individual volunteers, privates until they proved themselves, and only then if politically neutral.

Leedy said, "If you turn down the command, I'll appoint someone else. I need your decision quickly!" Fred knew he was best qualified, as he'd proven with all combat arms—artillery, infantry, and cavalry—could survive in the tropics, knew more about Cuba than most Americans, and spoke passable Spanish. But he was a realist about his lack of military training and knew he was unprepared to train a regiment from scratch.

But he'd never shirked a challenge, and said, "I'll accept your appointment as colonel of volunteers and command of a regiment", but was disappointed to learn it would not be in the island of Cuba, but the Philippine Islands.

Sears was upset when he learned of the article that led to his being by-passed, but he carried no grudge against Fred. In fact, he invited Fred to meet in the Topeka office of Senator Harris. He asked, "Have you studied any military books?" The army didn't yet publish official field manuals nor had the first field service regulations been written, so tactics and procedures books were generally written and published privately.

"No," said Funston honestly, "I've never read a single one."

Sears pulled several books from his shelves. "Here, take these and read them," he said as he began to write on a note pad on his desk. "And here's a reading list of other important books you should study and understand." Fred telegraphed Brentano's Booksellers in New York to have the others delivered "cash on delivery."

New regiments followed the lineage of the nineteen Kansas regiments in the Civil War. Therefore the first new one, Funston's, was designated the 20th Kansas Volunteer Regiment. Regular army regiments and volunteer regiments from states were filled with many Civil War veterans, especially among senior officers. Fred had one advantage over them—the Civil War involved fighting large units conventionally, or leading small cavalry detachments against Indians. He'd learned everything he knew of the art of war from a different perspective, as a guerrilla.

Key leaders in the regiment included Lieutenant Colonel Edward Little, with an extensive political resume as the private secretary to the governor, a former prominent Kansas lawyer, and United States consul-general to Egypt. Although without active military experience, he would command a battalion and serve as second-in-command of the regiment. The governor expected him to keep an eye open for political leanings. Majors commanded the other two battalions. Major Frank Whitman was a graduate of the U.S. Military Academy and currently a Second Lieutenant in the 2nd United States Infantry. Major Wilder Metcalf was a colonel in a disbanded National Guard regiment.

Funston began immediately to form and train the new regiment. When the governor called him to Topeka to formally present his commission as a volunteer colonel, he came straight from the field. He walked into the governor's executive chamber wearing muddy boots and a seedy civilian raincoat. His appearance that first day set the stage for his entire military career—muddy boots.

The regiment's officers were sent first to Kansas towns to recruit their own companies and battalions. Applicants were plentiful as Kansans shared the patriotic fervor that engulfed the nation. Former national guardsmen with experience took precedence if they met physical requirements and agreed to enlist as privates. Untrained recruits fleshed out the ranks.

Initial authorization was one thousand men, but a second call raised the total to thirteen hundred. The roster included three hundred former national guardsmen and sixty soldiers from the regular army. Company officers were elected, many comrades from the Civil War. Despite democratic methods, the end results satisfied Funston as former National Guard officers were chosen to command companies, and they appointed subordinate knowledgeable officers and non-commissioned officers. Three officers had Civil War experience, two were former enlisted soldiers from the regular army, and others had National Guard drill-time. But the regiment was filled with mostly untrained men led by a commander with no basic training.

The training challenge was greatest but he believed after several months of hard drills his men were good. Although some were discredited for misconduct, his method to eliminate an ineffective officer was to draw up both court martial charges and resignation papers, then give him a choice.

Once companies formed they were sent to Fort Leavenworth for clothing and equipment, and then to Topeka to camp at the State Fair Grounds in National Guard tents. A ceremony enrolling volunteer regiments into United States' service was set for May 13, 1898. As uniforms were in short supply, only those with National Guard or army-issued uniforms were allowed to stand in ranks. Funston was dismayed by the army's unpreparedness and contacted the War Department by telegram on May 8th, complaining about shortages of arms, ammunition, and uniforms.

He resided in a Topeka hotel and wore civilian clothes, not having an officer's uniform. He went to the fair grounds for the official ceremony but was halted by a tall sentinel in uniform, who informed him visitors weren't allowed. He announced he was the commander, not a visitor. The guard found this amusing and bent over to the short man in civilian clothes, and whispered, "Try the next sentry. He's easy." Exasperated, Funston summoned the officer of the guard to get in.

Three days after being federalized, the units marched to the Topeka railroad depot and boarded a Union Pacific train bound for San Francisco. However, the new regiment left without its commander. During his lecture at Fort Leavenworth, he'd met U.S. Army Colonel Hamilton Hawkins, who would command a brigade at the Battle of Santiago in Cuba; he was interested in Funston's experiences in Cuba and sent a letter to the War Department suggesting intelligence might be derived from an interview with him. Instead of accompanying his troops to San Francisco, Funston complied with a War Department telegram ordering him to Tampa where troops bound for Cuba were assembling.

§

Funston arrived in Tampa wearing civilian clothes, reported to General William Shafter, and was turned over to Lieutenant Colonel Arthur Wagner, his intelligence officer. He was expected to assist in planning for the invasion by contributing to a pamphlet about Cuba based on his experiences. Wagner questioned him at length and made copious notes for several days, however, the notes were of limited value since the planned

American campaign in Cuba would be near Santiago in the northwest of the island, not the southeast where Funston fought. Neither General Shafter nor General Miles was much interested in what he had to offer for those reasons, and were askance of his dress. When asked about that, he said, "I'd look pretty wouldn't I, trotting up and down in a colonel's rig, when all around are sure-enough soldiers—men who have fought their way up from the line in the regular army, who have been in the Civil War and in a score of Indian wars, who have the right to wear only a captain's or at most a major's uniform! Wouldn't I be a daisy, letting men like that salute me in soldier's clothes?"

He wasn't versed in military protocol around senior officers either, and junior officers were more interested in his combat accounts. Some questioned his artillery qualifications when he related how he employed guns in Gomez's army. Now, he saw an army going into Cuba unprepared, lacking experienced soldiers and officers, and realized a well-trained and equipped standing army was vital for national emergencies.

Arthur Wagner, the intelligence officer in Tampa, was a major change agent for the army. At the Infantry and Cavalry Service School at Fort Leavenworth he prepared two published seminal texts—*Organization and Tactics*, and *The Service of Security and Information*, both essential reading on the role of the army in national defense, education of officers, how to fight, and the over-riding importance of intelligence. Funston studied those from Sears' reading list as he prepared to lead a regiment, and he adhered to their tenets in the near and distant future.

He left Tampa in June to rejoin his regiment in San Francisco, traveling through Kansas to bid farewell to family and old friends. When his father, the Civil War veteran, asked him how he expected to command a regiment when he had no army training, he replied, "he had some books." Books always stood Fred in good stead, but noting in writing could prepare him for what lay ahead.

§

The 20th Kansas Volunteer Regiment traveled by trains to San Francisco. Many, who had not been issued new uniforms, traveled in summer clothing, including "ice cream" pants, seersucker coats, and linen dusters.

The bedraggled unit was a laughing stock when it first arrived. Funston traveled from Tampa, via Kansas, to San Francisco and found his regiment already in tents at Camp Merritt, in the western suburbs. He was pleased his commissioned officers were well educated, two-thirds with degrees from western universities, but the real strength was in top-notch enlisted men, who quickly learned to look and act like soldiers. But, he found as much disorder and confusion in San Francisco as he had in Tampa.

General Wesley Merritt was department commander and had his headquarters in the city. General Elwell Otis commanded Camp Merritt and lived there with the Independent Division of the Eighth Army Corps. "Miserable Camp Merritt," as men termed the place, had a magnificent view of the bay; it was a hastily built cantonment only four miles from city center and just north of Golden Gate Park, connected by a trolley line. City sanitation service was the only military justification for the site as a training center—city distractions too close to ignore. Sightseers, peddlers, and curious citizens were constantly seen at the camp of ten thousand men, mostly volunteers from western states. The 20th Kansas, 1st Tennessee and 51st Iowa Regiments were assigned to a brigade commanded by General Charles King. The division was a "feeder" organization to funnel manned, equipped, and trained regiments to the Philippines.

General Merritt, a veteran officer of the Civil War who commanded a division by age thirty, was considered kind and courteous; but General Elwell Otis, "Granny Otis," was different—civil and reserved, worked too hard, and took on details best left to subordinates, no sense of humor, and kept isolated in his office. James Blount, a southern statesman, described Otis as having the "mental caliber to command a one-company post in Arizona." Brigadier General King, commander of the volunteer brigade, was a medically retired active army captain, from a serious wound in the Indian wars. But he kept abreast of military affairs with a keen eye for detail and inspired others by his example. He was also a prolific novelist.

Many volunteers from western states were miserable at Camp Merritt because they had not been issued warm uniforms against cold winds and chilling fogs off the bay; blowing sand from beaches filled tents, clothing, and uncovered food. But easy access to street car lines brought visitors readily from the city, and tempted off-duty soldiers—mostly farm-boys and ranchers—to sample diverse enticements. However, San Franciscans were friendly and welcomed the troops. Camp Merritt was not ideal to prepare new volunteers for war. Space for tactical drills was limited there and at The Presidio, a former Spanish post, two miles away. But ships in San Francisco's bay reassured they'd be leaving soon for the tropics.

Funston was challenged preparing his regiment for battle in the city, but he tackled that as he had those in Death Valley, the Yukon, and Cuba—throwing all his energy, strength, and single-mindedness into it. By his delayed arrival from Tampa, primary training in guard duty, manual of arms, and close order drills was complete; some rudimentary battalion-level drills begun. Fortunately, Major Whitman, with his active army and West Point experience, was valuable as a trainer. Fred was a scrappy fighter in battle, but unprepared for prerequisite parade-ground tests.

He acquired an officer's uniform and studied military books, eager to learn details. His troopers responded to his personal style and storied past—his distinct limp a constant reminder their colonel was a combat veteran—yet he was a stickler for keeping the camp clean and neat. He closely followed progress of drills and quizzed men on details, checking their knowledge while learning from them. Kansans liked uniqueness of their colorful commander, such as his distinctive, multilingual profanity that spewed in torrents. But his stern temperament was mitigated by sympathy and understanding of their difficulties.

His presence set a tone for the regiment as accounts of his adventures circulated and were often embellished. Yet he was a simple farmer from Kansas like his hardy and loyal volunteers, and never pretended to be a polished West Pointer. The men of the 20th Kansas knew him that way and privately called him "Freddy." They knew Colonel Freddy would go out of his way to talk with anyone from Kansas, and inquiries about their food, training, accommodations, and news from home were genuine. They saw him slouch in the saddle like a cowboy instead of a rigid manikin. On parade, he rested his sword against his arm instead of his shoulder and they appreciated those small things as they did his condoning only competent officers to lead them. General Merritt saw rapid improvements of the regiment and publicly praised them.

§

Large quantities of cloth was suddenly available to dye army blue, cut, and sew into uniforms. But blue dye didn't hold and during sweaty drills, soldiers were also blued. Fortunately, this was resolved prior to the 4th of July parade, dreaded by soldiers because of cobblestone streets and lack of shade along the route.

The Independent Division was to march through San Francisco's streets on Independence Day. The 20th Kansas' deployment orders for the Philippines hadn't come, so their future remained uncertain—they'd have to march. Due to indecision, officers hadn't purchased mounts, but hired horses from local livery stables—some better trained than others. Fred got a horse so frisky it was barely controllable, similar to the one he rode to school in Kansas, but this one drew up lame on parade day. The only horse available was a "handsome black animal with arched neck and ugly eye."

As the 20th Kansas formed to march to the starting point on Market Street, Funston mounted his prancing charger. As soon as the band opened with the first notes, it bolted. "I might have tried to hold a cyclone," he recalled. The horse charged straight toward a tent and scraped him off under a fly in front. Thirteen hundred Kansas volunteers found this hilarious, but he considered himself lucky not to be impaled on his own saber. The horse ripped down the fly on top of them and both man and horse struggled to free themselves to peals of laughter. This before the parade even began.

The terrified horse cavorted to the starting point and more trouble as thousands of soldiers converged on the wide streets filled with blaring bands. Spectators were loud on the sidewalks, and unrestrained hooligans tossed firecrackers to excite soldiers and horses. Officers on horseback were fair game, despite the danger of raring horses in crowds of spectators on the curbs, but police made no attempts at control. At the head of his regiment, Funston on his skittish horse was a prime target for thugs with "cannon crackers." His horse darted from side to side and reared, until a hooligan made a bad throw, then lit another and ran with the burning firecracker to toss it under Funston's horse. He saw him coming.

"Right then and there murder came into my heart, and I made a hard and conscientious effort to kill him." He slashed with his saber. A desperate leap backwards spared the ruffian from a severed artery or decapitation. "I deeply regretted my failure," said Funston, willing to take his chances with a jury. Before the parade ended, his left arm was so tired from trying to control his horse that he sheathed his saber to use both hands on the reins. "I have been in but few battles in which I would not rather take my chances than to repeat that performance."

While Funston was getting more comfortable in the saddle of leadership, he still lacked something important in his life. Despite all he'd been through, he was still a boy at heart, full of adventure, fearless in the face of danger, yet he missed having someone to share life. He had fallen in love every few months in college and was discouraged about his prospects when he heard of his college friends marrying while he whiled away in Cuba. Life was good, but he needed a partner. That seemed virtually impossible as his regiment waited to deploy to a distant shore. But fortune had always smiled on Fred Funston….

NINE

The 20th Kansas drilled and waited impatiently for orders to deploy. Admiral Dewey sank the Spanish fleet and berthed his ships in Manila Bay, although the old walled city of Manila had not fallen to Americans or Filipino guerilards. Regiments sailed away, but those from Kansas, Iowa, and Tennessee chafed at Camp Merritt until moving to Camp Merriam on The Presidio Reservation, nearer the port. Training progressed to regimental-sized drills and Fred Funston was glad his voice was strong enough to make commands across the parade field. But he was so unschooled on drill and ceremonies he didn't always know if his orders were actually being followed.

One sunny day, the 20th Kansas was on the parade field as local citizens gathered to watch drills. He spotted one young woman on the sidelines standing with her gray-bearded father, and his adventurous heart skipped. He had been rejected repeatedly by beautiful women, but this time he hoped was different. He pointed her out to a Kansas friend and swore "he was going to marry that woman." He didn't even know her name was Eda Blankart.

Soldiers at drill were entertainment for people of the bay area and the notion they were going across the Pacific to fight against Spain made it that much more exciting. It wasn't coincidence that brought Otto Blankhart and his daughter to The Presidio that sunny day, but a chance to catch a glimpse of a Kansas man who had already made a name for himself in Colorado, Death Valley, the Yukon Territory, and Cuba. Gossip led to reviewing of published articles, which drove them to see for themselves. Just a glimpse—something to write in a diary, something besides music for a young woman with feelings. But he was shorter ... and older.

Most evenings after training were free at The Presidio, and San Francisco offered theaters, restaurants, and other opportunities, some more risqué, for soldier's to mingle with friendly local folks. Fred Funston was too busy training a regiment for war and seldom availed such opportunities. Ladies of both cities sent cakes and pies, even flowers, for troops in training—generously supporting them and, perhaps, hoping for something more. Fred's job was to keep his rowdy men focused more on fighting than fun.

Once he was inspecting guards when he saw Private John Steele walking post with one of the ladies' bouquets pinned to his blouse. General King approached as Fred yelled, "Steele, take that damned thing off!" Steele was rattled by so much high level scrutiny. He snapped to attention and saluted. King walked past, shaking his head. But when Funston left, flower petals were scattered over the sidewalk.

When Generals Merritt and Otis and King departed for Manila, Funston was made acting commander of the brigade of three regiments—Kansans, Iowans, and Tennesseans. Companies regularly practiced on ranges with live ammunition and on tactical fire and maneuver drills used blanks. Now in control, Funston drilled them even harder in preparation for war.

Then stunning news arrived—the Spanish-American war was over! Interest in daily drills waned along with hope of seeing action. During this uncertain time before deployment, men physically unfit for service were discharged and others released for personal reasons. Several officer replacements were lifted from enlisted ranks based on superior performance. But, those who wanted to deploy overseas, most of them volunteers, now assumed they'd be returning to the boredom of farming.

By October, the brigade was still mired at The Presidio undergoing spiritless daily grinds expecting orders to return to Topeka, Des Moines, or Nashville to be mustered out. Orders came, but not for Kansas—for Manila on the *SS Indiana* departing on October 27th. Time, which had seemed endless before, was suddenly short—and couldn't have come at a worse time for Fred Funston.

§

In the land of earthquakes, the world had shifted under Fred Funston in San Francisco. During that drill day at The Presidio he'd seen that stunning young woman on the sidelines of the parade field with an older man, apparently her father. However, there'd been no opportunity to meet her as it was considered forward and inappropriate to simply ride over and introduce himself. As the Blankhart's were intellectuals and had social standing in the communities of both Oakland and San Francisco, they were generally aware of Fred Funston's earlier exploits from newspaper and magazine coverage, plus the rumor mill of polite society. Curiosity was as much a reason for their visit to The Presidio that day, as enjoyment of watching men in training for battle—neither father nor daughter expected causal eye contact to go beyond that. Neither did Fred Funston.

Fred and Eda first met at a Sunday gathering at the Belvedere estate of Mr. C.O. Perry, a prominent San Francisco banker. Fred never placed much stock in college fraternal connections, but he and Perry were both members of the Phi Delta fraternity at the University of Kansas, although different years. Perry invited him to come to fulfill his fraternal obligations, but also to add a colorful character to a stuffy social occasion. Eda Blankhart had already attended two of these socials as a guest, chaperoned by her mother—an acceptable way for young ladies to meet respectable men—while Fred was always prevented by duties with the regiment. This one time, he relented and accepted the invitation.

He spotted Eda, the girl he had seen at the parade field, standing on the pier with her mother and younger sister, Mattie. They were all waiting to catch a ferry to Perry's estate for the afternoon tea party. He remembered her from The Presidio parade field and his heart skipped again at destiny's intervention. He'd said he found her "a stunner" then, and she was even more stunning this close. As they talked, he discovered they had much in common—like him, she was well-read, including his favorite Kipling poems and stories, she was conversant with politics like his father, a musician like his mother, and she was a Presbyterian. Fred ignored his history of rejection by beautiful women and mapped out a campaign to win over the lovely, dark-eyed debutant. First, he secured Mrs. Blankart's permission to call on her at home, and he called as often as possible in the few weeks he had left before shipping out.

Eda was enchanted by his old-fashioned ways and electrifying charms behind a handsome face, small frame, and polite manner. Although he was eleven years older, she only twenty-four, and three inches shorter, she was drawn to his presence, sensing something about this man that could change her life.

Like him, she was born in the mid-west and moved to California with her family when she was only weeks old. Her parents—Otto and Theresa Blankart—were well-to-do Germans—her mother actually a French Huguenot exiled to Germany. Both were musicians and taught music in San Francisco. Otto had studied violin in Mannheim and played second violin with the Jean Becker Quartette before moving to Illinois. In San Francisco they opened a music studio on Geary Street before moving to Oakland. Otto Blankart organized San Francisco's first string quartet while teaching in his studio and presented a long sequence of musical recitals. Theresa had studied piano in East Konigsberg, East Prussia, until contracting typhoid fever, limiting her ability to withstand the strain of competitive performance. Now she taught music at California College and continued there for twenty years.

Eda was also talented with the violin and piano. Newspapers described her as "a woman of marked beauty, great strength of character and a high degree of culture as a musician," with dark eyes and broad attractive facial features. She frequently played the violin at concerts or musicales in San Francisco and Oakland. At first glance, she appeared to be an unlikely companion to Fred Funston. She was vivacious, lively, and a refined member of upper-class social circles, and she wore flats when she was with him to not eclipse him in size.

During Fred's frequent visits to their 10th Avenue home in Oakland, he moved quickly. He had to—when deployment orders arrived, he was to sail in one week. On his third Sunday visit, he asked Eda to go for a walk and as they strolled along the shady, tree-lined avenue, he proposed. She said, "No!" But she confided in her mother and confessed she was in love with him, but rejected him due to their brief acquaintance and courtship—"How would it look?" She said, "I intend to wait for his return from the Philippines, and then if we feel the same way, I'll consider it."

Fred had been rejected before and was determined to overcome this one. On the following Sunday, he brought reinforcements—Major and Mrs. Wilder Metcalf, Lieutenant Colonel Little, Captain Clark and several other Kansans who could testify on his qualities and sincerity. Fred and Eda slipped away for another walk around the block while his friends vouched for him with Mrs. Blankart. This time he was more convincing with Eda while his teammates set the stage at home. Hand in hand, Fred and Eda announced their intentions to marry to everyone in the Blankart home—Theresa Blankhart, Eda's sisters, and Fred's friends. "It was a pretty sudden thing to all of us," Theresa Blankart admitted. "Though we had known Colonel Funston but a very short time, he never had any opposition from any of us. He was the most unassuming young man I ever saw.... He never talked about himself.... I could trust the future of my daughter with him, and I told him so."

Funston was to sail on October 27th. Theresa Blankart was alone to consider her middle daughter's surprise decision while Otto was in the east on business. She quickly arranged a quiet wedding at home for October 25th with the Reverend R.F. Coyle, minister of the First Presbyterian Church, presiding. Funston's good friend, Vernon Kellogg, professor of entomology at nearby Stanford, received an urgent telegram and made the hurried trip to stand as Funston's best man. Only those few, the original group of officers and a few of the Blankart's closest friends, attended the brief evening ceremony beneath a canopy of American flags, surrounded by stacks of arms, bunting, and pink flowers. Eda was adorned in a white organdie gown trimmed with white satin lace and ribbons and carried a bouquet of pink roses with one in her hair. Her younger sister, Mattie, was maid-of-honor. Despite the few people invited, society columnist from Oakland and San Francisco caught wind of the celebrity wedding and turned up on time at 10th Avenue in Oakland. The Funston's only escaped briefly, their honeymoon curtailed until they were reunited in Manila. Theresa Blankart recalled, "Though Colonel Funston was so quiet and unassuming, he was ardent as a suitor, reminding one of that other Lochinvar—so dauntless in love and so famous in war."

Otto Blankart tried, but couldn't make it home in time for the wedding or to say farewell to his new son-in-law. Although his romance with Eda Blankhart unfolded so quickly, Fred Funston had no misgivings—his best decisions always those he acted on without deliberation. "This was by all odds the smartest thing I ever did in my life," he said, prescient understanding of how this remarkable young lady would add to his future.

§

War never pauses for affairs of the heart, especially not a heart that beats for excitement and adventure, and not for a young woman who cast her lot with a soldier. When the *Indiana* sailed on schedule with regimental headquarters and the 2nd and 3rd battalions of Kansas volunteers, a huge crowd gathered on the dock to see them off on an eight thousand mile journey to Manila. After society columns covered the sudden union of Fred Funston and Eda Blankhart, the crowd was larger than usual, hoping to catch a glimpse of the prominent couple. Standing in the crowd was Mrs. Eda Blankart Funston, waiting for her absent father to return and give his blessing before she followed her new husband to the war zone. The Spanish-American War was officially over so no one aboard or dockside expected any real fighting, but that didn't diminish the excitement and anticipation of sailing overseas.

The Red Cross Society furnished luncheon as a send-off for the troops and requested Colonel Funston line up his men to eat before boarding. He refused, insisting preparations to sail must be kept on schedule. Instead the mid-westerners "double-banked" sandwiches for secret picnics with local sweethearts, sneaking kisses among stacks of freight on the pier. Funston escorted Eda and a few others to the ship, away from chaos on the docks, for private farewells. As he led up the gangplank he was confronted by a sailor guarding the portal to the ship. Fred ordered him to stand back. The guard refused. Funston swung a roundhouse and "laid him low," which created considerable excitement among gentile ladies and lurking correspondents. Soldiers also took notice. Fred huddled with Eda on the bridge for several private minutes like many others bidding long and passionate goodbyes. Suddenly he shouted to soldiers, "Say what you have to say, men, and say it quick!" Eda laid a gentle hand on his shoulder and whispered in his ear. He looked up meekly and again shouted, "You can take a little more time to say it!"

Finally, with soldiers on board and visitors back on the dock, General Merriam concluded his inspection and the *Indiana* glided from berth and pointed her bow to the Golden Gate with assistance of the tug *Sea King*. Eda Funston boarded the tug *Liberty* chartered by the Catholic Truth Society and rode alongside as far as The Presidio. She caught her last glimpse of her colonel as he stood on the windy bridge. The *Indiana* outpaced the tugs and raced for open seas under a fast bell, rigging thick with adventure-minded soldiers, starry eyes fixed on receding landmarks of home and recent girlfriends. A final salute was fired from The Presidio's big guns and the 20th Kansas sailed for the battle lines of Manila. Eventually, after a stop in Hawaii, the *Indiana* crept past Corregidor Island guarding the entrance to Manila Bay on November 30. Meanwhile, the *Newport*, with Eda aboard, was already underway at sea chasing a life time of shared adventures.

§

Several wives sailed on the *Newport* along with Eda—including those of Major Whitman, Captain Buchan, Chaplain Schliemann, and Lieutenant Haussermann. Eda had not been ready to sail on such short notice when Fred departed two days after their wedding, so she caught the next expedition, with War Department approval, and with the 1st Battalion of Kansans on November 8th. This afforded her time to see her father, Otto, since he had missed the wedding excitement. He gave his blessing.

Smedley Butler, a marine officer and future general nicknamed "Old Gimlet Eye," sailed on the *Newport* a few months later and described the ship as an asthmatic, broken-down old transport on its last legs. His voyage broke down twice between San Francisco and Honolulu and had to lie in the trough of a heavy sea for thirty-six hours each time. It was not a pleasant cruise for Butler but may have been only slightly less traumatic for Eda. Nevertheless, it was a grand adventure for a bride heading to a battle zone. She later skillfully reported on her experiences traveling to Manila aboard the *Newport* and her other observations while in the Philippines for *Cosmopolitan Magazine*.

§

Frederick Funston went ashore in Manila on December 1, 1898, to pay respects to General Elwell Otis, former commander of the Pacific Division and now VIII Corps. The corps occupied positions surrounding Manila using trenches prepared and occupied for months by Filipinos. Otis informed Funston his regiment could not disembark until a decision was made about which command they would be assigned. Also, there were insufficient barracks ashore until more were acquired, so Funston spent another week in cramped quarters on the *Indiana*. After a week, they disembarked to report to the first brigade, second division. On December 5th, the situation improved for Fred when the *Newport* docked with his first battalion and Eda, along with thirteen other American women. Funston first paid his respects to General Marcus Miller, brigade commander and veteran of the Civil War and Indian wars, and then struck out to find his young bride and her baggage. After comparing quarters, they returned to his slightly more comfortable quarters on the *Indiana*.

Next day, their first together, Fred and Eda set out early aboard a launch with Major and Mrs. Frank Whitman, to find adequate dwelling ashore. Funston had been looking for a place but was not satisfied. He and Whitman believed pooling funds could gain a more spacious place and be better for their wives with company in the house. The navy launch chugged up the Pasig River, skirting long native canoes and canopy-covered dugouts until docking at a stone quay near a broad, busy, paved street. They climbed into a two-wheeled carriage pulled by a small native pony, artfully dodging colorful vehicles on streets as narrow as the sidewalks. They found an American living in Ermita who had properties and rented them a suitable house. Eda was delighted it had a view of the Luneta, a bay-side park where Manila's elite promenaded in the evenings in Spanish tradition. But they had to wait another week in the hot confines of the *Indiana* before the roomy house was available to occupy.

Meanwhile, Fred was nagged by billeting shortages for his troops, as he was with his personal quarters. When arrangements were finally made, troops were drawn up the Pasig River in native boats pulled behind tugs, then poled up the muddy canals, and spread out into dispersed barracks. Headquarters and 2nd Battalion were in a large Spanish colonial administrative building in the Binondo district. The 3rd Battalion was housed in another warehouse in Tondo along with the recently arrived 1st Battalion on the *Newport*, until moved to a tobacco warehouse in Tondo. Battalions were separated but within minutes of each other. The Binondo district was the most disreputable of Manila and a likely flash point for trouble. Then, a smallpox epidemic broke out despite pre-deployment inoculations, and several men died, alarming the entire command. Fred moved them out of the barracks for weeks of airing, cleaning, and sanitizing. Despite rumors of trouble, men were chagrined by constant sentinel duties, broken only by barracks details and constant drills. Like their commander, they came to fight.

Fred and Eda escaped the stifling ship by moving into Funston's more comfortable commander's office in the barracks. Eda and Florence Whitman slept on folding army cots in the commander's office while Fred and Frank bunked in bachelor officer quarters. While they were busy with the regiment, the ladies were confined to the small space, gazing out the windows to take in local scenery. In three days, they moved into the house on Calle San Luis. There the ladies were busy taking pony-drawn cabs to scour Chinese shops for household goods and furnishings. Two Chinese servants cleaned and decorated, while Eda and Florence got acquainted with surly shopkeepers and pungent smells and steamy heat of Manila.

Then bad news hit. Higher authorities noticed the regimental and battalion commander living too far away and directed they move closer. By the end of December, they packed again to move to a new residence on Calle Analogue, three blocks from the barracks in Binondo. This house was even larger, and Fred's battalion commander and friend Major Wilder Metcalf plus the regimental adjutant, Lieutenant Walker, and quartermaster, Lieutenant Hull, all moved in with them. Chinese servants moved with them too, and by Christmas of 1898, Fred and Eda enjoyed a relatively normal life, including Kansas-style dinners and California cuisine at home—all with a Filipino-Chinese flavor.

The officers' orderlies and their horses also resided in the large house and courtyard, which included space for a pair of little Philippine bays Eda acquired to pull her small Victoria carriage through the narrow streets of Manila. The carriage was so small that when the top was set, she removed the seat cushion to sit upright. The *caramoto*, as Filipinos knew it, was frequently about town with Eda and Florence on a shopping spree during the day or with Fred and Eda sporting about after 5:00 p.m. In the evenings the happy couple often returned to the Luneta to join the promenades, listen to serenades by a regimental band, or simply stroll in gentle breezes off Manila Bay. Eda especially appreciated the sun setting across the bay, painting water and ships with undulating hues of color—reminding her of home, and painting, and music.

But as life seemed to offer the excitement she'd hoped for, she saw subtle changes in the attitudes of Filipino merchants, and pedestrians in town were growing surlier day-by-day. Paradise began to look a little rocky.

§

The navy frequently provided entertainment aboard ships in the harbor and Eda especially enjoyed the small social gatherings with other Americans—a reminder of San Francisco with extra pleasure. Gatherings of officers, diplomats, and their ladies were the height of societal activity for Eda and Florence Whitman. But during such tranquil times Fred considered the next phase of his life—marriage had changed the terms. His volunteer commission was indefinite and business prospects in the Philippines were more appealing than a Mexican coffee plantation. Eda told him she was certain he "could make a mint of money with timber, minerals, hemp, sugar, and tobacco produced in the islands." They hadn't discussed long range plans when they courted feverishly in Oakland, but Eda was determined not to have children until they "settled into a proper station of life." She found army life more exciting than business and encouraged him to pursue a regular army commission—and encouraged her family to subtly support her. She loved Fred, but was critical of his table manners and social etiquette—she could work on those. Another concern was regular drinking at the officer's mess, but this more disturbed her father, and his. She actually encouraged him to be socially active at the Manila Army-Navy Club. Fred couldn't fathom a single fault with Eda, and still considered marrying her, "the smartest thing he ever did."

He was happy in marriage, but never forgot he was a soldier, never lost sight of why he was there, or that the military situation was deteriorating. He was aware of Filipino's desire for independence and stayed attuned to treaty negotiations in Washington. Support for Cuban insurgents had made him sympathetic with the quest for freedom, but he would do his duty as an American soldier—political failures could rupture Philippine-American relations. The future swung on ambivalence in Washington, not aggressiveness in Manila. Meanwhile, General Otis formed fighting formations instead of administrative organizations. The clock was ticking—the time for volunteers to rotate home fast approached. But instead of redeployment orders, they were reorganized to fight.

General Otis concluded the Philippine center of gravity was northern Luzon—vital of the seven thousand islands which "dangled from Luzon like the tail of a kite." Luzon, central to his spring campaign, contained Manila and Malolos, the insurgent capital and was also the commercial center, shipping base, and vital business hub. The rebel army was primarily in Luzon along with its commander-in-chief, Emilio Aguinaldo. The Manila-Dagupan railway was the only modern transportation route to supply an army in the field other than on the backs of mules. The intellectual and industrial population was in Luzon—the focus of upcoming operations.

The new brigade commander was Brigadier General Harrison Gray Otis, editor and owner of the *Los Angeles Times*. This Otis, not to be confused with the corps commander Elwell Otis, had served in the Civil War in the same regiment with President McKinley. The Second Division was commanded by Major General Arthur MacArthur, distinguished in the Civil War as a regimental commander at the age of twenty and awarded the Medal of Honor at Missionary Ridge. MacArthur's division had two brigades, H.G. Otis's and another commanded by Brigadier General Irving Hale of Colorado, a future founder of the Veterans of Foreign Wars.

MacArthur didn't like politicians or journalists but was most comfortable around soldiers—officers or enlisted. He eschewed the press and was reluctant to grant interviews. He established headquarters in the prestigious San Miguel district in the former home of Admiral Montojo, commander of the sunken Spanish fleet, and studied everything published about Asia with a standing order for new books with Kelly Booksellers in Hong Kong. Funston admired MacArthur's broad military knowledge and experience, aware of his own lack of military training, but MacArthur knew Funston's background and treated him almost as a son.

MacArthur's Second Division manned an arc of outposts north and northeast of Manila. Regiments were housed in the city, except the 1st Nebraska in Santa Mesa. The division linked with the First Division under Major General Thomas Anderson in the south, Manila Bay and the Pasig River to marshes on the north. The 20th Kansas made the link at the marshes and extended to Manila-Dagupan Railway. At the railroad, they connected with the 3rd U.S. Army Artillery, fighting as infantry, under Major William Kobbe.

Funston kept seventy men on the outposts over a six hundred yard front on alert twenty-four hours a day. The railroad and a wagon road cut through his lines at right angles, complicating security. The road was lined with nipa houses, trees, and gardens obstructing the view. The standoff couldn't last indefinitely and there would certainly be trouble due to McKinley's decision to keep the islands—the only question, when and where. The situation was explosive with the 20th Kansas at the flash point.

American troops were under strict orders to bear insults and threats in silence, and not take the initiative. Yet they were targets, and they were in close contact, even as unarmed Filipinos were allowed to cross lines in and out of the city. Eda Funston noticed natives becoming gruffer and less helpful during shopping expeditions but life continued as normal.

§

Fred wrote his mother when Eda reached in Manila, informing her of that and what his regiment was doing to guard the city, the sights—including the largest cigar factory in the world. He assured her food from the commissary was almost as good as in Kansas, except milk and butter couldn't be found. Then he asked her to assure Mr. Winchester from Iola that his son, who was seasick on the voyage, was quite recovered.

Eda also wrote to her mother about her love for Fred and the high regard everyone had for him. "General MacArthur said he was just the kind of man the army needs," and as he was a volunteer, asked "if he would command his regiment in the march on Malolos." She wrote that Fred assured him he would "always go where duty called." MacArthur asked if he was afraid to go into the hottest part of the conflict. "Fred replied, more than before I was married." Then in the margin, she scribbled, "There! Dewey has just sent another shell beyond Caloocan."

In a later letter, she described an invitation from Admiral Dewey to visit *Olympia* for a social occasion. Major Whitman was ill and Fred had duties so neither could attend, but Eda and Florence Whitman were anxious to go as there were few socials in Manila. Fred accompanied them to the ferry where naval officers transported them to the command ship. Captain Whiting met them on the *Olympia* and introduced Admiral Dewey—who monopolized Eda—and invited them to return the following Sunday. Dewey told them "when inevitable fighting starts, you are welcome to bring their trunks to the *Olympia*." She continued about that, "I am just as anxious for a fight as Fred is and am not the least afraid. It is really most interesting and exciting to think that this will be—or is—all history, and I am helping to make it." She concluded by asking for a corset and her hair curling tongs. She also told her sister, "He wants to please me and make me happy.... Major and Mrs. Whitman laugh at him because he does everything just as I want it. I have only to say and it is done. I hope he will always be that way."

Approximately two hundred fifty American women were in the Philippines, including fifty nurses, most others military or diplomat wives. Eda was established as a leading lady among them—also with senior officers and many young and lonely lieutenants. There were no operas or theaters to attend, but teas, impromptu dances, charades, riding, boating, naval parties, promenades, and band concerts on the Luneta served pleasantly. *The American*, a local English language newspaper, and a subscription to the *Kansas City Star* and *Iola Register*, which arrived in infrequent bundles on mail ships, kept them informed. One of Dewey's shells, or the crack of a rifle, was a reminder they were in Manila, not San Francisco or Topeka.

§

Christmas was tense in Manila. Natives scoffed at Americans living in lowly warehouses—Spaniards always confiscated the finest facilities for themselves. Americans guarded all property, not just their own, a sign of weakness in the minds of those accustomed to brutal occupation. Meanwhile, Filipinos used terror tactics learned from the Spanish, including assassinations, to keep their own people in line.

In early January 1898, Funston, with Lieutenant Colonel Little, Major Metcalf, Captains Bishop and Boltwood, mounted for a reconnaissance along the road toward Caloocan. One hundred yards beyond friendly lines, they approached a Filipino outpost and requested to see the officer of the day. They were led half a mile further, not realizing then they were seeing terrain they would soon fight over. They relinquished swords and revolvers to the Filipino officer and were allowed to proceed through Caloocan, past a church which would be the objective of an assault in a month.

To fight complacency from repetitive drills and false alarms, Funston ordered men to hold three hundred rounds of ammunition in their knapsacks and canteens filled with water—he made random checks for compliance. As division officer-of-the-day he studied the entire line of defenses and checked friendly and enemy trenches, venturing close to insurgent lines—impatient to get on with the inevitable fight.

§

Trouble exploded at a stone bridge over the San Juan River in the 1st Nebraska Regiment's sector. On the night of February 4, 1899, Fred and Eda retired in the large house they shared with the Whitman's, Major Metcalf, and their orderlies. A quiet evening of reading brought early sleep, until Metcalf startled them, pounding on their bedroom door. "Come on out, Colonel! The ball has begun!" Tranquility became confusion and excitement. Private Todd Wagoner of F Company wrote, "The air was full of war, the big ball was about to roll. We had been brought here—for what purpose we knew not."

Fred quickly dressed but in the dark couldn't find his jacket and one boot. Eda scampered to help. He quickly managed a complete uniform, including sword and pistol, and dashed into the hall, shouting to orderlies "Saddle the horses! Hurry!" Metcalf led him to the window and they listened to the rattle of Mausers, no mistaking that sound. A clatter, erratic at first, swelled to a steady roar mixed with anxious shouting, doors and windows slammed shut, and people running through the streets. As suddenly as it began, the city fell completely quiet—the eye of a storm.

Orderlies brought horses around while hurried good-byes were spoken. Fred told Eda, "The fighting has started, but don't worry, it won't get past the outpost line. Stay here!" Then he rushed to the sound of gunfire. Men pressed through streets to regimental stations, infantry companies forming with barely stifled excitement. Funston later recalled, "But as they heard the ominous sound borne to their ears, I will warrant there was not one of them who begrudged the dreary months of drill at San Francisco."

Shortly, Burt Mitchell returned to tell Eda and Florence, "Prepare to go to the barracks, ladies. It will be safer there." Eda quickly packed a few belongings, a toothbrush, towels and necessities in a small case and instructed Chinese live-in servants on maintaining the residence. Eda and

Florence left with soldiers sent to escort them to the Kansas barracks, not knowing "whether for a few hours or forever."

On the way to the barracks, they passed a battalion marching to the front. Major Frank Whitman led—as commander, he had risen from his sick bed to lead them with a revolver in hand. He leaned from his horse and kissed Florence, whispering a fond goodbye. As he rode away, she called, "Be careful, Frank," as she was hurried along. Sergeant J.O. Morse wrote, "I thought how much harder was the part of these two women than that of the colonel and the major. And how much harder, too, for the women at home the fight would be than for the men who did the fighting."

Booming guns of the *Monadnock* sent shock waves through the air from the bay as shimmering signal flares lit the eerie scene. "I shall never forget that walk to the barracks," Eda recalled. "Every step seemed to add a century to my life." The barracks were quiet inside, except for the sound of firing along the lines and the clicking of telegraph keys next door. "I sat day and night at the operator's elbow, dreading, yet insisting on learning every bit of news."

While Eda and Florence Whitman settled, other ladies marveled at how Eda had presence of mind to remember to bring essentials, even a toothbrush, at such a time. "I watched Fred and how he's always ready at a moment's notice. We keep an emergency checklist in our heads." Sergeant Morse led them to a room and told them to "make themselves comfortable." The long sixteen by nine foot room was home for three months. In the center stood a "table strewn with books, magazines, cigarettes, matches, and articles distinctly masculine." A straw wall tapestry was pinned with photographs, shelves lined the other wall and a curtain served as a closet. White mosquito netting was the most important feature of the space. Additional folding cots were set up for seven ladies in a room for three sergeants. As soldiers returned from the front lines, Eda interviewed each of them for news. Then Mrs. Jesse Haussermann had her piano brought into Funston's office, now their parlor, and Eda sent for her violin to while away days and nights with music … while waiting….

§

While battalions assembled, dressed, and formed for movement, Funston climbed to the roof of the headquarters to observe fighting in front of the Second Division. The First Division was not yet engaged, but would be by daybreak. An order from brigade directed the regiment to proceed at once with two battalions to reinforce the outpost line. Funston left the 1st battalion in Manila as reserve.

Private Todd Wagoner of F Company said, "In the warm barracks quite a number of us had discarded our heavy woolen shirts and were unprepared for the hasty order to buckle on our cartridge belts, fill our haversacks with ammunitions and proceed at double time to the scene of action." The 2nd and 3rd battalions marched in column along Calle Lemeri in the dark, approaching the fighting. A one-gun battery of Utah artillery followed to support. Captain Adna Clark and Lieutenant Krause were on outpost and had acted promptly to first shots fired; their seventy men were fully alert when fire first struck their positions and returned it immediately. Todd Wagoner recalled going forward that "everyone seemed to be stooping toward the ground in search of something he had recently lost—and it might have been a piece of his nerve!"

Wagoner continued, "I can see our little colonel standing there with arms folded as he gave the order to go. He remarked as we started: 'Boys, you've got a nasty fight ahead of you, but I know you are good for it.'" Normally Funston spoke with a quiet voice but on the firing line he was loud and clear. As his column of a thousand reinforcements reached the front, Mauser rounds split the air overhead and thudded into the sides of nipa huts, roofs, and trees. Initial excitement faded with silence replacing chatter as unseasoned troops heard messengers of death whispering. Funston realized, "it was a new world for all but a few of them."

Meanwhile the reserve battalion in Manila was challenged by snipers and bolo-welding insurgent infiltrators, determined to take over the barracks and slaughter Americans. This was within easy earshot of ladies huddled inside the Kansas headquarters, holding their breaths and waiting for news.

Burt Mitchell, Funston's aide and first cousin from Iola, wrote home, "When the firing commenced ... I was sent to escort the wife of Colonel Funston and another lady down to the Kansas barracks in Manila, where they have remained ever since. The next day the regiment got to the firing line.... It was my first experience under fire, and when the bullets began to drop all around, my legs began to shake and my natural inclination was to dodge, but when I saw Fred riding up and down the firing line as if on dress parade it seemed to give us all confidence and we braced to the work wonderfully." Captain Bishop also wrote, "Colonel Funston realized that success depended on haste, and as he hurried up and down the line...we realized that we had the bravest colonel that ever led a regiment...."

At the front, Funston ordered the Utah cannoneers to set up in the road and return fire. He placed one company to the left of the road and three on the wider right side, ensuring the flank touched the boundary along the railroad tracks. He kept a battalion in reserve. Firing was intense from both sides for two hours before it slackened. Funston advised those not on sentry duties to sleep—morning would bring a new situation. Filipinos slung some artillery from captured Spanish pieces at them during the night, but morale was high, having made their first combat. Funston enjoyed camaraderie with men in action and laughed with them when they joked, calling "High Ball!" or "Low Ball" at the Filipino's ineffective artillery. He knew he could do better; he did far better in Cuba.

TEN

When shooting started, Funston led on horseback to the outposts. As he neared railway barns a loud blast sounded a half-mile ahead and a large cannon ball struck the ground in front, bounced into the air and passed low overhead, ripping through nipa huts like a cyclone. Before daylight, thirty-eight similar shots barreled in but caused no casualties. Later that gun was captured, a bronze, muzzle-loading Spanish siege gun over sixty years old. The shells were solid shot and had one landed among advancing columns could have taken out many men. Kansas men prayed their commander's historic invincibility protected them, too.

Those already on outposts defended for an hour as reinforcements marched through such shells and bullets. New troops dispersed along the line, finding cover behind rice dikes, taking turns catching shut-eye, although constant fire from cannons and rifles growled incessantly.

By daybreak firing diminished and two field pieces of the Utah artillery battalion were hauled up by hand to fire at the big Spanish gun. Funston and Major Richard Young were standing in the road talking when the big gun fired a shell in their direction. It came in low, snapped off a banana stalk near one of the Utah guns and plowed through.

Captain William Bishop's company was just right of the road when Private Charles Pratt was struck in the head with a Mauser round, first of the regiment to die in combat. Kansans were spared heavy combat in their first outing, but Funston got busy preparing for worse, checking artillery placements and reviewing infantry fields of fire, encouraging leaders and men, and verifying everything.

The brigade commander also checked and visited the regiment several times as he trooped the lines. The 1st Battalion, released from reserve, rejoined under temporary command of Captain Frederick Buchan. Lieutenant Colonel Little dropped his revolver in the excitement and was wounded in the leg when it went off, sending him to the hospital in Manila.

Kansans advanced to Lico road, parallel to their front, expanding the security perimeter before Brigadier General Otis ordered them to move forward five hundred yards across the road. The skirmish line rose on Funston's order and advanced rapidly without firing, concealed by trees and bamboo. In new positions, they prepared defenses while insurgents pounded them with heavy rifle fire. Five companies worked their ancient Springfield rifles as fast as possible, but the Civil War relics were .45 caliber single-shot rifles that kicked hard and obscured view with black smoke. The situation was precarious and Funston alerted Captain Bishop to get his men ready. He ordered trumpeter Barshfield to blow "Cease Fire!" All along the line, the clatter of metal-on-metal signaled bayonets being snapped on. They rose and advanced at a fast clip until Funston shouted, "Fire at will!" They pressed a frontal attack, firing and reloading as they walked, yelling, trampling fences, and blasting brown earthworks—Funston with them, firing his revolver.

Seventy yards out, Barshfield sounded "Charge!" Men rushed forward, still yelling, and quickly occupied the trenches when insurgents broke and ran. Captain Charles Martin's company got the worst of it with six men hit. Thirty dead Filipinos lay in the trenches. Sergeant Morse wrote home, "Colonel Funston is all right, only his nerve would have got him killed a good many times before now if he was fighting anyone who could shoot."

While Kansans celebrated and consolidated their new position, rebels fired on them from Blockhouse Number One, two hundred yards away. Companies became intertwined during the scramble to take the trenches but Funston organized a hasty attack of the blockhouse. That small group killed or captured the occupants and secured the building.

But thirty men continued further without orders, crossing a narrow bridge ahead of their company. When they drew heavy fire from a larger force they realized they were isolated and took a hasty defense in a shallow trench. Funston galloped alone on horseback across the bridge and stopped midway between the bridge and the men. He sat astride his small Filipino pony, arms folded across his chest, studying the situation as Mauser bullets whizzed by and naval artillery shells burst in the free fire zone. He couldn't be heard over the noise, so he raised his sword and signaled the men to follow him back over the bridge to safety.

His decision was fortuitous, as brigade ordered the regiment back a thousand yards for a solid brigade line for the night. As they rushed back to Lico Road, ten-inch naval artillery shells from the *Concord* burst around them—the ships unaware of the fluidity on the ground. Funston double-timed the entire regiment out of the field of fire, averting a near disaster.

When they reached Lico Road, MacArthur and his staff rode out to meet with Funston. He asked which unit attacked that sector of Filipino trenches. Funston proudly and loudly declared, "The 20th Kansas, sir! These Kansas volunteers are as good as any regulars!" MacArthur admitted their attack was as good as any he ever saw. Praise worked wonders for morale of dirty, sweaty, tired, hungry, and now bloodied volunteers.

Funston did consider them real soldiers but not yet seasoned veterans. That night, the first after combat, was spent sharing food, water, and experiences. No one had blankets since the quartermaster was busy shuttling ammunition to the front. Funston strolled among his boys, wearing the same faded blue shirt, brown trousers and canvas leggings they wore, only distinguished by his small size and the silver eagle on his collar. He saw "they seemed to worry themselves but little over the serious business ahead, and were inclined to let each day take care of itself."

§

The regiment resumed their original position south of Caloocan in a united division defense. As lines reformed, Funston found he had more space to cover than the previous night. He extended the left flank, keeping the right flank anchored against the railroad, to form an unbroken line of three battalions. He placed his regimental command post two hundred yards to the rear, just off the Caloocan road. He sent scouts out, who reported the enemy had not yet returned to the trenches.

Occasional small-arms fire kept outposts alert. Major Franklin Bell, intelligence officer for the division, requested Funston furnish a sergeant to accompany him on a personal reconnaissance for the division commander. He bristled at anyone else scouting his sector instead of doing it himself. Bell insisted this came from Brigadier General King, so Funston gave in. Major Bell was a heroic officer and strong supporter of Funston and they became close friends. But Funston wanted the same information so with several men he crawled through the dense woods to within a few hundred yards of insurgents fortifying positions. King received the same report from Bell.

That night, with outposts established, Fred had leaders use shifts to allow men to sleep. He prepared to sleep, too, when bullets interrupted the quiet, and the entire line opened up with Springfield's firing as fast as possible. While he scrambled for a bugler to blow "Cease Fire," one man was hit and his screams caused a panicked increase in firing. Funston ordered "Cease Fire!" but kicks, blows, and curses were necessary to stop the shooting. Funston seethed over twenty-five thousand rounds fired against an attack that never came—fire discipline one of his main principles.

§

Funston visited MacArthur at his command post at La Loma church to coordinate his regiment's activities with division plans. That day and the next were so quiet Funston sent Trooper Caldwell to Manila to tell Eda the situation was safe enough that she could visit the front, if she desired. He reasoned it was safe enough and would give her the opportunity to see troops in the field, expand her horizons, and have a brief talk with her husband. This was not an opportunity the audacious Eda Blankhart Funston could let pass. She married this man after a short courtship and followed him to a war zone to see the world. She wanted to see all of it.

Trooper Caldwell delivered Fred's note to Eda the following day. He had other errands but when he returned she was ready. Florence Whitman handed her a small pistol as she departed in her covered carriage, with an armed rider forward and another behind. She found passing over ground the regiment fought over fascinating as her escort pointed out key terrain features and battle scenes. She witnessed trees and limbs shattered by artillery, houses and nipa huts on both sides of the road riddled with bullet holes, scattered shell casings, all fresh as she rode through with her pistol in hand. When she reached the front lines, Fred wasn't there, but Dr. Smith and Dr. Rafter met her and made sure she was comfortable, keeping up an interesting conversation until Fred returned.

Prior to her arrival, Captain Christy had led a small patrol beyond the regimental front and got into a sharp fire-fight two hundred yards away.

Fifty insurgents advanced from trenches, pinning down Christy and his small patrol. Naturally, Fred went to investigate, crawling through woods, following the rattle of Mausers and Springfields until he reached Christy, sheltered by a depression in the earth within by a clump of trees. The patrol was outnumbered and in a hard fight to avoid being overrun. Funston crouched with them and considered how best to get them out. He ordered everyone to cease fire at once, and run all-out to a protected area out of the line of fire, where they reconsolidated and hurried back to friendly lines.

Eda heard the nearby fighting and was well aware Fred had to be involved. Orderlies rushed her to safety behind an earthen embankment as stray rounds whizzed overhead. "And there I stayed," she recalled, "with my pistol clasped tightly in my hand and feeling like a fool." Bullets snapped all around her, cracking overhead. This was no place for a lady, but it was the ideal place for a Funston.

Fred returned winded and found Eda there, safely ensconced within Filipino fortifications taken a few days before. He assured her the rebels were shooting at his patrol, not at her. After a more intimate greeting of hugs and kisses, he asked her to "please put the pistol away," and she stowed it in her buggy. Funston wouldn't let a little skirmish ruin her outing, so he escorted her on foot to brigade headquarters and introduced her to General Otis. Then they visited the 3rd Artillery and officers who were happy to see a pretty face to admire and talk with while Fred chatted with the commander. From their elevated position, Eda was able to view enemy soldiers through the field glasses she had given him as a Christmas present, and questioned what they were doing. Fred took a look and saw they were preparing to attack. The quiet interlude ended there and she readily agreed she was in the way of the war and should return straightaway to Manila with her armed escorts.

Safely back in Manila, she sat beside the telegraph operator at headquarters who informed her that a fierce battle broke out half an hour after she left. He said, "The fighting is so hot out there I can hardly hear my instrument." Eda wrote to her sister Elizabeth, "You can imagine how worried I am." But she had plenty of other fresh news to write about, enough to prompt her to begin an article for *Cosmopolitan Magazine* about the life of a soldier's wife. Eda kept up a steady stream of correspondence with her husband at the front, but also with her sisters and mother in Oakland, and with Ann Funston in Iola, Fred's mother she had yet to meet.

§

Funston sent a staff officer to brief the brigade commander on the recent patrol encounter and requested authority for a limited attack to neutralize the Filipino snipers. Permission was granted with strict limitations—attack only to dislodge the threat, but not pursue. Plans did not permit a general engagement.

Funston chose to overwhelm the position quickly and selected three companies for the mission. While the enemy position was known, the flanks and depth of other formations was unknown. Attempts to turn the flank could be disastrous, a frontal attack less risky.

On order, three companies rose with bayonets fixed and walked through the woods for a hundred yards. When they broke into the open three hundred yards from the dike, straw-hatted insurgents opened fire with repeating Mausers. Kansans held steady until ordered to fire, then raked the dike with bullets, forcing them to cover. Kansans continued under tight control with a favorable wind blowing away black smoke of Springfields. Eighty yards out, Funston ordered "Charge!" Infantrymen ran to the trenches with bayonets poised and poured into ditches. Hand-to-hand fighting broke out in a melee of close-order combat, bayonet slashes, butt strokes, and battering blows.

Kansans fought for a red silk *Katipunan* flag, embroidered with the white Philippine sun, riddled with bullet holes and drenched with blood. Funston had the war relic presented to the Kansas governor for display at the state house in Topeka.

Companies assembled quickly before a counter-attack led to the general engagement MacArthur wanted to avoid. Filipinos lost heavily—thirty dead in the trench where the heaviest fighting occurred. Unfortunately, First Lieutenant Alfred Alford of Company B was killed in the final assault. Alford was Fred's classmate at the University of Kansas and his loss hit hard. Sergeant Jay Sheldon was also critically wounded. Fred visited Sheldon at the aid station where the surgeon informed him his condition was grave. He tried to encourage him, but Shelton said, "It was worth being hit to have been in so fine a fight." He died the next day.

MacArthur reported on the attack in a telegram which said the fight was "most gallantly carried through...by Colonel Funston personally and his Kansas soldiers...."

§

MacArthur's first objective in the campaign was the nipa-hut village of Caloocan astride the railway, defended with well-built trenches occupied by four thousand fighters. In order to move north one hundred-twenty miles to Lingayen Gulf, the railroad must be taken and Caloocan was the first step.

MacArthur called a commander's meeting at his headquarters to resolve the irregular division line by advancing the 1st Brigade as in a wheel with the Kansans on flank making the greatest adjustment. This would relieve congestion and position units more favorably for an attack. Funston's orders were to move through the woods, take the town of Caloocan and trenches defending it. Attack was to begin in an hour but MacArthur had pushed his staff to mass supplies and reserves, and coordinate artillery and naval gunfire support in advance.

Funston had anticipated the move and scouted the area, drawing maps to fill gaps in the army map inventory. The target was to be plastered for half an hour by naval gunfire from vessels of the fleet and division field artillery. Shortly after 1500 hours the air overhead screamed with six- and eight-inch shells and the ground in front erupted with their bursts.

Just as the attack began, a veteran war correspondent for *New York World* and *Collier's Weekly*, Frederick Palmer, hurried to catch up with Funston. Funston asked about his rush, "Were you worried lest the rebellion should be over before you arrived?" Major Metcalf joined them as he continued, "If you had waited a year you would have still found it going." Metcalf nodded his agreement.

Battalions began the ground attack at the end of artillery firing. Funston deployed all twelve infantry companies in a skirmish line and they rushed quickly through the woods. Although rebels couldn't see them coming, they fired into the trees. They walked quickly for a mile and Funston had them hold fire despite sporadic sniping. Two hundred yards out, within range of the Springfields, he ordered them open up even before targets were visible. Soldiers fired as they walked, reloading as needed and Funston rode his horse behind until incoming fire was so heavy he dismounted and followed on foot.

Sergeant John Murphy was nearby, smoking his large, brier pipe, and only removing it to curse men who needed inspiration. As five companies broke into the open in view of the church, they came under heavy fire from the trenches. Funston ordered buglers to sound "Charge!" Filipino defenders bolted and trenches were taken.

Trenches were filled with dead and wounded rebels, who torched the town as they withdrew. Kansans, winded from exertion, pushed through, but the rebels escaped across the Tuliajan River. Some pursuers chased them too far and Funston mounted his horse and followed to a ridge half a mile beyond Caloocan. He ordered a new line there as his out-of-control skirmishers approached the next town, Malinta, a thousand yards north.

Rebels gathered across the river near Malinta, and fired on them at long range. Captain Orwig and his men were tired of dodging bullets and launched a return volley. Funston spurred his horse to chastise Orwig for wasting ammunition, shouting and cursing that the rebels were poor shots, and Mausers were ineffective at that range. Suddenly his horse slumped to the ground with a Mauser round in its neck! Laughter filled the ranks and he exploded even more furiously. A surgeon removed the bullet and the horse eventually recovered, returning to duty, but Funston needed longer to overcome his embarrassment—but this only added to his legend.

The regiment's new line had disadvantages. The left was on a narrow causeway connecting Caloocan with the larger town of Malabon, which ran along the left flank and gave insurgents a clear field of long-range fire. Casualties resulted from that direction until a six foot-high sandbag barrier was constructed. Bamboo and trees were too close and the ground cut with low ravines, allowing insurgents to get close without being detected. Malabon couldn't be taken without crossing the river.

Funston entered Caloocan church to assess as regimental headquarters. Inside he found a female camp-follower, an American nurse, rolling pillaged items in a blanket. Otis' had issued strict orders against looting, so he directed a sergeant recover the loot and chase her away. She refused to comply and Funston forced her out. She swore revenge—he'd not heard the last from her.

The fight at Caloocan raised the stature of the regiment when they captured a fortified camp and hoisted the American flag in less than two hours. Then they captured five dismantled railroad engines, fifty passenger coaches, and a hundred freight and flat cars, valuable to an army advancing along the rail line. First Sergeant Sampson wrote home, "Scrapping Fred...has proved himself to be the bravest officer in the line and one that the boys will follow through fire or water. When the fire is the hottest he moves about unflinchingly.... He has found a place in the hearts of all his men...."

Not only was the 20th Kansas tactically successful, but set a high standard of courage and aggressiveness like their fiery colonel. Funston effectively used supporting fires, flanking maneuvers, vigorous pursuit, excellent marksmanship, tight command and control, and personal leadership. Otis mentioned him in reports and dispatches, adding to his reputation and drawing comparisons to Teddy Roosevelt's charge of San Juan Hill in Cuba.

§

The 20th Kansas remained in defensive positions for weeks as VIII Corps waited for reinforcements from the United States. A general offensive was out of the question, leaving Manila unprotected, until defense of the capital was assured. While waiting, Otis restored normal commerce in Manila. Elite of Manila and Chinese commercial interests accepted American dominance, but lower classes were clinging to hope for independence.

The Dagupan Railway connected lush farm land of north-central Luzon with Manila. MacArthur set his command post in the abandoned residence of the general manager of the Manila-Dagupan railway, just off the railroad track and one hundred yards behind the Kansas regiment. Brigadier

General Otis camped in the open in the center of the brigade line. Funston occupied the Caloocan church.

The scavenger Funston ejected from Caloocan church returned to San Francisco and complained to newspapers that he'd kicked open a glass case and looted a gold-embroidered robe for his wife. She found a civilian fire engineer from a troop transport, a deserter and another scavenger, to back her up. Funston had also caught him looting and turned him over to the provost marshal. Chaplain McKinnon from the California regiment verified Funston's version, but anti-imperialists excoriated him anyway with such stories. Father McKinnon said, "I was present at the surrender of Caloocan…. It is true that churches were desecrated and their sacred vestments and vessels stolen, but not by American troops. … The looting was done by the insurgents and Chinese. When we entered the towns we found Chinese loaded down with these goods."

Funston said, "There may have been isolated instances I am not prepared to deny, but such articles as the soldiers brought home were usually purchased from Chinese or Filipinos who had themselves stolen them from the churches…long before…." Accusations created so much trouble for Funston that he vowed never to allow camp-followers, if he ever commanded field army.

While they awaited orders from MacArthur, Kansas and Utah Mechanics used railroading skills to refurbish small Filipino locomotives to haul material and resupply between their lines and Manila. Fred got permission for regular runs between the capital and the Second Division. Amateur railroaders ran the engine and string of cars so fast they terrified the local natives as they blew through. Crews lashed signs to the trains proclaiming them the "Kansas and Utah Short Line," and "Freddy's Fast Express."

§

During the pause, officers were permitted to ride the rails into Manila to shave, wash, change uniforms and spend a day, returning in the evening. Funston always went straight to Eda, busy between visits with sewing, music, and writing at least one letter a day to be delivered to her husband on his fast train, and another to Oakland or Iola carried on slow ships. Once, Eda and Mrs. Jesse Hausermann rode the train to the front to visit, dining on field rations at Fred's headquarters in Caloocan church. At such times war could actually seem a pleasant, romantic, adventure.

But while Fred was in the field, Eda and other ladies visited wounded soldiers in hospitals, who frequently mentioned them in letters home. Lieutenant Colonel Little, the battalion commander who accidently shot himself at the outset of the fighting, was still healing. He justified his embarrassing wound to reporters, saying he "stood unflinching, protecting the barracks where the danger was greatest, rather than on the safer front lines." He complained Eda Funston and Florence Whitman moved much too freely about the city without security, going to afternoon teas despite extreme dangers. The absurdity of this was not missed by the reporter.

Eda also wrote home of her hospital visits, "How many there were and how my heart ached not only for them, but for their mothers and fathers and wives at home. … Every time I tried to impress on the sick men that there was nothing I would not do for them if they wished it, their reply would invariably be that they wanted for nothing, except to have us ladies come in and chat with them occasionally, and this we did as long as we were able. … It was such a mixture of pleasure and pain."

§

The standoff, with routine exchanges of fire, took a bad turn on the night of February 22nd, 1899, when rebels caught Americans by surprise. Funston's left flank didn't stretch entirely to the bay, but ended where the wet marsh was indefensible. During the night insurgents fired all along the line, especially in the Kansas sector. A fake frontal attack allowed a thousand armed enemy troops to wade through the marsh at low tide and sneak into Manila to join several thousand militias armed with bolos. The consolidated force attacked Americans throughout Manila, raising terror there and among men on the outskirts with families in the city. Insurgents lit fires in nipa huts and burned hundreds of acres of Manila. Street fighting continued through the night and terrorists took over the tramway car barn, swarmed Tondo and Binondo, and attacked military police in the city center where Eda Funston and the other ladies prepared to defend themselves with guns and kitchen knives.

Eda had heard rumors of an uprising, but when it actually came everyone was surprised. It was Washington's Birthday, and Eda and Mrs. Haussermann were entertaining ladies and officers of a company of the Oregon regiment guarding the rear with a music recital. They were in the middle of *Schlumerlied*—Slumber Song, when firing woke everyone. From the window, the sky seemed on fire and shots cracked all around. Soldiers at the musicale formed in the street to join fighting mere blocks away.

The ladies packed their bags, prepared to flee at a moment's notice. Curiosity compelled Eda to peer outside the windows to look until several bullets cracked walls close by. They stayed put as firefighters beat out the blazes, and soldiers beat rebels from the city. As day broke over a more peaceful place, Eda led other ladies to visit wounded men in the hospitals.

Major Metcalf, at the front, took a Mauser round though his ear, leaving a perfect hole one inch from his skull, but it was a bad night for all Americans, awake all night, shooting, ducking, and worrying. At first light, a puff of smoke revealed the first of three accurate shots from a large gun on the summit of the hill overlooking Malinta. The Krupp, a breech-loading rifled coastal defense gun had been left by the Spanish, and Spanish prisoners forced into service to fire it.

Captain Edgar Russell, the division's chief signal officer, used semaphore flags to send a fire mission from the church tower to the naval vessels in Manila Bay. The *Monadnock* and *Charleston* fired on the Spanish gun, and it fell silent. It seemed naval gun fire disabled the gun, but actually the recoil from the third shot had only damaged the elevation mechanism.

Another story made the rounds that one of the ten-inch naval gun shells killed two dozen men of a Filipino battalion. However, it was learned later the round hadn't even exploded. The buried shell was excavated by insurgents, the fuse removed, and the round stood on end. When a crowd gathered to gawk at the large shell, a corporal accidently dropped a burning cigarette into the open mouth of the shell. The explosion slung body parts all over the area.

§

After the surprise attack, sniping and random firing resumed with several killed or wounded. The death of Captain David Stewart Elliott, a Civil War veteran, was disturbing to many of the Kansans. He commanded a company from Coffeyville where he was a lawyer, newspaper editor, and community organizer. His father had been killed in Kansas by Quantrill's raiders. Elliott died the next day with his two sons, serving in his company, by his side.

Soon after Captain Elliott's death, rebels waved a white flag and Funston went to meet them. They requested a meeting with the military governor, Major General Elwell Otis. Funston held them until permission was obtained before allowing them to proceed. While waiting, both sides relaxed during the temporary cease fire. Funston suggested that when the meeting was ended, he'd direct his men to hold their fire unless fired on first, so the constant and ineffective sniping could end. Rebel commanders agreed neither had authority to make a truce but both were willing to apply relaxed measures for a temporary ceasefire.

For several weeks trenches were quiet on both sides, but Funston warned his men not to expose themselves needlessly nor bunch up. But he sent for the band's instruments from Manila and began evening concerts that Eda would appreciate; insurgents also enjoyed listening atop their trenches. Soon, baseball teams were organized and games played in full view of gawking enemy spectators.

Slackened fighting was a good reprieve, too good. A patrol discovered zigzag trenches being dug during the pause and Funston waved a white handkerchief to confront the working party. An officer warned him away so he ordered a company to fire a volley at the new trenches—the truce ended. It had to end anyhow as regular army regiments had arrived from the states so troops were available to begin the long awaited offensive.

The Jayhawker regiment was the most successful unit of the Second Division—aggressive, competent, and professional, with high morale. Funston was widely respected by his men, his peers, and his superiors as the one who shaped it with his constant prodding, coddling, cajoling, hard drills and demands for high standards, and he was consistent—from mustering in Kansas, training in San Francisco, and combat operations in the Philippines. During all of this, he wed a beautiful bride who accompanied him to the war zone and was amazing in her own right. It was evident his reputation in Cuba was no myth, but only a sampling of what he was capable of achieving. He was regularly out front, in command of the situation, unafraid, and self-schooled in military art and science. Yet, he was approachable, modest, and concerned for the welfare of his men. In a letter to his friend, lawyer and businessman, Charles Gleed, Funston wrote of his fellow Kansans: "When I tell them to charge, the trouble is not to get them to come on, but to keep from being run over by them."

Weeks of fighting and marching, jungles and rivers, incidents and adventures were so varied and with such rapid transitions that to write of it is like "trying to describe a dream where time, space, and all the logical sequences of ordinary life are upset in the unrelenting brutality of war."

The task organization and disposition of units changed with the arrival of the newly arrived 22nd United States Infantry and the 2nd Oregon, designated as the Separate Brigade of MacArthur's division. The battle for Caloocan had been a regimental commander's fight, but the coming larger battle belonged to brigade and division commanders. The attack included nine thousand men over an eight-mile front, opposed by an equal number of rebels, well-armed, well supplied, and well dug in.

ELEVEN

The entire VIII Corps, including 20th Kansas, was still stranded outside the ancient capital city of Manila. Until the arrival of reinforcements, there had not been enough Americans to confront a well-manned, well-trained, well-armed, and well-supplied rebel army, under the popular Emilio Aguinaldo. The Philippine Islands lay eight thousand miles by slow ship from the west coast of the United States and recruiting new troops, clothing and equipping them, and training them prior to a lengthy voyage cost valuable time. Meanwhile, the McKinley administration was focused on driving the Spanish out of Cuba and leaving that country to self-governance. But, no clear decision was made regarding the Philippines. Washington grabbed a tiger by the tail and once Spanish hold was broken, had no strategic plan for what to do next.

When enough troops arrived they could breakout from former Spanish positions toward the rebel capital in Malolos. Fred Funston, after fighting with a rebel army to liberate Cuba, was now leading a regiment of occupation troops to occupy the Philippines. He accepted his duty in both cases and avoided amorphous politics. This was easy at first but eventually made him the focus a high-profile debate with famous anti-imperialists.

Fast success in clearing southern Luzon allowed a major strike to the north, with the Manila-Dagupan railroad as the main axis of advance, the seat of rebel government at Malolos the initial objective. MacArthur's plan called for Hale's and Otis' brigades, along with Funston's regiment, to make the main attack, overrun insurgent trenches, cross the river, then wheel left to Malinta to cut off enemy retreat. Wheaton's new Separate Brigade would follow the main attack to occupy the trenches just across the river. Hall's brigade would conduct a supporting attack. Both sides were evenly matched, but the insurgents were excellent defenders and had the advantage of dug-in breastworks.

§

Reveille stirred the Kansans early on the morning of March 25th, 1899, to begin the breakout. Otherwise, the day was normal as men prepared coffee and bacon, cleaned weapons, and packed gear. Across the river, General Antonio Luna and the best of the rebels were prepared for the anticipated attack. Luna's troops were primarily from native regiments, trained and organized by the Spanish, wore old uniforms, and had the same leaders, weapons, and organizations; they were well trained, except in marksmanship which degraded the advantage of their superior rifles. They were strong defensive fighters, dedicated to independence and courageous enough to die for it.

War correspondent Frederick Palmer followed Funston's regiment in the breakout. He reported the beginning of the attack: "With the first light, a line of blue figures rose in the morning mist—the longest line I ever saw.... Our left on the seacoast was supported by the fire of gunboats. We had nine thousand men in all—the 2nd Oregon, the 20th Kansas, the 1st Nebraska, the 1st Colorado, and a battalion of the 3rd Coast Artillery fighting as infantry. For the first time I was noting the stern intensity of the Americans in action to go straight to a goal."

The 20th Kansas was one segment of that long skirmish line extending across the Tarmac Valley from Manila Bay to the foothills and higher mountains. The first wave moved in a thin line with reserves and support troops behind. The entire line advanced until defensive fire was enough to drive them behind low dikes.

John F. Bass of *Harper's Weekly* also watched the division attack from La Loma Church. He wrote, "Heroism became a matter of course and death an incident." From a distance the battle assumed one perspective: "From La Loma church you may get the full view of our long line crossing the open field, evenly, steadily, irresistible, like an in-rolling wave on a beach.... Watch the regiments go forward, and form under fire, and move on and on.... Then gradually the power of that line will force itself upon you, and you will feel that you must follow, that wherever that line goes you must go also." Closer, battle takes another perspective as it becomes much more intense and very personal.

As they fought, the rebels were armed with superior Mausers with flat trajectory bullets reaching out to a thousand yards, while Americans had old Springfields, with low velocity and a high trajectory. At least, cartridges with smokeless powder had replaced black powder rounds.

Lieutenant Colonel Little recovered from his accidental shooting and returned to command the his battalion in the "relative safety of the front lines." Major Frank Whitman returned from sick leave to command his and the third battalion was under the steady hand of Major Wilder Metcalf.

Two battalions marched on line to the summit of the ridge past trenches occupied by new regiments, and started down the gentle slope toward the river. Brigades crossed a level, open, parade-ground type plain, as crackle of fire kicked dust from the dry ground and snapped overhead. Funston used the same fire and maneuver tactics practiced at The Presidio, advancing by companies, with one platoon rushing, falling prone, then the covering platoon rushing past.

Funston's horse, the bay wounded at Caloocan, was skittish under fire but he stayed in the saddle. On horseback he could see the enemy line was a series of disconnected outposts. He kept the attack moving until the front lines were close, and had the bugler sound "Charge!" Troops broke into a run and rebels bolted to the rear.

Company G attacked with their ever-present mascot, a bulldog from Coffeyville, Kansas, hometown of their dead commander, Captain Elliott. The dog, excited by the fight, ran up and down the line, barking, encouraging them, anxious to get at the enemy. The bulldog was in every battle and never injured. But, luck ran out when the company returned to Kansas. The K9 veteran bit a policeman who shot and killed him. Company veterans, ever grieving over loss of their beloved commander, almost rioted over the death of their faithful and much-loved mascot.

Filipinos traveled light, leaving supplies and equipment in their fallback positions. Americans carried heavy loads—rifle, bayonet, ammunition belt, haversack, mess kit, filled canteen, poncho, a day's ration, and at least a hundred pounds of ammunition—struggling in the heat to keep up the attack. Word, not an order, was whispered down the Kansas line: "Let's throw away our rations and blankets and go at them with guns, canteens, and ammunition alone." Journalist Karl Irving Faust stepped over cans of beef and salmon, blankets, and mess kits as he followed half a mile behind the attack. "With such a brigade of fighters, the Filipinos thought all pandemonium was after them...."

The road was the boundary between 1st Montana and 20th Kansas, but during the attack, two Montana companies crossed the road, pinching the Kansans' attack zone. Funston first squeezed two companies behind to prevent overcrowding, but galloped to the road to correct the problem. The offending officer refused to accept orders from the colonel of different regiment. Funston was furious and slung some choice words before galloping to complain to higher command. He found MacArthur and breathlessly vented to him. MacArthur said, "Well, well, Funston; is that all that's the matter? Let's not get excited about little things. It's better to wait for something serious." MacArthur was amused by Funston's grumbling in the middle of an attack, but sent a junior officer to straighten out the lines.

When he returned from complaining, the objective had already been taken. The attack resumed through rougher ground and denser woods. Lead units approached the river but maps were only crude Spanish charts. As they descended the gentle slope close to the river, heavy rifle fire met them. Kansans could not withdraw or stay in the open, so Funston ordered them to rush to the river line. Infantrymen hit prone firing positions and returned fire. While he considered next moves from horseback, James Creelman, another reporter, joined him. Both remained on horses but couldn't talk over battle noise until rounds cracked over their heads, forcing them to dismount. Funston recalled, "Only once, and that at Cascorra in far-away Cuba, had I seen bullets thicker."

Funston rode along the river, seeking a crossing site, but his horse's legs became mired in a bog. He dismounted and continued on foot, leaving the bay behind. When he reached a possible crossing, he motioned some men to try swimming across. Captain William Watson led several soldiers into the current and struggled to cross the shoulder-high river. Others followed with rifles raised overhead and as they reached the far bank, Filipinos withdrew.

Private Wagoner described the stronghold across the river: "still further beyond were tier after tier of them, bank of rice dikes rising at gradual elevations like a big amphitheater. The elevation of this incline was sufficient to allow all these Filipinos to shoot at the same time, without danger to the tiers ahead of them." Later, when infantry crossed into the trees, they couldn't find the rebels, even while under fire. Soon they discovered snipers lashed in the tops of trees and it was a "squirrel shoot," leaving dead snipers dangling from ropes.

Finally, soldiers extricated Funston's horse from the bog and returned him. Though fighting was over, Funston found a shallow crossing point and the regiment waded across and dropped exhausted. Karl Irving Faust had watched the attack. "It was a hot fight but the indomitable colonel and the unsubdued Kansans drove him back."

§

In Manila, Eda Funston sat beside the telegraph operator and wrote home, "They are advancing on Malolos. ... I am afraid for Fred because he is so dreadfully brave ... he runs right in front of his men, waving his hat...." Sergeant Ozias confirmed her assessment, "General Funston is spoken of as rushing at the insurgents with uplifted sword.... Funston was bareheaded, as were all officers, except a few who carried native canes as an aid to walking.... I am glad to tell of bravery not often paralleled in commanders."

Brigade headquarters caught up with the regiments and MacArthur called a halt for the rest of the day. Water was plentiful, stars overhead clear, the sky was dry and warm so troopers were content to camp for the night.

§

Crossing the river initiated Phase II of the operation. On March 26, 1899, the regiment stepped off heading west along a wagon road connecting the Novaliches ford across the Tuliajan River toward Malinta. Funston spotted MacArthur on horseback near the artillery and went to consult.

MacArthur directed him to deploy right of the 3rd Artillery and attack the enemy as quickly as possible. The 3rd Artillery, a regular army unit, was equipped with new Norwegian-made .30 caliber Krag-Jorgensen rifles, superior to Springfields carried by Funston's volunteers. The Krag was a repeating rifle with a magazine of five rounds for rapid fire and reloading.

It had less kick-back than the Springfield .45 single-shots and used smokeless powder. The regular troops advanced quickly, firing those modern rifles with remarkable effectiveness at exposed targets.

Funston pushed his battalions to double-time to a line of deployment to the right of the 3rd Artillery. By then, they were too winded to attack in good order. Maneuver space was limited but several companies came on line and began firing and advancing slowly. The distance to the enemy was too far for Springfields to be effective. Men fell, not from bullets but from heat exhaustion. Cursing and screaming by Funston and battalion commanders couldn't change that.

Captain Boltwood watched closely as heat took a toll. He encouraged men to find shade under trees when possible. Karl Irving Faust, the reporter still following the brigade, noted "that Boltwood and his men were like untamed panthers when the battle was on." Behind, reserve troops lay low, "for bullets are barking the trees all around them—yet they talk and joke as if this was only an April holiday."

§

The Second Division mission was to take the rebel capital in Malolos. The advance guard made first contact as they approached the town. Major Kobbe, of the 3rd Artillery, ordered his men to press on but many were squatting on the sides of the road roasting plundered chickens over small cooking fires. Reluctantly they left the chickens over the fires, cooking still unfinished, to continue the fight. Kansans considered it their duty to complete the chicken job for their brothers in arms, cooking and eating all of them.

The fight stiffened and Funston prodded his men ahead to assist their hungry comrades. The Kansans received sudden fire from their left front and Funston took Major Metcalf with him to scout the origin of the firing. They found a line of trenches in a stand of wood and bamboo. The space before it was open, crisscrossed by one-foot rice dikes.

Funston ordered the two leading companies ahead. They rushed into the open, deployed under fire, and attacked using rush-and-fire tactics until one hundred yards away. The bugler sounded "Charge!" Men stood, yelling, running, and then stopped just as quickly. The trenches were on the other side an impassible river eighty feet wide and ten feet deep, the Marilao, drawn incorrectly on the map. The enemy held elaborately concealed trenches while Americans scrambled for cover behind low dikes. Several men were hit, two killed, and Chinese litter bearers rushed under fire to recover them. Funston withdrew to safety to reconsider.

Brigadier General Otis rode up to consult with him. He disagreed with the decision to withdraw, and Funston led the two original companies back to the exposed positions. They raked the top of the trenches with fire and retook the positions without further casualties while Funston and other leaders ran along the river bank scouting for crossing sites.

Funston saw a raft moored to the opposite bank of the deep river, below the trenches on a ridge eighty feet above the water. The raft was directly across from Franklin Bell's troops. Funston called for volunteers to swim the river. Lieutenant Hardy, Trumpeter Barshfield, Corporal Drysdale, and Privates Huntsman and Willey stripped and plunged into the water. They swam the river, grabbed the raft, and towed it back across under supporting fire from the Kansas and Pennsylvania regiments, plus the field piece and the Colt automatic.

When the raft arrived, Funston jumped on with Lieutenant Hopkins and twenty-one other men. They poled across, sent out patrols on the far side, and bore down on the trenches above. They found a white flag waving, not because of their crossing, but because the artillery was destroying their protective cover; small arms fire made escape impossible.

Funston appealed to the brigade commander to bring his entire regiment across on the ferry-raft, but was overruled. Brigade consolidated on the south bank awaiting orders when the entire division front was restored. Meanwhile, the South Dakota regiment continued a heavy fight near the bridge. At 1600 hours, the brigade commander ordered the 20th Kansas and 3rd Artillery to cross the railroad bridge and deploy on the other side of the river.

James Wadsworth was standing near the railroad bridge when he observed, "a column of infantry came along, the men in blue shirts, sleeves rolled up, canvas pants flopping without leggings, felt campaign hats all out of shape—haversacks hanging across one shoulder, blanket rolls across the other, and most of the men bearded—a hard bitten crew." Then Wadsworth spotted a little man walking at the head of the column, "slender with a small pointed beard. I doubt if he weighed more than 115 pounds." Wadsworth hailed a passing sergeant and asked what outfit it was. "His contempt for my ignorance was conspicuous in his reply—'what [blank] outfit? I'll tell ya [blank]—this is the 20th Kansas!'" Then Wadsworth asked about the little guy up front. The sergeant replied: "Little guy? Say that's Colonel Funston, do you hear me?"

At this point, the Marilao River made a sharp bend north, then east. As Funston approached the railroad bridge he was met by MacArthur's adjutant general who said MacArthur wanted him to hurry in extending the line to the left on the other side of the river. The 3rd Artillery and Hale's brigade were already across, expecting a counterattack by thousands of enemy troops. The enemy was assembling along a two-mile long line with a reserve force behind. MacArthur believed they intended to counterattack during the river crossing.

Funston found railroad ties removed from the bridge, slowing footwork of crossing the high drop over a deep river. Filipinos opened fire from a distance and one man was killed, several wounded. Horses were swum across the river by orderlies. In constricted space, Funston put only two battalions on the firing line but shooting continued for half an hour until it suddenly stopped.

§

The brigade rested while engineers repaired the railroad bridge so trains could bring supplies from Manila and a build a wagon bridge for wheeled transportation to cross the river. Weather was intolerably hot and rest was welcome, fatigue evident though marches were slower and shorter.

By morning, the division reformed across the river. Near Bocaue was a line of trenches and advancing troops were soon met by Mausers. Kansans quickened their pace and returned fire. Major Metcalf, already shot through the ear, was hit again in the foot. He tried to continue but relented and returned to Manila for treatment. Six enlisted men were also struck.

Rebels withdrew and the next railroad bridge was seized before it was destroyed so several regiments crossed. Further up the tracks at Bigaa station, enemy troops used railroad cars to escape. Field guns opened fire on the train, creating mass confusion, but insurgents still burned Bigaa as they left.

When fighting ended, Funston shouted to Sergeant Whisner, "Jake, where did you get these fighters? They are the best I ever saw." Whisner laughed and yelled back, "Why Colonel, we have got plenty more like them in Kansas City." Then Whisner told a reporter, "He is the best little fighter in the islands. He walks up and down the lines when the boys are fighting, saying 'Keep cool boys. They can't hit you. Give 'em hell!' Then he will pull out his revolver and blaze away at the Filipinos. He is always in the thickest of the fight."

Kansans passed through the burning town of Bigaa and pressed on the insurgent capital at Malolos, but stopped at the Guiguinto River. Trenches on the other side were deserted, but the railroad bridge was burning. Troops hauled water in buckets from the burning town to fight the fire and limit damage. Banks of the river were too steep and high to cross without the bridge.

Twelve hundred yards ahead stretched an open and level rice field, beyond that a dense wood. Scouts went to check. A large, disciplined enemy force entrenched in the line of trees held their fire. When scouts returned without spotting them, the crossing began. Bell's 10th Pennsylvania and Funston's 20th Kansas crossed the railroad bridge together using both tracks simultaneously. Two field pieces and the Colt machine gun were portaged by hand to the other side and set up for action. Horses were left behind.

Funston and MacArthur stood on the north end of the bridge talking as they watched the crossing when a torrent of Mauser fire came at them. Major Strong, standing three feet from MacArthur, was hit first. Bullets zinged off the bridge as they dove for cover.

Both regiments hurried across and deployed. Two field pieces and the Colt went into action as battalions advanced in rushes. A rifleman next to Funston was hit in the head, and behind him, wounded men writhed in anguish with cries for "Hospital Corps!"

No more attempts to advance were made, leaving the afternoon to distribute rations and ammunition. The attack resumed the following afternoon. The brigade advanced slowly and cautiously, passing line after line of vacant defensive positions. That night they camped within three miles of Malolos.

§

Strategically, Malolos was unimportant to Americans, yet they expected strong defense of the Filipino's revolutionary capital. Scouts reported defenses were strong during the night. But when daylight lit the town, trenches were empty. Fearing a trap, scheduled artillery preparation began at 0700 hours and continued for half an hour. Near the first line of parapets, Funston halted his regiment and sent scouts out. They found the positions deserted so they and waited for the brigade to catch up.

MacArthur sent scouts from division headquarters toward Malolos and conferred with Funston on the railroad tracks, considering the apparently vacant rebel capital. MacArthur asked if he would take another look, disbelieving it was actually deserted and fearing a trap. Funston put Lieutenant Colonel Little in charge took Lieutenant Ball and a dozen men with him. He rode up a narrow road into the city mounted on a small native pony. Snipers fired on the patrol but they pressed on.

Funston was joined again by James Creelman, the irrepressible reporter. Funston wouldn't be stopped by a few snipers, so he dismounted and ran toward the city, shouting, "Give 'em hell, boys!" Springfield's cracked against the stone wall and he shouted "Now, for them!" He charged with sword and pistol in hand, with dramatic showmanship. Men scrambled over the wall and into San Fernando Plaza. A company of rebels fired on them and the small Kansas detail returned fire. The rebels never intended to stand and fight. Kansans took the public square, the Hall of Congress, and Aguinaldo's residence and headquarters which were all ablaze.

He learned from Chinese workers Aguinaldo departed days earlier, leaving a small rear guard to delay them. He sent word to MacArthur the city was clear and was soon joined by all of the regiments and the brigade commander. The American flag was quickly raised. Capture of the capital was a bloodless victory for the division, but through it all—Caloocan, Tuliajan River crossing, Malinta, Polo, Meycauayan, Marilao, Bocaue, and Guiguinto—the campaign long and hard-fought against a formidable conventional army. Breakout from Manila was complete, but war was still on.

The New York Times reported the "troops behaved splendidly. They advanced steadily against successive lines of trenches, through woods and jungles, suffering from the most frightful heat." That afternoon they enjoyed a feast of coconuts, bananas, and a well-earned rest. Meanwhile, Lieutenant Charles Crawford, appointed to West Point by Edward Funston in lieu of his son, graduated. He was brevetted a captain for gallant service in battle at Santiago, Cuba, and was on orders to the Philippines. Newspaper correspondents conjectured whether the plebe who had taken Funston's place at the Military Academy would be assigned to the unschooled colonel's regiment. He wasn't.

Had Funston gone to West Point he would have missed two years of fighting as a guerrilla in Cuba, consequently promotion to volunteer colonel and command of the Kansas regiment in the Philippines—and he'd never have met Eda. Fortune smiled.

Jayhawkers were proud they were first to occupy Caloocan and now were first in Malolos. The governor of Kansas quickly cabled his congratulations to the regiment. Funston moved the battalions through Malolos and into defensive positions a mile north of the town along the railroad line. When outposts had been established and the entire division positioned, they again waited.

TWELVE

Second Division didn't capitalize on success at Malolos for three weeks while consolidating new positions, preparing for counterattack, and securing extended lines of communications with the support base in Manila. Rest was welcomed by men suffering under stifling heat without tropical-weight uniforms, and exertion of fast marches and rushing attacks. Fifty men were overcome by heat, including Funston, who dropped utterly exhausted.

The brigade commander, Brigadier General Otis, resigned his commission to return to his business in the United States. He believed, as did many, the enemy was on the run and the war nearly over. Before he left, Otis said of Funston, "He's the greatest daredevil fighter in the army, and he'd rather fight than eat. I never saw a man who enjoyed fighting so much. He watched every chance in a scrap and never missed an opportunity."

Brigadier General Lloyd Wheaton, who had commanded the Separate Brigade, took over Otis' brigade. Wheaton had shown the courage and aggressiveness that characterized him in the Civil War. Funston admired him and said, "He seemed to enjoy fighting for its own sake, and had a positive contempt for danger." Funston also said Wheaton "despised a coward" yet was "most generous in his recognition of every gallant action by members of his command...inclined to stretch a point to give others the credit...."

While Americans rested, General Luna, didn't rest. His large and well-armed army was still full of fight although withdrawing into the northern mountains of Luzon. American connections with Manila were extended and vulnerable, especially the railroad which could not be entirely protected. In addition to normal sniping, Luna developed a plan to attack.

MacArthur directed the Oregon and Minnesota regiments to secure the routes to Manila by stationing companies at critical points such as bridges or junctions. Luna made multiple surprise attacks during the night and the simultaneous surprise attacks stunned dozing Americans.

Alarming Morse code messages rattled into the headquarters one after another from Marilao, Bocaue, Bigaa, and Guiguinto, before telegraph lines were cut, then battle sounds filled information gaps. General Wheaton responded immediately with some men on foot by following the railroad tracks and collecting more along the way. He routed the rebels with his quick response at four locations and mustered an armored train car equipped with several Gatling machineguns near Guiguinto. The car, without an engine, was pushed along the tracks by sweating soldiers. Some bridges and rails were damaged but engineers quickly repaired them.

Eventually the division prepared to resume its advance, crossing the Quingua River, then came on line at the Bag-Bag. They waited all day, listening to small arms and artillery resounding like a distant thunderstorm.

By morning, lines were restored and the 20th Kansas followed a cart road just west of the railroad. MacArthur accompanied the brigade as Chinese coolies pushed the four-car armed train—two flat cars and two box cars. The first flat car was armed for direct action with a naval six-pounder and three machineguns while the other carried supplies and ammunition. Box cars housed the crew.

§

After marching several miles, the Kansans came to a field of young corn, and beyond was a railway bridge over the Bag-bag River, defended by rebels in earthworks. Funston discussed plans with MacArthur and Wheaton while the armored train approached. Wheaton ordered him to have a detail guard the train and its guns. Suddenly the guns on the train opened up on enemy trenches joined by rifles of deployed infantry. The rebels returned fire for half an hour. Finally, Wheaton ordered Funston to seize the bridge for a crossing with all guns and artillery in support.

The narrow zone of attack accommodated only one company, so Funston directed Captain Boltwood to move his company forward, concealed by the cornfield. While they advanced in rushes, Funston, Sergeant Major Warner, and Trumpeter Barshfield ran beside cornfield with horses on leash.

Funston stood with his horse, watching, cracking his whip against his riding boot. When troops reached the bridge, supporting fires stopped and they spread out to fight from the open. They were unable to stop rebels from dropping the farther span of the steel bridge into the water.

Funston shouted, "Who goes across with me?" He was answered by a chorus of volunteers.

"It's a swim," he said, and the chorus replied they all could swim.

He selected ten and ran to the embankment at the end of the bridge. They had to cross the river and secure the other side in order to use the bridge, which was two hundred feet long with a sixty-foot section lopped off the far end. He believed they could snake across and wanted find out, so he picked four of the ten and left six to cover them. Lieutenant Ball, Sergeant Enslow, Trumpeter Barshfield, and Corporal Ferguson removed boots and dropped arms and ammunition, then followed him onto the bridge. He swung down to reach a steel rod running diagonally from the top of one stanchion to the water line at the next. Others followed him down the rod to the water. Funston dropped first, sank ten feet and came up sputtering. They swam forty-five feet to the other side and rushed the trenches, dripping wet, barefoot, and unarmed. Fortunately, rebels in the trenches were dead or disabled from train guns. They grabbed Mausers and ammunition to fight and waited for more to come across.

Funston was sopping wet and climbed back over the bridge to a group of admiring men, but there was no backslapping or cheering. He looked like he had been "pulled from a watery grave," said one man who offered him his boots. Funston said, "I only need dry socks."

"I have a dry pair for you, sir," he replied.

"Good boy," said Funston, but "they must be yours." Funston pulled on the dry socks, then his wet boots with brass spurs, but refused dry clothes. "They'll be dry in a little while," he said.

"How'd it feel going across there, Colonel?"

"Kind of ticklish," he said. "But they're poor marksmen." The chaplain offered his hand before he joined his regiment, deployed along the river bank. Later when questioned about leaving his regiment to swim the river, he said, "I just forgot myself and couldn't help it."

The moon came up clear and full and shone down on them all night. Their camp fires were cheery, bamboo fuel popping like Springfield rifles. But not everyone slept. One company shouldered muskets at sundown for outpost duty. Tomorrow they would cross over the larger Rio Grande.

§

John Bass, special correspondent for *Harper's Weekly*, was embedded with MacArthur's division during the push. Had he not witnessed the crossing of the Rio Grande, events might have been questioned, but he saw the story developing. "The crossing of the Rio Grande and the taking of the strong insurgent positions on the other bank was not, like the actions of the previous days, due to the combined movement of more or less large bodies of men. It was due to the individual efforts of a few men. Strategy and tactics were not concerned. Generals and general officers had nothing to do with it. The colonel of the Kansas regiment planned it, and he and a handful of American soldiers executed it. Military writers will probably never mention the crossing of the Rio Grande except, perhaps, with mild protests that military rules were broken; that the risk was too great and the chances of success too slight. In the living history of men, however, Colonel Funston's crossing the Rio Grande will stand out as the most daring act of the war."

The brigade came to a standstill short of the town by the deep and wide river Rio Grande. The breakout and pursuit had become a series of hard river crossings against well-organized defensive lines. Division engineers constructed a foot bridge over the broken span of railroad crossing over the Bag-bag. The entire 20th Kansas carefully crossed the scaffolding next day along with the most of the 1st Brigade. Terrain around Calumpit was constricted by converging rivers and the lagoon. The mission of forcing passage was assigned to Brigadier Wheaton's brigade while Hale's supported from along the Rio Grande. MacArthur came forward for firm control and timely decisions as the situation developed.

Reconnaissance parties crept to the river line and engaged rebels on the far side to ascertain their strength. This position was the strongest the division had yet encountered. The river Rio Grande de la Pampanga was four hundred feet wide, very deep and fast flowing, the opposite shore defended by four thousand well-armed insurgents in elaborate earthworks constructed with strong overhead cover, dirt supported by steel rails and wooden ties removed from the bridge and tracks, and parapets reinforced by bamboo revetments. Trenches were interconnected for relocating troops unexposed. Three captured Spanish artillery pieces and a Maxim gun supported.

Twentieth Kansas found shelter a bit back from the river. Captain Flanders' company occupied a brick railway freight house one hundred yards from the near end of the steel bridge and knocked firing holes in the walls to fire across the river. The enemy responded with artillery, missing its sight, which lobbed twenty shells at the building without a hit. But, an overshot round landed near where Funston conferred with Brigadier Wheaton, Major Young and Lieutenant Ball. Wheaton sniffed at the annoyance while Young and Ball ducked, covered with dirt but unhurt. Moments later Ball was hit in the face with a stray bullet.

Funston rushed to the freight house and organized troops to take a burned rice mill on the river bank. Otherwise not much progress was made although rifle fire and cannons continued all day, showing the difficulty of crossing the powerful river.

The night was the cool but Funston saw his commanders "were deeply concerned over the situation, and thought it was up to someone to do something...." He volunteered to assail the bridge with a dozen men. MacArthur was not optimistic but allowed it—if only a few men could get across they could secure a foothold for others.

He set two hundred Chinese laborers through the night digging trenches to approach the bridge safely. Rails and ties had been removed and stringers eight feet apart held up the skeleton of a bridge, so he wanted each man to scurry through the trenches with a long plank to span gaps in the bridge, and then lay them to cross one stringer at a time. Covering fire from infantry and artillery would keep the rebels' heads down.

Funston's fifteen volunteers worried if stringers were missing they couldn't span the gaps with their planks, leaving them stranded in the open on the bridge. Corporal Ferguson, a scout, offered to inspect the entire length of the bridge prior to an attempted crossing. This was dangerous, but Funston knew Ferguson was the best man. Funston and Captain Flanders crawled with him to the near end of the bridge. He removed his shoes, stripped to his shorts, and shimmied hand-over-hand beneath the bridge, using angle irons and reinforcing rods for hand and footholds. A slip would splash him into dark, swirling waters forty feet below.

They waited nervously for two hours in the dark under the end of the steel carcass until Ferguson returned with bad news. Some stringers on the far side, nearest the enemy, had in fact, been removed and they couldn't cross using planks. Funston sent a runner to inform Wheaton and MacArthur. Meanwhile, more volunteers wanted to join the assault if a way was found. Funston sent scouts along the banks in both directions looking for a raft or boat of any kind. A barking dog and cackling chickens alerted the far trenches that something was afoot. Flashes lit the other side of the river and bullets zipped and popped. Plan two was abandoned after midnight and the small group fell to the ground exhausted and discouraged.

Sniping resumed with the blazing sun but fortune smiled—in daylight, some Kansans spotted a partially burned raft downriver from the bridge. Plans One and two had failed, but plan three took shape—if someone could swim a rope across to the enemy side and tie it off, the raft could be used to ferry troops. Several volunteered for the suicide mission but Privates William Trembley and Edward White were chosen for their courage and known swimming skills.

During the previous pause, each company was issued twenty-five new Krag-Jorgenson rifles. One hundred of the best sharpshooters were picked from across the regiment, spread along the river bank and told to protect the river crossing. MacArthur put division artillery and all machineguns at Wheaton's disposal to support the risky undertaking.

White and Trembley stripped behind a clump of bamboo, tied the end of the long rope around one's waist, and they plunged into the fast flowing river. Dragging the rope through water made the swim hard and slow even as it paid out by handlers on the shore while soldiers pounded the parapets with rifle fire, Gatling guns, a Hotchkiss revolving cannon, and artillery pieces.

In Funston's own words, "As a melodrama the whole scene was a howling, or rather a roaring, success. The greatest lover of the sensational could not have wished for anything more thrilling. The two men battling slowly across the current, with the snake-like rope dragging after them; the grim and silent men firing with top speed over their heads into the trenches on the other bank; the continuous popping of the revolving cannon, a gun of the pompom type; the steady drumming of Gatlings and the constant succession of crashes from the big field-pieces, their shells flying harmlessly from the armored trenches on the other bank, or hurling steel rails and wagon loads of earth into the air; the thin film of smoke rising along both banks of the river, and the air filled with dust thrown up by striking shells and bullets, made a scene that could not fade from one's memory in many a lifetime. There was now being carried out one of the most difficult of military operations, forcing the passage of an unfordable river in the face of an entrenched enemy."

The swimmers reached the bank exhausted, still dragging the wet rope, at the base of an earth work already battered. Artillery fires stopped as the naked swimmers reached shore but sharpshooters placed well-aimed shots very close. White's and Trembley's situation was precarious—separated from comrades by a wide and raging river, naked and unarmed, mere feet from hundreds of rebels, and in broad daylight. They needed somewhere to tie off the rope. They searched frantically for something solid, but the only hard fixtures were connected to parapets above. They made mud balls, dummy grenades, and tossed them over the top, driving several insurgents to run, only to be brought down by snipers with Krags.

The two men made a noose at the end of the rope and gathered slack, dashed to the nearest trench, slipped the lasso over a bamboo upright and ran back to the river bank. Kansas riflemen raked the top of the parapet to discourage anyone from cutting the rope.

As the partially-burned ferry raft was loaded and readied for the first crossing, two men ran to the water with a small dug-out canoe they found hidden under a house. Corporal Kerfoot and Private Tyler grabbed White's and Trembley's clothes and weapons and shoved off. Halfway there, the dug-out turned over and dumped men, clothes, and equipment in raging water. They swam out, but clothes and weapons for the naked swimmers were lost with their own rifles and ammunition.

The larger raft was loaded with eight men, including Funston. He was aware he was leaving the regiment behind but unwilling, and unable, to leave the small detachment alone on the other side. Raft riders pulled on the rope until they joined the swimmers on the enemy side of the river. Two men pulled the raft back for another load, so only six could cross at once.

Funston took head count after several ferry trips. He had Captain Orwig, Lieutenants Whisner and Hopkins, and forty-one enlisted men armed with Krags and two hundred cartridges each. He left a small detachment to keep the ferry running with orders to have new arrivals organize, defend the flanks and rear of the landing site, and secure the bridgehead. Funston formed skirmishers along the riverbank and moved upstream. When they attacked, he had them yell to give the impression of a larger group. But they ran into a small, deep stream, the Rio Francis, which emptied into the larger Rio Grande. Trenches had been deserted but those across the Rio Francis were swarming with rebels, protected by thick overhead cover and side trenches.

They were stymied again by the size of the stream but when they moved inland they disturbed a nest of rebels in thick bamboo. They fired on them and were supported by artillery, machineguns, and infantry across the river. Shrapnel from shells screamed overhead before impacting very near—a short round worse than the rebels. Although four thousand rebels were on this side of the river, they directly faced about six hundred.

Suddenly the odds became worse. Several men yelled, "It's the Maxim. We're goners!" Funston saw the Maxim and crew under a stone culvert, firing across the river. Those on the other side of the river couldn't hit the gun from there.

Funston shouted, "Cease Fire!" and then told them to fully load their magazines. Then they stood and fired at the Maxim all at once. When firing stopped the Maxim crew was dead or disabled.

The enemy was withdrawing but firefights were still underway. Funston's party found several dug-outs and crossed the Rio Francis tributary, scrambling up the other side in small groups even as one boat overturned, dumping those into the swirling water.

MacArthur and Wheaton watched the attack from the freight house while controlling supporting fires. When the Rio Francis was crossed, Wheaton crossed the wrecked structure carefully with troopers, rifles slung, using both hands for support. They laid more planks over stringers, creating a shaky foot bridge. Other companies followed, pursuing rebels toward Apalit.

The battle of Calumpit was over. Friendly and enemy wounded were collected and sent to Manila, enemy dead buried in trenches where they died, and hundreds of rifles and thousands of rounds of ammunition gathered. MacArthur's official report read, "The successful passage of the river must be regarded as a remarkable military achievement, well calculated to fix the attention of the most careless observer and to stimulate the fancy of the most indifferent."

Funston's reputation was solidified with his older peers, superiors, and his regiment. Frederick Funston, William Trembley, and Edward White were awarded Congressional Medals of Honor for forcing the crossing of the Rio Grande and the major victory in the Battle of Calumpit. Edwin Wildman, an American journalist reporting on the operations also observed the crossing of the river and called it "totally outside all the tenets of military tactics and a gamble of an adventuresome mind that offered hardly a chance in a thousand of success." But it was typical of Fred Funston.

Theodore Roosevelt sent a personal letter to Funston from Oyster Bay, New York, in which he mentioned attending a reunion of the Rough Riders in Las Vegas. During his remarks he had made Funston's exploits the theme of his talk. "I knew your career before you enlisted," he said. "I had the greatest sympathy with the spirit of adventure which drove you to Alaska and to Cuba and which has graven your name for all time on the American honor roll for what you have done in the Philippines. ... Besides being an adventurer, in the best sense of the word, and a natural soldier, you are a practical believer in civic life also—in honesty, courage and horse sense—all three qualities being so indispensable that the lack of any one renders the other two pretty near useless. I like your style."

Success changed everything. His name was now recognized all over the United States and also changed the nature of the war from conventional to unconventional. The message received by General Antonio Luna was it was time for guerilla war.

§

After the hair-raising crossing of the Rio Grande River, Fred was more concerned with resting and refitting his Kansas regiment then basking in glory. Several days were needed to ferry artillery and supply trains while the damaged bridge was repaired. He allowed his men to rest, ordering only necessary outposts and light patrol duties, tightening internal lines by pulling outposts back so fewer were required. Men chatted, slept, and tried to stay out of perpetual monsoon rains. Fred acquired two native houses in nearby Apalit for off duty men to shelter from the rain.

When men were cared for, he rode "Freddy's Fast Express" into Manila to spend a couple of days with Eda, and visit the recuperating Major Metcalf. When he returned to the front, it was clear something would happen. MacArthur soon issued orders to march north to Santo Tomas.

Wheaton's brigade had bivouacked near Apalit and pushed out from there, following the railroad bed with the 20th Kansas west of the tracks. Leading units made initial contact in open terrain. The countryside was sliced by numerous waterways, lagoons, and ravines—one deep and sluggish lagoon was traversed by a railroad bridge defended by several hundred rebels. A hand car with the mounted Gatling gun hammered their defenses from the tracks. Wheaton encouraged the crew to fire faster and faster until a grizzled sergeant saluted him and said, "Sir, we are out of ammunition!"

Lieutenant Krause led his company to the bank of the lagoon, intending to rush the bridge. But it was dismantled as usual, so they spread out and laid down a heavy base of fire. Funston called Captain Albright to the bridge for orders, but a bullet zinged off the bridge and struck Albright's thigh. He cried, "This is certainly one hell of a birthday present."

Funston got two companies across the wrecked bridge a few men at a time. Wheaton told him to push along the tracks toward Santo Thomas station and find out the situation there. Scouts reported General Luna was assembling a large force for a counterattack against the small patrol that crossed. Luna led the charge himself, with a three to one advantage. Quick warning from the scouts allowed time for a hasty defense and the two companies made a valiant stand in a battle that lasted only five-minutes. But Lieutenant McTaggart and a private were hit and died. General Luna was also hit in the abdomen—the engagement was brief but very costly.

§

Hasty defense allowed the regiment to defend against the rebel's larger force, while loss of the wounded Luna, his dispirited fighters withdrew. Funston called for Captain Howard Scott's company to drive them away while two others defended the railroad. He wanted to press the pursuit, oblivious to Mauser rounds cracking all around. Then a bullet smashed Funston's left hand, bashing his field glasses.

Lieutenant Burt Mitchell recovered the scattered pieces of his binoculars, a Christmas present from Eda. When he saw the hand he called for a corpsman. The bullet had passed through the meaty span between his thumb and index finger and was dripping blood. He hadn't realized at first he was hit, but Mitchell's response and the smashed glasses were real enough. He refused to look, asked, "Is there anything left of it?" Mitchell assured him it was a clean shot. He stared at the gushing blood and blamed himself, "What a fool thing to do!" Mitchell and the corpsman bandaged his hand while he looked away.

Wheaton arrived with his staff, and ordered infantrymen firing from flat on the ground to stand and attack. Funston, already angered by his wound and the stalled attack, disliked anyone giving direct orders to his men. He ran with his bandaged hand waving in the air to stop the attack—too late. Three companies were already rushing forward. Since he was already running, he joined the attack with his hand throbbing and bleeding. Wheaton fired his revolver and pushed them on until the enemy broke and ran. They pushed through Santo Thomas and fell back during the night to consolidate.

As darkness gathered, the wounded were collected for transport to Manila. MacArthur said, "Well, Funston, you got it at last. I am glad it's no worse." The wounded were crammed into a jostling ambulance wagon pulled by four small ponies over the washboard wagon road toward the Bag-bag River Bridge. At midnight they reached the railroad where a train coach would take them to Manila—that ride another hour, and cramped.

At Caloocan station, a soldier handed him a telegram from Colonel Thomas Barry: "Congratulations. Shake, if your wounded hand will permit. No man better deserves the star." Funston was promoted to Brigadier General of Volunteers. He was elated by the news, forgetting the pain in his hand and anxious to share the news with Eda.

§

A reporter from the *Chicago Tribune* stepped off the train at the flag station for the Santa Fe Railroad at Carlyle, Kansas, hitched a ride to a farm four miles north of Iola, to deliver a message in person. He found the "farmer's friend," Edward Funston, tilling his field. The reporter informed him his son was being promoted to brigadier general. "I suppose there is no mistake this is true?" Funston asked. When the reporter confirmed the dispatches, he turned toward the house and walked away, the reporter following. "I must tell Fred's mother," he said. "She has a right to receive the news first."

The quiet, retiring woman joined them in the former congressman's study, surrounded by a large desk and shelves of books. She was small, less than one hundred pounds, and seemed fragile standing beside her husband at six foot, two inches, and over two hundred pounds. "This is the young man who brought the news of Fred's promotion," he said, introducing the reporter. She nodded her head respectfully; tears filled her brown eyes but a smile crossed her face. The reporter observed, "Her silence was as eloquent of praise as the restrained expressions that fell from the lips of her herculean husband...."

Edward continued, "He came all the way from Chicago to tell us that Fred was a brigadier general." She smiled even wider. "But he does tell me that Fred is talked about a great deal about in Chicago."

"I hope they speak well of my boy," she said, trembling slightly. "If they knew him as well as we do, they would know he deserved it." The reporter assured them everyone knew he was a great soldier.

"Yes, Fred's a good boy," said Ann Funston. "But I wish he was back at home again."

Edward Funston moved to the window, looking out at the half-plowed field. "If Fred comes back alive...." He looked back at Ann, confirming they were thinking along the same lines. Nothing more said on that.

The reporter shifted the subject to politics, acknowledging there was talk of making their son governor of Kansas. The former Congressman always preferred the United States Senate. Ann brought them back to reality. "We'd better wait until he returns to talk of these things," she said. "He'll come back to us, too. I'm sure he will."

The reporter noted, "the tinge of sadness never once was lifted from the atmosphere. While father and mother evidenced their elation the shadow of apprehension was always present."

The New York Times re-filed the *Chicago Tribune* article, prompting letters to the editor with various opinions about Fred's prospects in politics. One letter, signed only "Kansan," gave some history of the 20th Kansas Volunteer Regiment and their commander. It also added, "Fred is a soldier, pure and simple. He is a natural cavalryman.... To elect him at office would be to spoil an excellent officer to make a very poor politician."

In Oakland, the Blankarts received the news of Funston's wound first by telegram. Theresa Blankart said, "We are quite anxious about it. We know that whenever there is any fighting he is always right out at front in the most dangerous place. Eda says his men adore him, and that every time he comes in the soldiers go out and cheer him."

§

Fred Funston knew promotion would move him out of the 20th Regiment he loved and into higher command. Yet he was concerned that his regiment have the best possible leader to replace him. The Kansas governor had ultimate authority but he believed his recommendation carried weight. He asked the twenty-eight officers in the regiment to confirm his choice of Major Wilder Metcalf as regimental commander. Metcalf was his most trusted combat comrade and MacArthur called him "Funston's strong right arm." Kansas Governor Stanley had replaced Governor Leedy in a recent election and concurred with the recommendation. Metcalf was still convalescing with a wounded foot, but Funston pinned his eagles on his collar as a full colonel.

Funston's crossing of the Rio Grande had captured the nation's attention and the War Department enjoyed some favorable publicity in an unpopular war. James Blount, an officer of volunteers in the Philippines from 1899 to 1901 and subsequently a United States District Judge in the islands, reflected on Funston's crossing of the Rio Grande. "The desperate bravery of the performance, like so many other things General Funston did in the Philippines, was so superb that one forgets how contrary it was to all known rules of the game of war." Major General Otis endorsed him as an "able leader of men," and MacArthur pushed for even more recognition of the man he considered almost a son.

§

Eda was ill and had taken to bed to await a doctor while in temporary quarters in the barracks. Heat and heavy humidity in Luzon had finally caught up with her and she was physically exhausted. While Fred was in the field she'd been active touring the relatively quiet city with other ladies. They visited wounded boys in the hospital regularly, entertained officers in the rear with music and refreshments in the evenings.

Before Fred arrived, a telegram reached her at the barracks where she was staying, informing her of his wound and that he'd be on the next train. She was worried she wouldn't see him right away but when the doctor arrived, he assured her the wound was minor and promised to meet the train. When the train arrived he examined him quickly and escorted him to Eda's bedside before going on to the hospital.

She remembered, "Soon I heard the voice which above all others I longed to hear. Straight to me he came and never, never, shall I forget that moment. After I had satisfied myself that I really had him again safe and alive, I was ready to hear something of what he had to relate. The first thing he did was to show me a telegram from headquarters informing him that he had been recommended for a brigadier generalship."

Fred's presence helped her recover more rapidly and she was able to escape the confining barracks and return to their quarters in the city. She was weary of the lonely life of a soldier's wife, and his long absences in dangerous situations made it even worse.

Fred reported to General Otis, still wearing a sling, for duty in his new rank. Instead, Otis ordered a medical board report, which confirmed that if the wound was exposed to field conditions before it was properly healed, would certainly become infected. "Confound it!" he stormed. "I was a big fool to wear that sling." So he dawdled with Eda and Wilder Metcalf until both officers were medically cleared to return to duty and she was better.

As Colonel Metcalf was recuperating and on crutches while Fred carried his arm in a sling, Eda recovering as well, the three spent two weeks on convalescence together.. They dined together, took carriage rides through the familiar city streets, enjoyed the promenades at the Luneta, and relaxed as tourists. The war slipped into the background for a time and Fred visited the Army-Navy club and carried on with British officers aboard the *H.M.S. Powerful* anchored in Manila Bay. His only duty was to report to the military hospital daily to have the bandages changed and the wound checked for infection.

Finally, he was too impatient for a sedentary life and with medical clearance reported to duty still wearing a sling for his hand and a star on his collar. He was given command of Wheaton's old brigade in MacArthur's division at San Fernando. Metcalf took command of the 20th Kansas, though still on crutches. Fred was proud of his wound leading Americans in combat, different from scars of more serious wounds fighting with Cuban insurgents—this one earned in service to his own country, the Purple Heart, a symbol his Civil War father would understand and appreciate.

Leaving Eda behind again, Funston rode out on a commander's reconnaissance, accompanied by a few scouts, into the town of Santa Rita. He found the population hiding outside the town. Using his best Spanish he persuaded town leaders they meant no harm. He accompanied the mayor out of town alone and led a long procession of Filipinos back into town shouting praise of Americans. Soldiers were surprised and amused by the bizarre scene. Trenches were cleared and the town put back to normal. Then Funston returned to headquarters in time for an insurgent attack in the northwest sector. He led eight companies of Kansans to reinforce the picket line and the insurgents melted away again, still smarting from their earlier defeat.

§

By the first of June, Eda was again in a debilitated condition but convinced her doctor to accompany her to San Fernando on the morning train for a brief consult with Fred before returning on the evening run after exchanging news and views.

Back in Manila, Eda was again alone in the big house with only one invalid soldier for protection. She invited Mrs. Schliemann, the chaplain's wife to come and stay one night with her. After that night she persuaded the chaplain to join them there as well. But, after three weeks, both Eda and Mrs. Schliemann fell ill. The doctor advised Eda the house was contaminated and unsafe. He insisted they move out at once. The Schliemann's moved back home, and Eda moved into a spare room of Dora Devol, wife of Major Carol Devol, the quartermaster, where she lived for the nine months she remained in Manila—waiting, writing, and considering the future.

THIRTEEN

San Fernando was pleasant enough for Brigadier General Fred Funston to wait while the railroad was repaired, replacement officers assigned, and he acquainted himself with new responsibilities. The town wasn't destroyed as many others were and had fine houses and buildings. A fertile plain stretched beside a rugged mountain range with pleasing vistas. Routine was slow-paced like the idyllic setting. He kept strong outposts with two battalions on the outskirts of town. Sniper fire and an irritating 3-inch Krupp field gun reminded a war was still on.

Tranquility ended when MacArthur gave a mission to take care of strong enemy trenches near Balacor. A mile from the outpost line a deep, dry ditch extended for a half mile. Each morning the Montana regiment sent a patrol to clear the ditch in case rebels were there. Usually the ditch was empty, but one morning the patrol was engaged and forced to withdraw.

MacArthur wanted it cleared out. Kansans estimated enemy strength as high as four thousand, requiring the entire brigade to deal with it. After heavy rain delayed the start, the brigade marched out in a column of fours. When they reached the trenches, rebels appeared to lack flank security so Funston ordered both regiments deploy while he led a reconnaissance patrol to see for himself. He decided to roll up the flanks in a pincer—hitting both ends at once.

He had the Utah field guns holding the attention of the middle while two Montana battalions attacked the right, two Kansas battalions the left. One battalion of each regiment kept the center under fire. Major Bell guided the Kansans into position since he'd scouted that area. Heavy rains covered their approach.

Funston's attack cleared both ends of the ditch. The fight cost Kansans two killed and six wounded, including Second Lieutenant Parker, a Civil War veteran. They found forty-eight dead Filipinos and took fifty-three prisoners.

§

A few days after the scramble for the ditch, MacArthur asked Funston to scout along the road leading north from Bacolor with only eighty men. He wanted to take more as the enemy outnumbered them. MacArthur refused, "If I give you a force of any size, you will bring on a pitched battle.... Examine the road, and if you encounter any considerable number of the enemy, come back."

As he left to organize the mission, Captain James Lockett, one of MacArthur's aides, stopped him in the hallway. He'd overheard the conversation, and said, "If you go out there with eighty men you will get the hell kicked out of you. I am going out to the Montana regiment, get it under arms, and when I think the firing has lasted long enough, come out and pry you loose."

Funston wanted forty of the best from each regiment, all armed with Krags. They reached Bacolor unchallenged. Funston posted Lieutenant Murphy and the Kansans to observe from the church tower while the Montana detachment advanced. He left orders that if the advancing group was attacked, the Kansans would counterattack. They would scout the road for only one mile so the reserve was never far away.

Three-quarters of a mile out the Montanans observed rebels and stopped. Funston moved up to see for himself. He ordered Montanans recon-by-fire to entice the enemy to return fire and ascertain their numbers and firepower. His answer came quickly—they were strong and well-armed. As American firepower increased, so did the rebels'. The ground opened with new fighters popping up along the front, preparing to attack.

Funston saw several hundred reinforcements coming and realized the futility of any attack he could make. The enemy's left was anchored in the trench but the right was massed and about to overrun them. It was time to withdraw—horses were sent back with wounded men by Chinese litter-bearers.

Small arms fire ripped overhead as the Kansans protected the left, about to be ravaged. All reloaded to fire and withdraw in bounds, covering each other.

Rebels, determined to decimate them, stood and charged, yelling and firing, closing the gap fast. While those on the left were thwarted by expert marksmanship, the horde on the right launched a colossal wave, closing fast. Funston said, "Never before had I seen the Filipinos take the aggressive, and I was astonished beyond measure."

Montanans had brought only one hundred and fifty rounds each for the short patrol. Kansans had more but redistribution was impossible under the circumstances. Captain Lockett kept his word and led the rest of the Montana regiment across the field from San Fernando, firing rapidly and giving some relief to the beleaguered patrol. Suddenly rebels stalled and gave way.

Funston credited the outcome to courageous actions of commanders and small unit leaders, including those leading detachments outside a normal chain-of-command. Their courage, flexibility, and initiative combined with strong discipline were major factors in success—plus the initiative of Captain Lockett. Superior marksmanship, courage, and initiative carried that day.

§

While Emilio Aguinaldo retained his position as *El Presidente*, he never relinquished his position as commander-in-chief of the rebel army. From his mountain command post he issued last ditch orders to dislodge Americans from San Fernando and drive them back to Manila. This was a turning point in the war, a determination whether the war would remain a conventional war of two armies in the field or whether it would devolve into something else. Brazenly, Aguinaldo sent a note to Funston, "You did well at Calumpit, but next Thursday we will retake San Fernando."

Aguinaldo never personally commanded operations against Americans, rather conceived strategic direction and broad plans. In this case, he intended to surround San Fernando with seven thousand troops, rush outposts in coordinated attacks, enter the town, burn it, and drive Americans out. The attack was set to begin in the darkest of night, led by commanders acting independently. The plan was complicated, uncoordinated, without unity of command on the ground—a risky operation, a desperate, last-ditch gambit to regain control of the war.

The concept depended on surprising outposts and passing through the picket line quickly before reinforcements arrived. In San Fernando, highly flammable nipa huts would be set afire, creating confusion and hesitation to use rifles inside the town, giving advantage to attackers. If Americans were routed at San Fernando, the war could be transformed.

However, command and control of the operation was inadequate, the attack disorganized at the outset, and no unit reached the line of departure on time, some not arriving until after daylight, or after the fight was over. Surprise was lost along with the initiative.

An impending attack was realized when Captain Howard Scott of the Kansas regiment returned from a patrol half a mile past his outpost. He heard verbal commands of an enemy preparing to attack—the Tagalog words cryptic, their meaning clear. He briefed Funston, who sent a report to MacArthur and warning orders to battalions to immediately reinforce outposts. As daylight came, first shots broke out near the old sugar mill at Bacolor. A crescent-shaped battle line of nearly eight hundred men appeared in the faint light. They charged, firing wildly. That the rebels were making a coordinated attack at all was a strategic surprise even though tactical surprise was lost.

Kansans stood above their trenches, unafraid of ineffective shooters, taking careful aim to drop them, inflicting heavy losses, but not enough to stop them. Montanans faced a similar situation, but got a break when attackers sought cover in a sunken road, a deep ditch, clumps of bamboo, and ripening rice crops.

Both regiments were fully deployed and Funston considered a counterattack. Before he could launch it, a group of attackers worked their way close and charged across the open. They perished in a storm of bullets, but efforts by the Kansans to take and hold the ravine also failed.

Major Bishop assembled two companies of Kansans and charged seventy yards to seize the sunken road, thick with enemy soldiers—hand-to-hand fighting. This broke the back of the attack and the sunken road was a scene of carnage. Even Funston admitted it was "not a pretty sight." Two native priests in robes with crucifixes in hand were among the dead. Funston considered, "their presence and exhortations on that occasion had no little to do with the unusual pluck and dash shown by this particular force."

§

The war in the Philippines had changed. In an interview with Funston by Roundseville Wildman, the consul in Hong Kong, he was reported to say, "I believe that there should be a little less gunpowder and more diplomacy." Later he denied saying that, but the truth of the statement resonated. Other transitions were in store for Fred Funston and the 1st Brigade. Kansans and Montanans were ordered to Manila to return to the states—volunteer discharge dates already passed months before.

Eda was especially anxious about getting home for their first anniversary, but wrote to her mother that "Fred is still away. I think of nothing all day but Fred and me going home." But on July 4th, a traditional celebration was held in Manila with buildings and vessels decked in bunting and flags. Regimental bands began playing right after reveille, national salutes booming from the ships guns, and even young Filipinos joining in street parties. In Manila, the Declaration of Independence was read frequently and firecrackers and rockets burst everywhere. The 20th Kansas organized a banquet beginning with oxtail soup, shrimp salad, vegetables, fish and chicken, and ending with a wide selection deserts, sauterne and cigars. Toasts and short speeches followed. Eda celebrated with friends while Fred kept constant vigil over San Fernando until the last possible moment, clinging to what he did best.

Montana and Kansas volunteers consolidated in Manila to prepare for passage back to their states. With his mind turning to Kansas, Fred reflected on milestones the regiment surpassed from initial muster in Topeka, through training at Camp Merritt and The Presidio, shipment to the Philippines, initial engagements, and the breakout north as far as San Fernando. He considered his 20th Kansas Volunteer Regiment a good one which became even better during a year and a half of service. They had only two desertions shortly after muster, but lost thirty-five from disease, and in battle lost three officers and thirty enlisted killed, ten officers and one hundred twenty-nine enlisted wounded. But at the end, he saw reluctance to volunteer for missions outside the lines, reality of going home weighing on hearts and minds.

To his men he was one of them, a "bullet eater," willing and eager to be at the front with them, always at the decisive point of action. On the battlefield, fighting came first; everything else was to support the fight. His propensity was to lead attacks, make river crossings, scout enemy positions. This led some in the regular army to disparage him as just a high ranking infantryman or cavalryman, a "Boss Scout." In reality, he was a leader unafraid, a commander who wanted eyes on the target before sending men into battle. He was as comfortable with enlisted men of his regiment and brigade as he was with general officers. Promotion to general only made him a soldier with more assets. His colorful language and appreciation of a soldier's situation, willingness to share it, and pungent and earthy sense of humor drew them to him, as he was drawn to them.

The *Kansas City Journal* (Missouri) published an editorial, republished by *The New York Times*, reflecting on the demonstrated changes in the 20th Kansas Regiment. The article pointed out Funston's initial arrival in San Francisco from Tampa, when the regiment was at "odds and ends," when most of the men clung to the idea they were on a "picnic." He commenced at once to "hammer the regiment into shape." His hard discipline and training made him unpopular at first, but "the Kansans were not fit to go until Funston had battered the picnic idea out of their heads." Numerous letters poured in to the Journal back then, criticizing him as a martinet. "But look at the letters which are coming from these self-same men since the 20th has gained its battle glory. They idolize their little colonel and vie with each other in praising his deeds of valor. ... He holds their supreme confidence and most fervid admiration."

His reputation as a scrapper spread across the United States, but especially in Kansas, while San Francisco also claimed him and his beautiful Oakland bride as theirs. Funston was frequently mentioned by Theodore Roosevelt and they continued to correspond after the Rio Grande operation. Career opportunities in business or politics awaited him as a civilian, and he'd shown little interest in a regular army commission, although Eda encouraged him to consider it. He wanted to earn a good living, as he now had two people to support and, the possibility of a child in their future. But Eda wanted their future firmly established before starting a family.

The brigade's two volunteer regiments, Kansans and Montanans, were replaced by the regular 9th and 12th U. S. Infantry. Before the brigade redeployed, Funston was struck down by a recurrence of his old hip injury from Cuba, his limp more pronounced and painful as infection flared. Emergency surgery was required in Manila. He whiled away two weeks with Eda prior to surgery by going shopping, lunching with Metcalf, and hanging out at the Army-Navy Club. In the evenings he enjoyed the Luneta with Eda, dining with her at home or with friends. Then, he went under the knife again. At first the results seemed successful and he was back on his feet. But the wound abscessed again and he endured another surgery. This time the results seemed more successful with infection defeated.

Four hundred eighty sick and wounded men, including sixty-seven Kansans, departed on the hospital ship *Morgan City*. On board they spoke lightly of their wounds and scars, but had high praise for their officers. "Of Funston, they are proud as if he was the personal property of each man…and how Major Whitman, with a sick leave in his pocket…remained with the regiment." And they were glad Major Metcalf was made a colonel…the most popular officer, after Funston, in the army…."

Prior to departure of the healthy Kansas and Montana volunteers, Funston was ordered to return with the Kansans to muster out of service as a volunteer officer. Fred and Eda vacated their house in Manila and boarded the British ship *Tartar* along with officers and men of the 20th Kansas bound for San Francisco. They stayed over for three days in Hong Kong to have barnacles scraped from the hull of the ship in dry dock. Fred, Eda, and Metcalf enjoyed sights in the British colony, visited prominent Americans there, and dined at the best restaurants. British army sergeants threw a banquet for the Kansas regiment and staged a rifle shooting match, which the British surprisingly won. The Kansas band reciprocated with a lively serenade at the Theatre Royal.

Unfortunately, during their stay in Hong Kong tempers flared—prescient of things to come. Fred Funston attracted fierce loyalty, but also heated dissent. Captain Boltwood, an elderly officer and Civil War veteran had courageously commanded a Kansas company. Funston was aware of closet detractors but not the full extent until that evening. While the *Tartar* sat off shore at Hong Kong he was having dinner with Eda and other officers in the officer's mess. Boltwood complained loudly about him and the regiment. Shocked by such disparaging words from an officer, he slammed his chair backwards as he leapt to his feet and shouted, "I will not permit you or anyone else to criticize my conduct!" Boltwood rose to meet him as Funston lunged for him. Colonel Metcalf intervened and stopped a brawl. As regimental commander, he ordered Boltwood from the mess while Eda escorted Fred to their stateroom with a gentle hand and soothing words.

Metcalf stemmed the fight then, but on home turf Funston and Metcalf discovered seeds of discontent had already spread a virtual minefield of words. A cabal of officers, including Boltwood and Lieutenant Colonel Little, Major Whitman, and Lieutenant Hall, conspired to undermine him with allegations—executing prisoners, denigrating fellow officers, and lying about achievements. Metcalf gathered evidence countering the charges and army investigators interviewed over two hundred soldiers, completely clearing him. However, he was hurt by the allegations, both personally and in the press.

The *Tartar* continued a meandering journey home and while underway, Funston agreed to speak with reporters. He pinned a "bit of yellow cloth," a sunflower, to his blue blouse, tossed his cap on a table in the cabin and settled into a comfortable corner. He refused to speak of General Otis, but lavishly praised MacArthur, Wheaton, and Lawton. When asked why they were not permitted to do more, he smiled, shrugged, and said only, "Well ... you know." He complained "what we need over in that country is cavalry.... You can't catch these fellows with dismounted troops." Then he praised the commissary department under Major Devol and even gave credit to newspaper correspondents: "They didn't sit in Manila and get information from the headquarters, but were always right out in front."

The ship cruised along the coast of Japan with beautiful vistas of the islands on display en route to Yokohama and Tokyo Bay. Fred and Eda enjoyed more leisurely sight-seeing and a dinner party hosted by the American consul in Tokyo that lasted past midnight curfew. After a pleasant respite in Japan, many days of tossing seas and seasickness followed. The *Tartar* crossed the International Date Line, passed through the Golden Gate, and arrived safely in San Francisco Bay at last.

§

Home is one of the most comprehensive words in the English language. That single expression represents the wood, brick and mortar, picket fences and flowers, home cooking, mother, father, wife and children, old friends and jobs—life as it should be. Volunteers had turned their backs on all these to accept their country's call and fight its battles.

Despite rains and dark clouds hanging low over the bay area until midnight, clear and sharp conditions arrived with the British steamer *Tartar* and hospital ship *Morgan City*. Kansas Governor William Stanley and an exuberant group of citizen representatives had traveled by rail to San Francisco to meet their boys when they docked. As the *Tartar* dropped anchor, Kansans mingled with loyal San Franciscans on the docks, others boarded several small tugs circling the *Tartar's* hull. Quarantine regulations kept them from swarming the ship, but cheers, waving flags and shouted messages of encouragement clearly showed their pride.

As tugs drew alongside the *Tartar*, a merry fusillade of fresh red apples was hurled to the boys to welcome them back to "God's country." Among those laughing and catching apples on the upper deck was Eda Funston, her black gown standing out amidst army blue and khaki. She blew kisses in return, especially aimed for her mother, father, and two sisters. "Oh! Do let me get hold of that mother of mine!" she cried as she rushed into the arms of the gray-haired lady, standing speechless with emotion. Eda introduced her father, a big man with flowing white beard, to her husband for the first time. Some reporters were allowed into her stateroom after the initial greetings and introductions. Upon questioning, Eda admitted that she had "seen many things that saddened her" but would not have traded it for a "million dollars. Yet, sometimes, I feel a thousand years old."

Fred's celebration was cut short when he received word that his classmate from the University of Kansas, Will Snow, had drowned in choppy waters while the *Tarter* was plowing into the bay. He was a San Francisco newspaperman and was anxious to meet his old friend and get an exclusive. Snow, the son of the chancellor of the University of Kansas, had hitched a ride on the launch *Sybil* to meet the ship before it docked. Just after shouting to a soldier, "Ask Funston to come to the rail. Tell him Will Snow wants to talk to him," he slipped on the wet deck and plummeted into the water while the tide was swiftest in the Golden Gate. Snow fought desperately to keep his head above the ragged white caps while the launch was still lashed to the larger ship. He drowned in the rough, cold waters, so near his old college friend. It was a hard blow to San Franciscans, who knew Snow as an avid and fair reporter, harder still on Fred Funston.

But before they could free themselves from official duties, Funston and Metcalf met privately with Kansas Governor Stanley and then held a press conference to make their return official. Funston took some questions, giving his views on the fighting spirit of the Kansans and the situation in the Philippines. At eight that evening, he led a regimental march column through cheering citizens up Market Street to Van Ness, and then down Lombard to their camp at The Presidio where snowy white tents and real mattresses, large dining halls with tables and chairs, and best of all, milk and butter, awaited them. Funston wore the same boots that served him throughout the campaign, still stained by Luzon mud. Behind him limped Colonel Metcalf, a yellow sunflower pinned to his khakis as it was to the chest of every man.

On Van Ness, Funston and the Kansas and California governors wheeled into line beside General Shafter. Eda stood beside him; she knew many of the men by name and dabbed away a tear as she saw the sun flowered women of the Kansas delegation departing buses to welcome her husband and his men. After the parade, Eda was spirited by family to Oakland while Fred was surrounded by children at the corner of Van Ness and Sutter. "We want to say to our papas," said one boy, shoving his hand out, "'shake the hand that shook Funston's.'" He pumped hand after hand. "Say, General," shouted a red-headed boy. "How's the swimming in the Philippines?"

"Wet!" he replied to a roar of cheers and laughter.

"When I'm big I'll be a soldier," lisped a little lad of about six, still clinging to his mother's hand.

"If you do, you'll be a good one," said Funston as he broke loose to board a trolley heading to the Occidental Hotel. Hundreds tried to follow him and he was unable to completely escape until behind closed doors of the hotel.

While Colonel Metcalf handled details of the 20th Kansas' demobilization, Funston oversaw arrangements for both regiments. More than three thousand people gathered at Mechanics' pavilion to honor the 20th Kansas with concerts and dinner sponsored by the Y.M.C.A. and hosted by Iowa volunteers. Eda relaxed in Oakland with her parents and sisters before continuing the journey to Kansas, to meet his parents and neighbors in Iola. Fred spent his limited free time with them and divided the rest between official duties, with Will Snow's father—the grieving Chancellor of the University of Kansas—luncheons with Governor Stanley at the Occidental Hotel, and visiting old friends.

Oakland held yet another parade and celebration on October 13th. General Shafter and civilian dignitaries led the procession in carriages, but the center of attention was Funston and the East Oakland girl with him, their carriage filled with flowers from school children. Red Cross ladies arranged long tables for dinner at the Tabernacle. Fred and Eda were escorted to the platform and he thanked the people of Oakland and praised both Montanans and Kansans. "I want to say that there never was an army better housed, better fed, better equipped, better disciplined.... The hospital service is so good that within three hours...a wounded man is receiving the attention of a surgeon." When he was finished, the crowd clambered to hear from their Oakland girl, bringing Eda to the front to also thank the people of Oakland for their gracious support. After this, Fred and Eda cancelled all further public engagements, yet the constant stream of visitors to the Blankart residence was endless.

Reporters still snuck through barricades for "tiny talks" with Eda. When asked about being the wife of a hero, she said, "Fred and I don't realize the importance of it all... I would love him just the same if he were only a corporal.... I have seen wounded soldiers brought into the hospitals on stretchers and I have visited the hospitals, and the things I saw there I can never forget.... One could not bear up many more months under so terrible a strain as that was."

Then, Fred received a telegram at The Presidio announcing that President McKinley had selected him from a list of officers for extension on active volunteer duty as a brigadier general in the Philippines. Funston considered carefully, in consultation with Eda and friends, before cabling his acceptance, but he requested ten additional days for leave to visit his family in Kansas. Both his acceptance and approval of leave were acknowledged quickly. "I had not expressed any wishes on the subject, but was not averse to returning to the islands, though I thought the insurrection could not last many months longer."

Although he accepted his new assignment, Funston hadn't decided to make the army a career—he had other alternatives. Yet he liked the excitement in the Philippines and was eager to get back into the action. He'd come to believe in the American cause in the islands and it was in line with his abilities. Eda enjoyed the life of a soldier's wife, although she'd at times struggled under the weather in the tropical environment and suffered some illnesses. His next tour of duty was expected to be only for a year and she'd soon recover enough to visit him there. She found the idea of being an army dependent overseas as romantic, exciting, and liberating as her courtship, marriage, and first voyage. But this was still only temporary.

Kansas governor Stanley and William Sears, the lawyer from Topeka whose command had gone to Fred, arranged special Union-Pacific passenger trains to ferry all the Kansans home. Each man received his monthly pay, foreign-service bonus and transportation pay prior to departure. Colonel Metcalf addressed them officially before they anxiously shuffled trunks and baggage to the depot. Fred and Eda boarded the first car with Mrs. Stanley, Mr. and Mrs. Allen. At Mojave, California, they had breakfast and switched to the Santa Fe line to pass through Las Vegas. A band awaited the troops at Raton, New Mexico, for a dinner serenade, and then on to La Junta, Colorado, where the men were split between four trains to cross the high Rocky Mountains heading east. Snow on the mountains delayed progress but when the first trains reached Kansas, it was plain at every stop Jayhawkers were overjoyed to have their men home. Schools and colleges all along the line closed, business suspended, and people flocked in thousands to greet the trains.

As trains approached Emporia, a cannon in the park signaled arrival and stores closed. Within fifteen minutes the Santa Fe depot was crowded to overflowing, with lines along both sides of the tracks. When the train stopped, men poured out of the cars to talk and shake hands, some meeting families there before continuing on to Topeka. Fred stood on the front steps of the car, shaking hands with well-wishers and admirers. Then Eda was discovered on the rear steps wearing a blue silk shirt, black skirt, mink collar and black velvet turban with ostrich feathers. Women and students peeled away to meet her at the back of the train. Fred mounted a farmer's wagon to make a few remarks—with hat in hand expressed gratitude of all for their homecoming and asked for jobs for his boys. He hurried to join Eda in their car and the train continued to Florence and then Topeka.

When the trains reached Topeka, thousands overflowed the platform and spilled onto tracks, slowing locomotives to a crawl. Whistles screeched, cannon boomed, dozens of bands were on hand in a musical fest competing with cheering crowds. The entire town was wrapped in red, white, and blue bunting and other decorations. Soldiers leaned from every window, waving hands, hats, and shouting and cheering. Hardened soldiers leaped from cars into waiting arms of strangers, friends, relatives, wives and sweethearts who hugged, kissed, and cried. Mothers and fathers pushed forward to find sons. Citizens gathered from all over the state as almost every town had sent a company of men with Funston to the Philippines. Topeka was the final mustering out stop for the troops before returning home.

Fred and Eda rode in the last Pullman of the first train into Topeka. As soon as the train stopped, the crowd rushed them. Half a dozen strong Kansas infantrymen held them back to prevent trampling. One woman spotted Eda from the platform and passed her baby up to be kissed. As soon as she had kissed that one, a dozen more came forward. Fred tried to hustle Eda safely out of the car while a half dozen strong soldiers protected them from zealous admirers. Fred and Eda were half-carried upstairs into the Santa Fe depot dining room. Soon ebullient citizens compelled him to leave his sanctuary for a welcoming ceremony and banquet that lasted until the last of four trains appeared that afternoon.

The last train arrived to continuous, deafening celebrations. Colonel Metcalf formed the regiment for a parade, led by an honor guard of Civil War veterans of the G.A.R., members of the National Guard, civic organizations, and thirty-two separate bands with over a thousand musicians sprawled for over two miles. Colonel Metcalf rode his horse in the lead, followed by Lieutenant Colonel Little. General and Mrs. Funston rode in a black Landau carriage drawn by four black horses, all trimmed in white. The parade continued to the Kansas state house.

Laudatory letters from the President and Secretary of War were read extolling the achievements of the storied 20th Regiment of Kansas

Volunteers. Chief Justice Frank Doster introduced General Joseph Hudson who presented Funston a ceremonial sword specially ordered from Tiffany and Company in New York, costing contributors over $1,000. Funston accepted the gift with brief comments and was followed in remarks by Colonel Metcalf. Still another lavish banquet was spread that evening for the officers, the general, and his lady.

The 20th Kansas was formally mustered out the following day, well beyond their scheduled end of service date—most heavy fighting was past their legal service time. When General Otis had asked Funston how long the volunteers could hold a critical position under attack, he replied, "Until the regiment is mustered out, General!"

Although troops were returning to home towns, families, and work, Fred was in demand as the state's hero. In a few days, he and Eda broke free of the official demands in the state capital and rode the train to the Allen country seat. Ten thousand people met them at that station.

Charles Scott convinced Fred to allow him to take the elaborate sword in advance of their arrival, engendering even more excitement. Fred managed to get Eda through the jostling crowd and into their carriage to ride to the city park for another official welcome and banquet. The inevitable speeches were delivered from the steps of the courthouse late in the afternoon. Fred stressed that the men were the real heroes and deserved the most praise. Finished, and impatient with ceremonies, he took Eda's arm and led her to the carriage for the long awaited reunion with his parents and family in Iola.

During leave he was scheduled for other events in Kansas City, several talks and banquets along with Colonel Metcalf, Lieutenant Colonel Little, and other former staff officers. All his time was not spent in banquets and lectures, however. He ensured Eda met his friend William Allen White, Charles Scott, and others from the Kansas community. He also had to prepare for his departure to return to Luzon.

An elegant reception was hosted by Mrs. Frank Hodder for Eda, with gaslight and chandeliers, American beauty roses and lace, serving maids pouring coffee and chocolate, and an orchestra in the nook under the stairs. Meanwhile Fred attended an elaborate banquet at the Kansas City Knife and Fork Club at the Midland Hotel with line officers from the regiment and prominent citizens. Following remarks by Funston and Metcalf, souvenir menus were presented for autographs. Later in his hotel room, Fred called for a barber while talking with friends and reporters. "I've been on the farm for several days and this is the first opportunity I have had of caring for my beard."

He stayed home until the day after Christmas, when he and Eda left on the Burlington to return to San Francisco. Since they were travelling alone, many didn't recognize him in civilian clothing, but Eda attracted attention with her tall stature, dark beauty, and flowing shawls. While in the lounge, a fellow traveler asked if he was the general. "Yes," he admitted. "I stop off today in Denver with Mrs. Funston and leave for San Francisco the next day.... As soon as the fighting is over, I'll return to Kansas." Then he checked the passing landscape from the windows and commented on the beauty of the sunset over Colorado's mountains, mentioning the fond times he'd spent in those same mountains hiking, hunting, and fishing.

In Denver the Funston's were the houseguests of Mr. F.L. Webster and attended a banquet with veterans of the 1st Colorado volunteers. Aboard the train the following day, he was still disgusted by an episode of the evening before. "What kind of men were the officers of the 1st Colorado that they didn't immediately leave the banquet hall when their colonel was hissed?" He tossed aside a soiled towel in the Pullman sleeper and sat on the leather divan. "It was disgraceful. I know McCoy and his record as a soldier.... Five or six women who came to the Philippines with the volunteers created more trouble than a regiment of Filipinos.... They wanted the men to be pampered ... instead of being treated like soldiers. Because discipline was maintained they attacked the officers."

War Department orders required him to go directly to Manila, making it impossible to accept New York Governor Theodore Roosevelt's invitation to visit Oyster Bay. After taking Eda home, he prepared to board the *Indiana,* the same ship he had taken originally, to return to Luzon. This time Eda remained with her parents at their home in Oakland. Lieutenant Burt Mitchell accompanied him again as his aide, with another enlisted aide. Mitchell was commissioned into the 40th U.S. Volunteer Infantry as a regular army officer at Fred's request. But while he was returning to Manila, the situation there was changing.

FOURTEEN

While Fred was home with Eda and the Kansas boys, General Otis launched an offensive aimed at destroying the rebel army and taking control of Luzon. His three-pronged attack aimed to capture Aguinaldo before he retreated into the mountainous north. The plan called for MacArthur's division to pin down the rebel army in the central plains while Wheaton's division staged an amphibious assault in the rear at Lingayan Gulf, one hundred fifty miles north of Manila. Henry Lawton's cavalry would close off the mountain passes to the northeast. It was a good plan but too slow—Aguinaldo slipped through. A narrow escape at Tirad Pass cost Aguinaldo the life of one of his best aides, Gregorio del Pilar.

Upon returning to Manila, Funston reported to General Otis, still commanding all forces in the islands, and was reassigned to the Second Division, still under General MacArthur. Division headquarters had moved to Bautista, near the northern terminus of the familiar Manila-Dagupan Railway. This time Funston was assigned the 3rd Brigade, scattered over several provinces. Brigade headquarters was at San Isidro and the scattered units included 22nd and 24th U.S. Infantry, headquarters and two battalions of the 34th Volunteers, Troop G of the 4th Cavalry, and a squadron of Philippine cavalry made up of Macabebe infantry scouts.

Units were fragmented into small garrisons over the large brigade area, indicative of the changed nature of the war. Aguinaldo also broke his army into provincial commands, where they cached weapons and blended into cities, barrios, farms, and jungles with new missions of guerilla warfare. Aguinaldo maintained strategic control from his mountain hideouts while his generals commanded districts and guerilla bands.

American volunteer regiments had returned home and been disbanded, replaced by twenty-five regiments of federal volunteers of the regular army. Seventy thousand American soldiers were scattered among hundreds of small garrisons to stabilize the islands and counter guerilla attacks.

Near the end of December 1899, Funston, Captain Smith, and Lieutenant Mitchell left the railhead at San Fernando on ponies for two days ride to brigade headquarters in San Isidro. The countryside was quiet and the three rode armed with personal carbines, revolvers and without security escort to visit garrisons along the route. Towns seemed normal, people working the fields, getting on with lives, watching and waiting. Rice was abundant and locals were as prosperous as they ever had been, keeping distance from combatants on both sides.

Headquarters garrison at San Isidro had a battalion of the 22nd Infantry and Troop G of the 4th Cavalry. Funston's regular visitation program familiarized him with the region. Intelligence reports of guerilla bands prompted him to organize a mounted detachment of twelve men initially—eventually twenty-five—as command escorts and headquarters scouts. They were screened based on horsemanship, marksmanship, courage, and reliability. The first detachment was commanded by Lieutenant E.L. Admire of the 22nd Infantry and Corporal Hull as senior non-commissioned officer.

Headquarters scouts were constantly on the go, either escorting Funston or on scouting missions. They fended for themselves and their horses anywhere, and for as long as necessary, therefore not constrained by logistics. They stayed as mobile as true cavalry, frontier troopers of the Wild West.

When he set out with his scouts to inspect garrisons initially, he was accompanied by Mitchell and Hull. They moved rapidly for security, covering one hundred forty roundtrip miles in nine days, including a day in each of the garrisoned towns. Upon return to San Isidro, Funston heard reports of increasing guerilla activities.

§

Funston learned by questioning locals that the insurgent commander of the district was General Panteleon Garcia, his nemesis from Caloocan a year before, and previously Aguinaldo's chief of staff. However, Garcia was reportedly ill and hiding, leaving operations to Colonel Pablo Padilla. The district had fifteen hundred men with rifles, mostly concealed in caches.

Since boundaries of American and Filipino regions didn't correspond, the principle of "know your enemy" was made more difficult.

Gapan was near San Isidro but not garrisoned. Scouts and informants reported rebel officers were safe there, living with families, weapons concealed nearby. Funston ordered the town surrounded by eight hundred men. Searches left no houses, stables, wells, outhouses, or cracks and crevices unchecked but few weapons were found. Some men were captured with papers revealing them as insurgent officers. All but one was sent to Manila as prisoners of war. That one, Doroteo del Rosario, carried a secret letter from the 35th U.S. Infantry identifying him as a double agent. Funston consulted higher headquarters and released Rosario, but later found he was actually a principal agent for insurgents—pretending to help while leading patrols astray.

§

MacArthur decided to extend his reach north to the city of Baler, on the east coast of Luzon and directed Funston to find a land route to the town. But after eight day trying to cross rugged mountains, men and beasts found the route impossible and turned back. MacArthur wasn't satisfied so another route had to be found, this time crossing the mountain range east of San Isidro. This expedition required ten days to traverse a hundred miles over equally difficult terrain but the straggling convoy finally entered Baler.

A small stone church stood in the center of town, scarred by the hopeless last stand of fifty Spanish soldiers under siege over eleven protracted months. An account of those days was recorded by a last survivor and found in the church. Funston used the diary to conduct lessons with his officers using the trenches, redoubts, approaches, the wells, church, and rows of graves, examining offensive and defensive strengths and weaknesses—teaching a lesson in military history and tactics to his men.

Scouts and a company of the 34th Infantry escorted the pack train over the return route to San Isidro, leaving Major Shunk and a company to garrison the lonely and isolated town. Funston and his headquarters officers gratefully sailed home on a steamer dispatched to deliver supplies for the garrison.

§

While Funston was at Baler, insurgent activity increased with sharp encounters east of San Isidro. Funston, Lieutenant Wolfe—a newly appointed second aide—and Burt Mitchell, rode with a troop of the 4th Cavalry toward the mountain slopes overnight. At daybreak they surprised a rebel patrol and captured one with a Remington. He was interrogated and described a line of sentinels protecting the main camp in a narrow canyon, where a strong outpost was posted to block the only approach. He agreed to lead them to the camp if he'd be released on arrival.

At dark the guide led, arms tied behind and connected to a picket rope held by a soldier. The night was gloomy and rainy. They reached a well-traveled trail after midnight and advanced quietly. Just before daybreak, the guide whispered they were passing through the first line of sentinels. Then they entered constricted canyon walls and saw a small fire flickering ahead. The walls of the canyon were perpendicular, the floor no more than twenty feet wide, barely enough for five men abreast. The guide was released as promised and Funston and Koehler made plans to overwhelm the outpost, and then storm the main camp.

Private James Murphy, wounded at the Battle of Santiago in Cuba, was an experienced scout and took point with Funston and his aides closely behind. Officers carried carbines in addition to their revolvers. Enemy sentries stood guard but were not alert, talking and leaning on their weapons. They were disposed of quickly.

Riflemen fired down the narrow valley toward the camp and received a fast return volley. Funston's new aide, Wolfe, dove for cover and fell into a six-foot hole after being shot through one lung and an arm. Murphy also sank to the ground moaning, one arm nearly severed at the elbow by a ragged ricochet. Someone quickly applied a tourniquet above Murphy's wound. Others grabbed burning wood from the fire as torches to see how to recover Wolfe from the pit. He suffered when they dragged him out. Funston knelt beside Murphy as daylight topped high canyon walls, and said, "This looks mighty bad but I hope you can pull through."

Murphy said, "Well, General, if I can't I'll die like a soldier."

Litters were slung between two ponies to carry the wounded to medical treatment in San Isidro, escorted by Lieutenant Mitchell and the scouts while Funston searched for insurgents. Wolfe eventually recovered enough to return to the United States but Murphy died an agonizing death.

Funston stalked for days without results and came up empty. As they neared Gapan on the return trip, they saw a man in uniform—a Macabebe scout—running for his life with both arms bound behind him. He stammered that his companions were captured by rebels and held nearby. Captain Koehler attacked, and three rebels were quickly killed, three officers in civilian clothes captured. Two scouts were found horribly injured with bolo slashes across their heads, face, and shoulders. A sergeant caught two insurgents red-handed, chopping the helpless men with their hands bound.

The rebels admitted they were officers of Lacuna's band. They couldn't refute obvious facts, and Funston invoked provisions of General Orders 100, the law governing conduct in war signed by Abraham Lincoln in 1863. He conducted a brief inquiry and pronounced the death penalty—both hanged. He reported this to MacArthur's headquarters and his decision was upheld.

§

In April of 1900, General Otis asked to be relieved and returned to the United States. Arthur MacArthur succeeded him as commander of the Division of the Philippines, with headquarters in Manila and reorganized mobile tactical organizations on a geographical basis into four departments divided into districts. General Lloyd Wheaton commanded the new Department of Northern Luzon and Funston's 3rd Brigade, Second Division, became the 4th District of Northern Luzon. Regiments retained their lineage and numbers but were scattered about in garrisons in small detachments or sometimes with one or two companies in one place. Their mission was to stabilize the archipelago and suppress bands of rebels.

Days of large formations moving in mass against a consolidated enemy were ended. Funston rode out with his scouts on several occasions but without much success. Battalion and regimental leaders mostly patrolled, searched, and destroyed camps or supplies when they found them, sometimes engaging in brief skirmishes with guerilla bands.

Funston ran an expedition with Lieutenant Mitchell and eighteen headquarters scouts under Lieutenant Admire. They rode strong American horses, recently arrived to replace the smaller native ponies. Instead of going back into the mountains, they turned toward the flat country west and north of San Isidro, hoping to catch some guerilas in the open on their faster mounts. They forded the familiar Rio Grande at daybreak and struck out north into unknown territory.

On the second day, they hit a grassy plain dissected with trails running in all directions. Funston and Mitchell rode just behind the point man, the main detachment five hundred yards further back. Ahead, they saw a shaky bamboo bridge spanning a wide ravine. As the point man approached the bridge two armed men ran from the far end. Beyond them a dozen more formed in line to open fire. Only the three Americans on point were visible to the skirmishers. The ravine curved sharply back, just beyond the bridge, enabling guerillas to get close to the bridge on that side. Funston had Mitchell race back to the main body, take six men and ride along the ravine to protect the flank while the others crossed the bridge.

Funston told Lieutenant Admire to follow him across with the scouts, but only one man at a time as the structure didn't seem strong. Funston "gritted his teeth" and spurred his horse over the ravine. Others crossed as quickly and came on line. The rebels fired rapidly, standing their ground.

As soon as all scouts were across, they drew revolvers and charged at a gallop, firing wildly as they clung to fast American horses. Rebels held out until they were sixty yards away before falling back, firing as they retreated. Big American steeds instantly overcame them. But new horses were spooked their first time under fire, rearing and plunging, so riders' primary concern was just staying in the saddle.

Funston selected a man with a Krag as his target and set out after him, ignoring an officer with a revolver until he fired point blank—missed, but so close powder singed his beard! Funston pointed his Colt .45, fired, and severed the officer's hand at the wrist. He continued after the man with a Krag, reloading as he ran away. As Funston's horse thundered upon him, the rebel turned, fired, and missed. Funston also missed from his rearing horse—four times. The rebel missed five shots, emptying his magazine.

The rebel ran again and cleared a four-foot ditch, but Funston's horse balked. With one round in his revolver, he couldn't get a clear enough shot but the rebel reloaded again. Funston steered around the ditch to run him down. The rebel aimed from forty feet away. Funston fired first, his last bullet, and hit the Filipino in the forehead, killing him instantly.

§

San Jose was garrisoned by several companies of the 24th Infantry under Major Keller, who found out about an insurgent camp in the mountains ten miles east. Keller briefed Funston upon arrival and they schemed to surprise the camp with a night march. They started out after dark with one company of infantry and mounted scouts led by an Ilocano guide. The company was all black soldiers led by a white officer, and they were in high spirits even in heavy rain, slippery mud, and a grueling climb.

The raiding party reached the camp at dawn and found it deserted. They camped during the day to rest the men and allow horses to graze. While resting, another Ilocano approached and offered to lead them to an insurgent cache in the hills a day's march away. The company of infantry was sent back to San Jose as mounted scouts could move faster. The Ilocano guide rode his own pony as the route alternated between grassy uplands and gloomy jungle forests, sometimes following trails or breaking new ones. This guide was more competent than the first but scouts were in unfamiliar territory. Rain stopped, skies cleared, and visibility increased.

Scouts dismounted and left horses under guard, following the guide on foot with carbines ready. A forty-foot perpendicular cliff loomed ahead, a rattan ladder hanging along the face. From the bottom, several roof tops could be seen above, and then a fleeting glance of a lone sentry disappearing. A few shots discouraged him as a scout scampered up the swaying ladder. Funston crowded behind, then the others one at a time.

On top, they were amazed by their find. Sheds were filled to the roofs with records of the Philippine government, evacuated from Malolos when it was overrun, including letter-press books, copies of orders and correspondence, hundreds of official letters and telegrams, boxes of official stationary, forms, and a million postage stamps. Among the letters were some to and from Roundseville Wildman and Admiral Dewey, plus many from businesses in Manila trading with rebels. They found vast quantities of ammunition of all types, gun powder, petroleum, bolts of cloth, tents, dynamite, reloading tools, and miscellaneous other items and supplies.

They spent hours sorting and deciding what to destroy and what to evacuate. Some scouts went to the nearest garrison to fetch twenty-six mules to haul away the most valuable items. Documents and stationary were most important for exploitation and given highest priority. Blank stationary proved useful later as part of a deception operation. What could not be portaged was piled into sheds and burned. Blown explosives made a column of smoke hundreds of feet up.

§

After discovery of the warehouse spoils, the 4th District returned to normal tactical expeditions, search and destroy missions, and scouting for intelligence about guerilla activities. All garrisons carried on this way, but primary scouting was accomplished by Funston's headquarters scouts and Troop G of the 4th Cavalry. They needed a breakthrough to end the war.

Spies informed Captain Smith, Funston's adjutant, of the location of Panteleon Garcia, commander of rebel bands in central Luzon. Smith took a detachment of cavalry, crossed the Rio Grande during the night and surrounded the house where Garcia was sleeping. He was captured along with his adjutant, Hilario Tal Placido. With one ace in the hole, Funston's troops ran his hand. Ten days later, Colonels Pablo Padilla and Casimerio Tinio were captured. Erosion of leadership provided information in disrupting the insurgency while chipping away at the best of the guerrilla force.

Captain C.D. Roberts of the 35th Infantry in the adjacent 5th District was scouting when his patrol was overwhelmed by a larger guerilla unit under Tecson. Three of his men were killed and one wounded. Roberts and two soldiers were captured and taken into the mountains along the border of the 4th and 5th Districts.

Funston received telegraphic orders to attempt a rescue. He started out in the evening with his headquarters scouts, a cavalry troop, and a detachment of mounted soldiers from the 22nd Infantry. They moved fast and arrived at a rendezvous point and camp site at Stony Point just after daylight, but it was occupied by insurgents. The countryside was too rough for horses to charge so cavalrymen dismounted and rushed the rocky precipice on foot. Insurgents withdrew.

Funston left pack mules under guard and the cavalry mounted for fast pursuit. They set out at a fast trot, cavalry in the lead with two riders on point, following the trail taken by the enemy. Fifty guerillas prepared to make a stand on a steep grassy ridge. Cavalry dismounted again, deployed, engaged, and drove the guerillas off the summit onto the reverse side. As Americans reached the top they saw a larger force of one hundred men a mile away, marching to counterattack. Rebels had set a trap. Funston realized they were in danger of being cut off from their pack train—or the pack train was in danger of capture, so they made a run for their horses and secured the pack train at Stony Point.

The cavalry troop was short of ammunition and the pack mules were loaded only with rations. Some scouts were sent to San Isidro to summon a company of the 22nd Infantry and more mules with ammunition. When reinforcements arrived they were ready to make another run at the ridge. Cavalry screened an adjacent zone, while Captain Godfrey took the ridge with his infantry and scouts in a sharp, brief action. They reconsolidated and redistributed ammunition on the summit during a short rest before starting out in pursuit, scouts leading. Godfrey followed close behind with the infantry. Funston assessed the risk and directed scouts to move fast, ignoring the flanks and the peril of ambush in favor of speed. He told them, "If we are not willing to do this we might as well be in Manila."

Fire discipline of the insurgents was usually as poor as their marksmanship, taking on targets prematurely and out of range, but these were better led. Scouts had nearly crossed the open area and infantry were well out of dense woods when the tree line seventy yards ahead burst with fifty rifles in a well-timed volley. Riders dismounted and hugged the ground. On command, they rose and deployed on line, and laid down a strong base of fire. The enemy, entrenched in a deep furrow, maintained a persistent rate of fire across a yawning ravine. Scouts pushed up the trail, to flank the ravine. Godfrey and Private Ethridge were hit and killed instantly before the flank was turned but the enemy disengaged and fled. into the deep woods.

A detachment of the 35th Infantry of the adjacent 5th District was on an operation and ran into four hundred rebels under Pablo Tecson. They suffered an appalling defeat and another man was captured. General Wheaton, commanding the northern Luzon department, ordered General Grant of the 5th District to drive the guerillas out. He ordered Funston to gather as many fighters as available near the boundary to support Grant's operation. Funston found eight hundred men around San Isidro and reached the rendezvous in thirty-six hours after a grueling night march.

The task force of thirteen hundred infantry, cavalry, and artillery, proceeded toward the mountain strongholds. Tecson left behind a delaying force of forty men, who put up an effective fight from deep spider holes. When they withdrew, they burned sheds and barracks, leaving one building intact—the one housing Captain Roberts, the wounded American prisoner.

§

General MacArthur developed a stable of excellent officers, with future potential including Funston, John Pershing, Peyton March, Franklin Bell, William "Billy" Mitchell and others. Funston viewed MacArthur as the "ideal general" and MacArthur considered Funston almost a son.

At his level, Funston learned many lessons about the population and how important strong support could be to both sides. From his experience as an insurgent in Cuba, he worked to implement those lessons in his counterinsurgency operations. His thoughts and actions were not fully detailed or written out, but rather implemented by instinct—the way he operated. But his reflective observations provide some details of the importance of building crucial relationships with the population. Therefore, he seasoned this phase of the war with "pleasant social relations between officers of the American garrisons and the better class of people in the towns." Frequently, companies spent days on missions in the countryside then returned to towns for dinners, social gatherings, enjoyable dances and music, often at homes of local Filipinos—always aware of potential traps or rebel raids.

Filipinos were gracious hosts at social occasions. While their country was occupied and their own countrymen fighting as rebels, community leaders, shop-keepers, and others retained a quiet sense of humor, and remained courteous and reserved by nature. Often their genteel charm stood in sharp contrast to the rough, good-natured, and boisterous personality of American soldiers, farmers, or cowboys.

Funston outlawed taking chickens, pigs, grain, or anything of value without adequate compensation to owners. This was well understood by soldiers and when violated, punishment was expected. From his point of view, rebels didn't operate under a legitimate government, although they'd established a republic. In his district, military laws involving the population were leniently enforced, except in cases of capital crimes.

His counterinsurgency campaign exploited conditions unique to his area of responsibility and capitalized on enemy weaknesses—his concern was physical security, intelligence, rapid response, and preparing citizens to defend themselves. Funston relied on charisma and led by example, ran field operations based on informal contacts for information, and used his instincts for guerilla operations. He was lenient regarding terms of surrender, amnesty, rewards, and made friendships built on trust—pragmatic and flexible to exploit every tactical opportunity. He maintained a social network with former guerrillas to gain information about organizations, tactics, and methods from which he could anticipate future plans. He created a native secret service by paying for valuable information, hiring reliable local guides, and paying bribes as needed. He was aware his spies were vulnerable and went to great lengths to keep them anonymous, and rescued or protected them from retaliation.

§

Funston had returned to San Isidro after several days of chasing Pablo Tecson when he received a telegram from Major Wheeler, commanding the 34th Infantry garrison at Penaranda. One of Wheeler's local spies had informed him that Lacuna and four hundred men were in the village of Papaya only two miles from there. Wheeler planned to go after him immediately and burn the town. Funston believed more troops were needed and directed him to wait until he arrived with a troop of the 4th Cavalry and headquarters scouts. They saddled up and set out immediately.

As they approached, Lacuna spotted the scouts. He formed his men for battle and waited. Funston peeled off twenty cavalrymen to block escape over the ford across the stream, while the main element moved along the stream, concealed by trees on the banks. When they were set, Wheeler advanced with dismounted infantry and headquarters scouts. As the infantry broke into the open a fierce firefight developed.

Rebels stood their ground, fighting hard but firing ineffectively. Eventually, they pulled back with their wounded across open terrain. Funston's new American horse was still unruly under fire and Major Harris' horse bolted at a full run with him on his back. Major Wheeler's horse was killed while those of Admire, Mitchell, and Lyles broke free and raced off to be corralled by rebels. Mitchell had lashed his expensive new raincoat to his saddle—Lacuna wore it through many monsoon rains.

§

In San Isidro some officers and noncommissioned officers were joined by their wives. Funston sent for Eda, now sufficiently recovered to sail over to visit. She arrived in Manila with her sister, Mattie, in November of 1900. Fred rode to Manila to escort them to San Isidro, where Eda would experience being under fire again, Mattie for the first time, as rebels never let up. Rebels even set part of the town afire, something Eda was familiar with from nights in Manila—and a harbinger of worse days ahead. Funston commented on their stay in his understated way: "The American women who lived in San Isidro in those days had some experiences that in these times do not ordinarily fall to those of their sex...."

Funston was always a stickler for sentries staying awake, alert, and strictly following guard instructions--lapses could well result in loss of life. En route back to his headquarters with Eda and Mattie, he was challenged by a sentry. "Halt!" Funston and his party complied, knowing they would be shot if they didn't. In the dark, the sentry commanded, "Dismount!" Funston identified himself as the commanding officer, but the sentry was well trained. "I don't care if it's President McKinley," he replied. "You dismount or I'll blow your ugly head off." Funston dismounted, waded through the mud and congratulated the sentry on following orders.

Eda wrote home her travel to San Isidro with Fred and Mattie. "He jumped off his horse, got into the carriage with me and heading home took me to visit much of his district." She continued, "You can't imagine how strange it would be to be driving home at night…and be halted by sentries! 'Halt! Who's there?' and the answer, 'Funston.' Then the sentry orders, 'Advance and be recognized.' And then we advance and are recognized. You are as though you are living in a book."

Hardly any letters were posted by Eda or Mattie without a detailed description, sometimes drawings, of the various spiders and insects of San Isidro discovered unexpectedly crawling or prowling about the house. Mattie wrote her father about how she missed the electric lights, complaining that gas lanterns were awful. She wrote that Mrs. Devol, wife of the quartermaster, had sent a hammock from Manila, but generally it was difficult to get things needed or wanted. The only fresh food was eggs, chicken, bananas, and a variety of native beans. But prisoners made things like screens, chairs, mats, tables, cabinets, and hats—Eda purchased a light weight, comfortable hat for both of them. Mattie closed that letter in time to get it to the steamer before it sailed.

For devoted Presbyterians of German stock, Christmas was a reason for celebration anywhere in the world. Eda and Mattie set about bringing the best of the season to the small frontier garrison. They enlisted two other wives to help, and invited staff officers from Funston's headquarters and from the hospital. Winter is the hottest time in the islands but they were not deterred by that. Their first thoughts were for a tree but none of the scraggly type locally available was appropriate and a banana tree simply wouldn't do, so that idea was dropped in favor of a regular party. Using a roll of red crepe paper, they cut out heart-shaped favors and decorated the table with a large bouquet of red flowers.

Peanuts were abundant so the ladies sat in a circle and shelled and salted them before boiling them in olive oil over an alcohol burner, and then added peanuts to melted chocolate candy from the commissary. But the main idea to enliven the party was individualized gifts for each attendee. Funston was away hunting the black renegade Fagan but would return by Christmas. So Eda stuffed a doll sewn from black cloth with cotton hair and a miniature military uniform. She tied a small rope noose around the neck of the deserter doll. Funston was elated by his gift and declared it a "good omen." Each attendee received a unique gift along with an original, funny, jingle that was read aloud to considerable laughter.

Their Christmas turkey was a small native chicken, enhanced with canned tomatoes for soup and salad, canned apricots in place of sherbet, and the day was toasted with "canned Champaign." Afterwards, local natives invited them all to an entirely unique Filipino hop or *rigadon*, for singing, dancing, and a unique and memorable Christmas was shared between cultures. The local band was quite good but heat and humidity limited on enthusiasm for dancing.

After Christmas, Mattie wrote her father that their locally procured piano had arrived and she was very excited to play it until she discovered it was the worst "old rattletrap she had ever heard." The keys were loose and the ivory coming off—worse than the one stored in their attic in Oakland—but it was a piano and they were glad to have it anyway.

§

The counterinsurgency campaign had become a war of attrition, wearing rebels down and reducing the threat. American losses were light but every weapon captured from the enemy was important. The islands were isolated by expanses of oceans as the navy made rebel resupply almost impossible. Insurgents could replace loses of fighters by impressing farmers from their fields, but a lost weapon could not be easily replaced.

Lieutenant F.W. Alstaetter of the corps of engineers took three engineers and eleven cavalrymen to examine roads between San Miguel and San Isidro. Lacuna overwhelmed them in a surprise strike. Alstaetter put up a valiant fight until he finally surrendered, out of ammunition, and with one man killed and three wounded. Lacuna sent an escort to return the dead and three wounded to San Isidro but retained the others as prisoners. Two weeks later, he released the enlisted soldiers but held Alstaetter.

Later, Funston was patrolling the flat land between the mountains and the Candaba swamp and captured Lieutenant Colonel Manuel Ventus, one of Lacuna's subordinates. His wounds required hospitalization. Funston wrote to Lacuna, although he didn't have authority for a prisoner exchange, but said he'd be willing to release Ventus if Lacuna would release Alstaetter.

A few days later, Alstaetter was escorted to an outpost by rebels and when Ventus was able to travel, Funston released him.

After that, Funston made a sweep with his scouts and a troop of the 4th Cavalry when they approached a cluster of small houses. As they trotted into the hamlet, lead scouts drew fire at close range, but every shot missed. Rebels burst from the houses, firing while running away. One officer streaked down the bank and into waist-deep water while Funston and a scout emptied their revolvers at him. The scout jumped his horse off a fifteen-foot ravine into the water in pursuit, but the rebel officer reached the far bank and fled into the woods, making a narrow escape. That officer was Lacuna.

§

A spy informed Funston where the ignominious Tagunton's band was hiding. He took twenty-five mounted men of the 22nd Infantry to scout the area, and spotted a saddled pony standing alone on the opposite side of a wide ravine. A sentry shot at them, followed by a fusillade. They returned fire with revolvers. Major Brown was armed with a new Colt automatic, invented and sent to the Philippines for a field test.

A heavy-set Filipino officer tried to mount his skittish pony but couldn't get on the animal spooked by firing. Mitchell found a route around the ravine and gathered some men to cross to the other side. More Filipino riflemen emerged and laid down a heavy volume of fire until all resistance suddenly broke off. Only one enemy soldier was killed along with the officer wearing insignia of a Lieutenant Colonel.

The oversized officer was the notorious Tagunton. A dispute ensued over who had fired the killing shot. The surgeon settled it when he dug from the man's chest the steel-jacketed bullet of the Colt .45 automatic. Funston's only regret was that Tagunton could not be brought in to die at the end of a rope.

FIFTEEN

Counterinsurgency in the Philippines dragged on, with dissent at home becoming more virulent. Anti-imperialists led the charge against American occupation, opposing advocates of manifest destiny. Letters from soldiers alleging army abuses added columns to newspapers aligned with anti-imperialists. Pressure increased to end the fighting, but no way had yet been found to do that responsibly.

The whereabouts of the elusive guerrilla leader, Emilio Aguinaldo remained a mystery. Rumors rampant, most believed he was either in the great valley of the Gagayan River in northern Luzon, or in the extensive and massive mountains on either side that same valley. Aguinaldo took extreme measures to protect the secrecy of his location as he personified the spirit of the revolution. Only a bold stroke could change the dynamics of the stalemate.

Guerillas dispersed and reassembled only to fight, then faded back into the landscape under control of local chieftains. Aguinaldo exercised general control of the rebellion, but the unanswered question was how he did it. Funston and other senior officers were convinced the rebellion could only end with a strategic blow at the heart of the insurgency. Such a strike would necessarily lead to Aguinaldo's death or capture.

§

An Ilocano named Cecilio Segismundo met with his leader, "Captain Emilio," in the northern reaches of Luzon. He was given a pouch of correspondence to hand-carry south to the command post of General Lacuna in central Luzon at a secret location. Some mail was for Lacuna, some addressed to other key people. Lacuna would send couriers to places known only to him for distribution to other cells. Some personal letters would simply be dropped into the regular postal system for delivery to family members. Compartmenting information about names and locations of key people kept it out of American hands.

Segismundo set out on his long and difficult mission with a security escort of twelve armed rebels. His journey took him first along the ragged coast but then became even more difficult when crossing the rugged mountains. As they approached Baler they ran into a detachment of the 22nd Infantry. Segismundo lost two of his detail there.

Survivors resumed their march through a pass over a mountain range to the west and finally reached the outskirts of Pantabangan after twenty-six grueling days. They stopped to rest, exhausted and hungry. Segismundo had once been the mayor of Pantabangan, now under American control, and he knew the present mayor, Francisco Villajuan, who was neutral to both sides. Segismundo contacted him anyway for food, water, and advice. His friend strongly advised he turn himself in to Americans and work for them, but Aguinaldo's loyal messenger was not eager to become a turncoat.

Lieutenant William "Billy" Mitchell, later the army aviation pioneer and father of the air force, had befriended Villajuan and questioned him about Aguinaldo. Villajuan told him he sometimes heard news and promised to report what he heard. After the mayor talked with Segismundo he sought out Mitchell to report what he had learned but Mitchell was away on leave. So he consulted Lieutenant J.D. Taylor, commanding the garrison at Pantabangan and Mitchell's senior officer. Taylor realized an attempt to capture the courier would likely result in his escape, so he negotiated through the mayor to convince Segismundo to surrender.

Segismundo finally did—physically and emotionally drained from fighting for a lost cause. He informed Taylor he had come from Palanan, that Aguinaldo had been there for several months with only fifty soldiers, and he used messengers to communicate. Taylor was excited about his discovery and knew Funston would be.

He was in his office in San Isidro working on routine matters with Captain Smith when a telegram summarized the facts—the rebels had surrendered and the commander claimed to be Aguinaldo's messenger with letters to Baldomero Aguinaldo, Lacuna, and to others. The top-level letters were encrypted but the signatures resembled Aguinaldo's using fictitious names.

This changed everything—Funston was immediately energized and directed the courier be escorted to San Isidro with the correspondence. He fed Segismundo and talked with him in Spanish and he believed him. He turned his attention to the correspondence, but Segismundo was no help with that since important letters were encoded and he didn't know the key to the code.

He brought in Captain Smith and Lazaro Segovia, a Spaniard who worked as a secret service and intelligence officer. They stripped off shirts in the stifling heat and surrounded a table with pencils, pads of paper, and a jumble of encoded letters. The cook made strong coffee for a long night. Segovia, fluent in Spanish and Tagalog, finally cracked a key word-- ammunition. Using the seven characters in that word, he slowly untangled messy sentences in a jumble of Spanish and Tagalog, and then translated into English—a tedious process but excitement was growing.

Once the code was partially broken, letters were interpreted; they became ecstatic finding explicit orders to subordinates written by a secretary but signed with fictitious names—"Pastor" or "Colon Magdalo." They toiled until noon to assemble a complete picture but Funston realized they were exhausted and encouraged them to sleep. But his mind wouldn't rest and he tossed on his bunk while piecing together a plan.

§

One letter kept working in Funston's mind—one to Baldomero Aguinaldo, commanding rebels south of Manila. He was directed to relieve Jose Alejandrino of command, then to direct Lacuna, Mascardo, Simon, and Tecson to send a total of four hundred men to Palanan. These should be hand-picked and use routes selected by their commanders.

Before day, Funston sprang from his bunk and sent for Segismundo, and informed him that he intended to capture Aguinaldo and expected his help. They discussed routes to use. Segismundo assured him all trails were closely watched and any attempt by sea would be detected by lookouts on the coast—Aguinaldo would simply vanish again.

This was discouraging, but he said he intended to reach Aguinaldo anyway and again tried to sleep, but he couldn't stop thinking and by morning he had a plan. He recalled Segismundo and asked if this was possible. "The man clapped his hands together, jumped from his chair in great glee, and said it would probably succeed."

Funston planned to slip a force into Palanan pretending to be the reinforcements Aguinaldo requested. He sent it to General Wheaton, who called him to Manila for approval, and then to MacArthur. MacArthur also approved and arranged for Admiral Remey to provide a small vessel to transport the expedition part way up the east coast of Luzon. Funston then returned to San Isidro to complete his plans.

This operation would tax limits of human endurance, traversing rugged terrain along the eastern coast for over a hundred miles. A ride part-way by ship would cut the distance but was still daunting. If deceiving Aguinaldo failed, the raid would fail and they would likely not survive.

He had captured letters and official stationary of Lacuna the previous year, which could be used to develop the ruse to get into the protected area. Stationary captured in Lacuna's camp had Brigada Lacuna rubber stamped at the top. Samples of his signature were plentiful and a former insurgent practiced it, and then forged it at the bottom of several blank letters.

Funston selected Captain Harry Newton of the 34th Infantry to go with him as he had some experience at sea, had been stationed at Baler, and had once been to Casiguran, the only other town along the route. Lieutenant Mitchell, Segovia and Segismundo would go. Funston chose Hilario Tal Placido as the pretended leader of the expedition. Placido was the former insurgent wounded and captured at Caloocan, and was already known to Aguinaldo. He had taken the oath of allegiance and proved his value and loyalty, but was overweight and Funston worried about his stamina. Two other former insurgents were Dionisio Bato and Gregorio Cadhit. The chosen few returned to Manila to prepare to sail.

Funston took Eda and Mattie, who was still visiting, with him from San Isidro to Manila to stay with friends until his return. After all, if he failed to return, they'd certainly return to San Francisco on the first available ship. She knew the plan and swore secrecy, knowing leaks could endanger her husband's life. Despite her confidence in Fred, she was greatly unsettled about it all and he was glad she to have sister close through the ordeal.

General Wheaton selected Macabebe scouts as Aguinaldo's purported reinforcements from Lacuna. They were Aztecs brought to the Philippines by the Spanish, now loyal to Americans. They would pretend to be insurgents and speak only Tagalog. The company was commanded by Captain Russell Hazzard and his brother Lieutenant Oliver Hazzard. On board ship, the scouts were armed with captured weapons and ammunition from the Manila arsenal, and second-hand indigenous clothing and equipment. American officers dressed as enlisted prisoners of war.

Admiral Remey chose the gunboat *Vicksburg*, commanded by Commander E.B. Barry, to support the mission. Secrecy was critical—only MacArthur, Wheaton, Funston, the officers on the expedition, a small group at San Isidro, Segovia and Segismundo, plus Eda Funston, knew of the plan. Despite tight security, the mission was leaked and cabled to media in the United States while the operation was in progress.

§

When plans and preparations were complete, Funston saw Wheaton and MacArthur before casting off. MacArthur was a bit unnerved by the risks and said, "Funston, this is a desperate undertaking. I fear that I shall never see you again." Then, he delivered more untimely bad news—a War Department cable directed Funston return to the United States immediately to muster out of volunteer service. MacArthur asked for a delay to complete this mission, although this mission might result in his death.

His reaction: It "filled my heart with bitterness, and nothing but a feeling of the loyalty that I owed to my division and department commanders made me willing to go on with the apparently thankless and all but hopeless task."

In the dark of night, the *Vicksburg* slipped out of Manila Bay and participants were briefed for the first time. Commander Barry and his naval officers were first. Next, Funston, with Segovia as interpreter, informed Tal Placido, Bato, and Cadhit, the former rebels under Aguinaldo. They were stunned! He reiterated their oaths of allegiance and promised cooperation would be rewarded, but punishment hard if not. Every man had a crucial role. He trusted them with his life!

Macabebes' loyalty was unquestioned but they were simple native soldiers, were not well educated—pretending to be the enemy was a tall order. Funston asked First Sergeant Pedro Bustos, a decorated soldier of the Moro wars, if they would stand by the Americans. He replied, "I cannot speak for the others, but I am a soldier of the United States." Macabebes were quizzed on their roles to ensure they understood and didn't lapse into old habits. The cover story was that a party of ten American soldiers was surprised while making terrain maps. Two were killed, three wounded and left behind. The others, those on this march, surrendered and were prisoners. Weapons were exchanged, clothing and equipment switched, and for all practical purposes the Macabebes became guerillas.

The *Vicksburg* sailed around the southern end of Luzon and turned north along the Pacific side of the island, to make a port call at Antimonan. Lieutenant Mitchell went ashore to purchase native banca boats for a run at the coast further north during the night, but none were available there. The *Vicksburg* continued to the small island of Polillo where they obtained three bancas large enough to take the raiding party ashore in one lift. The boats were heavy to pull aboard so were towed. Two Macabebes stayed in each boat to steer them apart and prevent lines from becoming entangled.

Six days after leaving Manila, the *Vicksburg* turned north along the eastern coast, but winds rose to gale force, and seas ran high. One banca was swamped and sank. The two riders hand crawled along the ropes to another boat and cut the sunken boat free. By that afternoon the seas were so rough all six Macabebes were hanging onto the sides of water-filled boats. After two hours, they were rescued in life boats and the cumbersome bancas were sunk. Landing plans one and two had failed—an inauspicious start.

Plan three was to land raiders in small navy boats at night and hope for the best. Funston scribbled a draft of a bogus letter to Aguinaldo, posing as General Lacuna, which Segovia smoothed out for authenticity. In it, he acknowledged Aguinaldo's other letters and thanked him for his promotion and gave details of the current campaign to build trust.

The second letter was the Trojan horse. It mentioned orders from Baldomero Aguinaldo, as new commander of Central Luzon, to send one of his best companies. It said the company was under the command of Hilario Tal Placido, and mentioned that Placido had been captured and taken an oath of allegiance to the Americans, in case Aguinaldo knew that already, but that he was violating that oath. He introduced the Spaniard, Lazaro Segovia, as second in command. The rest of the letter was trivia down to the signature line. These letters were secured until an opportunity was found to dispatch them.

The *Vicksburg* slinked into Casiguran Bay in thick fog. All lights were extinguished and navy boats quietly lowered into the water. Surf was light in the bay and oaring to shore went smoothly in the rain. They carried only one day's rations. American officers were dressed as privates with campaign hats, blue shirts, khaki breeches and leggings. They lost two Macabebes when one cut his hand on a bolo and another got cold feet and hid in the ship's netting. Eighty-nine men landed on the dreary coast to begin a life or death venture—they wouldn't be taken alive.

Major W.C. Brown, Funston's inspector general in the 4th District, had been present during the decoding of the letters and rode with Captain Barry aboard the *Vicksburg*. Doctor Macpherson was also aboard for official business at Baler. Brown and Captain H.C. Hodges of the 22nd Infantry went ashore at Baler to deliver the ninety-nine-year sentence of a rebel tried by military commission for burying a prisoner alive.

§

Raiders tried to stay out of the rain as much as possible until dawn. In daylight they marched inland for fresh water and built small fires in the rain to boil rice. After a quick breakfast they started the long march alongside the bay without trails to follow. According to plan they landed approximately where a march from Nueva Ecija would take them. Sinews of the coastline forced wading of streams flowing into the sea at high tide, crossing mangroves lapped by the waves, adding fatigue to sea sickness.

At noon they found a banca to ferry six men upstream to Casiguran, a town with rebel sympathies. A letter addressed to the mayor said Lacuna's troops were going north and needed a guide, housing, and provisions. Hilario signed it and Segismundo, Cadhit, and two armed Macabebes carried the letter to the vice-mayor—the mayor was away.

The vice-mayor sent a guide to escort them around the bay and along a good trail through a dense forest. An excited crowd awaited them—a parade of victorious soldiers of the revolution. The village band played and Macabebes enjoyed themselves. Segovia worried lest they enjoy themselves too much—a lapse would expose their treachery. The prisoners were the first Americans they'd seen and were marched through the plaza.

Segismundo arranged to house officers and prisoners in the same building, enabling secret talks. The vice-mayor needed several days to collect provisions for their march—no rice, only cracked corn, fresh fish, and sweet potatoes. Fish wouldn't keep. Funston didn't want to spend time to gather additional provisions as they had a pre-established date to meet the *Vicksburg* at the end of the mission at Palanan Bay on March 25th. Any delay would ruin the operation, so they continued after only two days with what they had—food shortages increased their risk.

Despite native wine and pretty girls, the scouts stuck to their stories. But disquieting news came as a shock—General Tinio had already joined Aguinaldo with four hundred well-armed men. Funston and Segovia concocted another letter informing Aguinaldo they were coming and mentioned Americans prisoners. The vice-mayor sent some men ahead to deliver the letters.

The longest part of the march resumed in a driving rain, with twelve men of the town carrying the food—mostly cracked corn, a small quantity of dried caribou meat, and six live chickens—and an Ilongote guide. They'd be on short rations for the most difficult part of the journey.

They followed a muddy trail to the beach until the guide deserted, but a man from Casiguran thought he could lead—a mixed blessing, as it forced careful adherence to their cover. At the beach they followed the coast with multiple detours over mountains when cliffs reached the sea. Flat beaches were soft with deep sand and mud, and beset with large boulders to climb over. They waded sixty streams in incessant rain, soaking and spoiling their scarce food.

Each day, they started at first light, marched until 1000 and stopped for breakfast, resumed at 1300 and continued until dark. The second and final meal of the day was a duplicate of the first—never ending stew—already at half rations. They were ravenous with hunger, and unable to sleep on the ground in the rain. Small fish, snails, and limpets scratched from rocks were mixed with corn but made the stew more revolting. On the fifth day there was none. When they walked, they staggered, dazed, starved, and straggled for as much as a mile, reeling as they went. Segovia suffered from an abscess in one foot and hobbled badly.

Funston admitted, "It was plain that the end was at hand, but we were approaching our destination. It seemed impossible that the madcap enterprise could succeed, and I began to have regrets that I had led all these men to such a finish...." He was also beleaguered by MacArthur's distressing news—the army no longer needed him. And he thought of poor Eda waiting for some word in Manila, praying it would be good. As the bedraggled men stumbled toward Palanan, it seemed hopeless—they might have to fight Tinio's four hundred and Aguinaldo's fifty.

Near the end of the day they saw someone on the beach. Segovia ventured alone to meet him. Stragglers gradually caught up while they waited. The stranger gave him a letter and he limped back with it in hand. As he passed, he whispered to Funston, "It is all right. We have them." Relief was palpable. They were ten miles from their objective and had actually made contact—the deception plan was working.

The letter from Simon Villa, Aguinaldo's chief of staff, ordered no prisoners to the base. The column hobbled two miles further to the designated place but found it was not a town, only a feature where the trail met the beach. They found an old man and a few Negritos completing two small, grass-covered, open sheds, one for the prisoners, and one for the guards. It was dark already and they rested, still without food.

Funston schemed with Segovia during the night—how to circumvent orders to leave them behind. They also needed food before they were too diminished to continue. Hilario wrote a letter reporting their arrival at the rendezvous point, but stating food was badly needed. One of the Negritos left with the letter. Enough cracked corn arrived by daylight for breakfast. And the old man shared good news—Tinio's four hundred had not arrived.

Back in Casiguran, Major Brown went ashore to inquire about the "captured" American prisoners to judge progress of the raiding party, but the residents were spooked by the gun boat and fled. Those who would talk lied that no Americans or guerillas had been there. Brown suspected a cover-up but left without confirmation.

Nine days after landing, raiders began the final stretch without Funston. "Prisoners" were confined on the beach, under the guard of a complicit Macabebe corporal and nine scouts. On the trail Segovia signed a letter and sent it back to the prison-keeper saying a messenger on the trail said Villa wanted the prisoners after all. The corporal showed the letter to the old man, who just shrugged. Scouts and prisoners set out on the trail two hours behind the others.

The trail was muddy under the triple-canopied jungle and Americans were weak despite cornmeal for breakfast. Mitchell and Funston were in the worst shape; the Hazzard's were younger and more accustomed to rigors of living with the scouts. Funston stopped to rest every few hundred yards. Then they were surprised by a Macabebe sergeant and a private running, out of breath, arms signaling them to hide. As soon as they did, a rebel unit passed, going to take charge of the "prisoners" at the beach. They resumed their march with greater haste before insurgents discovered the prisoners missing.

§

Funston and the other "prisoners" lagged the main body. A mile from Palanan two rebel officers met the phony rebels and escorted them inside the security zone. The Palanan River was one hundred yards wide and quite deep, the town nestled on a hillside on the far bank. The only way across the river was in a banca. Hilario and Segovia crossed first, instructing others to cross quickly and form into ranks on the other shore.

Hilario and Segovia hurried to Aguinaldo's house to report and found him surrounded by seven officers with revolvers. They were warmly received by Aguinaldo and told their canned stories about travel from Lacuna's headquarters. Segovia kept an eye on the window to see when the scouts arrived. Finally, the ragged formation marched uphill where the fifty-man security guard stood in neat uniforms, armed with Mausers to honor them.

Weary Macabebes were nervous in this drama with them as main actors. Segovia stepped outside to the top of the stairs and signaled Cadhit that this was the moment. They had loaded their weapons before crossing the river and stood at "order arms," facing the honor guard. Cadhit saw the signal and shouted, "Now is the time, Macabebes. Give it to them!"

They fired a ragged volley that killed two insurgents, wounding the bandmaster. Aguinaldo heard the firing and rushed to the window annoyed, thinking it was celebratory fire. "Stop that foolishness," he shouted. "Don't waste your ammunition!"

Funston had been emphatic that Aguinaldo should be protected. Hilario grabbed him around the waist and wrestled him beneath a table, throwing his body over him. Segovia ran into the room as officers drew revolvers. He fired first, hitting Villa three times and wounding Alhambra. Villa and Santiago Barcelona surrendered. Alhambra and the other officers jumped through a window into the river and escaped. Hilario told Aguinaldo, "You are a prisoner of the Americans!"

Funston and the other Americans with their "guards" had reached the river when the shooting started, climbed into the banca and paddled frantically across. Funston, running on adrenalin, hobbled toward the house, but Segovia met him coming downhill. "It is all right," he said. "We have him." Funston continued to the house and introduced himself to Aguinaldo, verifying he was a prisoner of war to be treated with respect.

Aguinaldo was dazed, "Is this not some joke?" He assured him it wasn't.

§

Colonel Villa's wounds were treated but he was clearly agitated. Dr. Barcelona acquiesced, relieved it was over. Macabebes were elated and congratulated each other and their American officers with back pats and laughter. Aguinaldo's security guards vanished, leaving behind eighteen rifles and thousands of rounds of ammunition.

Deception was over. Funston took charge again and the Hazzard brothers resumed command of the Macabebes. Aguinaldo, Villa, and Barcelona were confined in a comfortable room, under guard. Searchers found weapons and documents revealing how Aguinaldo stayed in touch with subordinates from his remote command post. Filed with other letters were the fakes from Lacuna and from Hilario.

Sufficient food was found to feed the hungry men but civilian inhabitants of the town fled with Aguinaldo's guards at the first shots. Funston ordered no property be destroyed. Lieutenant Mitchell recovered his small camera from a "guard" who carried it for him, and snapped some pictures.

Funston later recounted his experience with Aguinaldo. "Aguinaldo, whose gameness and general bearing won our hearts, wrote and handed to me a brief note congratulating me on the outcome of the perilous expedition. In fact, the pleasantest relations were soon established between captors and captured."

They had one day to rest, only one spare day built into the extreme mission, before the *Vicksburg* was due in Palanan Bay to meet them. Early that morning they set out for the beach, two miles away. The column arrived first but soon spotted smoke from the steamer. Captain Newton used a bed sheet to send a semaphore message, "We have him. Send boats for all." The prompt reply from the navy: "Well done."

Wounded and prisoners were brought for treatment in Manila, using the banca to float the wounded downriver. The surf was rough, but Commander Barry took the first bucking boat to shore. With difficulty, all made it to the *Vicksburg* without anyone drowning, although soaked, and sailors cheered each arriving boat. Since Captain Barry had gone ashore to meet Funston, Major Brown met Aguinaldo and Lieutenant Mitchell as they arrived on the first boat. A sailor escorted Aguinaldo below for dry clothes. The voyage to Manila took three days and prisoners were invited to eat in the officer's mess or sit on deck in suitable weather. During a meal, Aguinaldo pushed his knife and fork aside, and humbly addressed them, expressing appreciation for their courteous treatment. Early on the morning of March 28, 1901, they slipped into Manila Bay with lights out.

At 0600, Funston left the *Vicksburg* in her steam launch with the executive officer of the ship, Lieutenant Mitchell, and the three principle prisoners. They steamed straight up the Pasig River through the city of Manila and docked at Malacanan Palace, where MacArthur lived and had his headquarters. The normally formal MacArthur was awaken by an aide and descended the stairs in pajamas and a robe, prepared for bad news. He looked quizzically at Funston, who said, "Well, I have brought you Don

Emilio." MacArthur asked where he was. Funston told him, "Right here in this house."

MacArthur hurried back upstairs to dress, directing a large breakfast be set, and told Funston to bring Aguinaldo and wait with him there. MacArthur returned fully dressed, and cordially greeted them. They sat down together for breakfast and MacArthur saw Aguinaldo was uncomfortable. He assured him his family would be brought immediately, and ordered special quarters prepared for his "guest" and his family. After breakfast, he prepared an official dispatch to Washington and another for public consumption. Manila went wild with excitement. MacArthur gave Funston full credit in his official report, recommending him for promotion as a regular army brigadier general. Vice President Roosevelt responded with a warm congratulatory telegram directly to Funston, declaring his feat "unequaled in the annals of American history."

He hurried to find Eda, as she had waited with the secret sealed in her heart for three full weeks, never hearing the fate of his husband, always fearing the worst. Within a few days, MacArthur showed Funston a cable from Washington announcing he was to be appointed a brigadier general in the regular army instead of being mustered out. McKinley and Congress had approved MacArthur's recommendation, jumping Funston over a hundred senior regular army colonels. Segovia, Segismundo, the three Tagalogs, and all the Macabebes were financially rewarded for their heroic efforts. But it was not over for Funston—only a new beginning.

Theodore Roosevelt penned his congratulations to Funston for capturing Aguinaldo on March 30th, 1901 from Oyster Bay, New York. "I take pride in this crowning exploit of a career filled with feats of cool courage, iron endurance and gallant daring.... I cannot recall any single feat in our history which can be compared to it.... I feel that you have given us one of those careers which must be an inspiration for all Americans who value courage, resolution and soldierly devotion to duty.... You have given us good reason to feel that you are fit to perform striking feats of generalship on a much larger scale...." Roosevelt continued to mention some of the problem areas around the world and the future possibility of the United States finding itself pitted against a big military power. "...I hope to be serving under or alongside of you."

§

All business in Iola, Kansas, was practically suspended as news of Funston's feat reached the small farming town. A messenger carried the newspaper to Edward Funston, where he was in his field husking corn. He leaned against his wagon and said, "Well, this is certainly gratifying." Of course Edward and Ann Funston already knew about the mission despite the clamp of security. Even while it was underway the press had leaked news of the operation as the trek to capture Aguinaldo had barely begun, endangering the entire mission and raising concerns at home. Only Aguinaldo's isolation and slow arrival of news, combined with slow and secretive communications between Manila and Palanan kept him in the dark. Edward said, "This was the first time I ever saw his mother worry."

At the house behind the white picket fence, Ann was read the article and headlines several times. She was proud, but mostly relieved by her son's safety. "I never lost faith in Fred's lucky star but I had a feeling this time that he was risking his life and everything on high stakes and that the end would be disastrous."

Iola went wild and that night a delegation of several hundred citizens brought a band to visit the Funston's home to celebrate. Ann's brother from the next farm brought his family to join the celebration. Their neighbors were the Mitchells—Burton Mitchell was Fred's cousin and his personal aide, also one of the raiders. Both families and the entire population of Iola were ecstatic about the anticipated homecoming of their favorite sons.

Edward deliberated, "We were puzzled why his wife let him go, and my wife had been congratulating herself because Fred's wife was with him down in that island, to keep him from making any desperate attempts like this, but I expect he went out the back door and she found out afterward when he was gone."

Burt Mitchell's mother said, "At first I hoped that Fred had not gone, and then I prayed that Burt was not with him, and I have neither slept well nor enjoyed a meal since the first report of the expedition! ... I knew he would follow Fred, and now I am glad he did. I would not have had him anywhere else."

In Oakland celebrations were more muted, but Theresa Blankart told an inquiring reporter, "We are overjoyed to know that General Funston has returned safely to Manila. We cared more for that than we do for the glory he has won...." When asked if they had received a letter or dispatch from him, she said, "...he is too busy to write and the letters are all from our daughters. ... We are not likely to, for he is not one who blows his own horn."

SIXTEEN

Fred Funston's life was a crescendo of ever increasing high notes tempered with physical pain. Praise of his bravado crossing of the Rio Grande, tremendous success on the great raid, marrying the talented and beautiful Eda Blankhart only highlighted some of his accomplishments. Everything changed after this, as he started a career inside of folds of the army instead of as an interloper. He was the youngest brigadier, yet had arguably the most combat experience of any serving officer. Yet for someone who thrived on excitement, Funston wondered if anything in his future could come close to his past—if his dramatic raid was the zenith of his life, the nadir must lie in the future. While he still had important work in the Philippines, he was on a spiral into the doldrums of peace.

§

Aguinaldo was set up in a nice residence near Malacanan with his family and enjoyed frequent visits from personal friends and American military leaders. A detail of guards were assigned, as much to protect him as to guard against escape. After deliberation, Aguinaldo prepared a proclamation urging his subordinates to give up the struggle and accept the sovereignty of the United States, as he had. Operations continued to mop up guerilla bands and many laid down arms and came in from the mountains of central Luzon. A week after the raid, Funston returned to San Isidro and opened communications with his primary nemeses, General Lacuna.

His first attempt to persuade Lacuna began with a long letter outlining conditions, citing the surrender of others, and stressing Aguinaldo's proclamation. Lacuna was noncommittal at first, but he offered to consider a specific proposition. After several more exchanges, Funston and Lacuna agreed to end all hostilities in the 4th District. He would be allowed to concentrate forces at Papaya while Funston would hold all his troops inside their garrisons.

Next step was a personal meeting. Funston, with his aides and a dozen scouts, rode ten miles to Papaya without a white flag or security of an advanced guard. They rode quietly into the insurgent camp, dismounted, and left horses with the scouts. They were met by Doroteo del Rosario, the insurgent captured by Funston and released on the basis of a letter saying he was a secret agent. They were escorted past a twenty-man honor guard into a large, grass-roofed shed, where Lacuna waited with coffee and cake.

Lacuna was splendidly attired for an old guerrilla, wearing a new uniform specially prepared for the occasion. He normally spoke Tagalog, but was also fluent in Spanish, so they talked in a common language. After pleasantries they got down to business with Funston explaining that all his officers and men could surrender if they turned in their arms and ammunition. They'd have to take the oath of allegiance, and all crimes against Filipinos would be overlooked and left for Filipinos to resolve. Any crimes against American prisoners would be prosecuted by military commission. Funston made clear these instructions were from higher headquarters and therefore non-negotiable.

Lacuna agreed that all of his men, except Fagan, Funston's most wanted, would march to San Isidro to comply with those terms. Lacuna led them as agreed, and formed in the public square. Americans, and the few wives present including Eda, filled the streets alongside local natives. The ceremony was brief and three hundred seventy-nine rifles and thousands of rounds of ammunition were stacked. Seventy-five more rifles were to be delivered from caches later. Funston escorted Lacuna to his headquarters to administer the oath of allegiance privately.

Lacuna was the last rebel leader in the Department of Northern Luzon to surrender. General Wheaton sent out a dispatch announcing a termination of the state of war in that district. An era of good feelings quickly followed with frequent inter-cultural social functions. The population was friendly enough to provide a sense of normalcy. Social calls soon began, encouraged by Funston, between rebel leaders and his veterans to recount old battles and discuss conditions, decisions, and results. The dramatic peace was good—too good to last.

§

During the relative calm of the truce with insurgents, General Frederick Grant of the 5th District and Colonel Thompson of the 6th, returned to the United States. Grant, the son of former general and president Ulysses S. Grant was no more a fan of Funston than he had been of blacks being admitted to West Point. His welcomed departure facilitated reorganization, combining all three districts under Funston's new, enlarged command. Funston moved his headquarters to San Fernando, less than an hour's train ride to Manila. His new command now contained fifteen thousand troops. But his position in the new command was primarily administration, supply, and discipline of Americans troops and prosecution of former criminal insurgents for war crimes, as well as policing bandits and civil criminals.

In days following the truce with Lacuna, quiet occupation meant reduced military operations, affording opportunities for trouble from native agitators, deserters, and civil criminals. Bandits ran unhindered with no effective local police or constabulary to contain them. The military stepped in again. Military commissions were established to deal with trials not applicable for military court martial or civil courts. Funston described commission trials: "Military commissions, though governed by the rules of evidence that prevail in civil courts, and while at all times guarding the rights of the accused, pay no attention to technicalities, and brush to one side everything that it may seek to bring in to obscure the main issue, which, after all, is whether the accused is guilty or not."

David Fagan, the black American deserter, had served under Lacuna and had executed prisoners. Funston kept the Christmas doll Eda made for him on his desk as a reminder to bring the man to justice. Fagan had become a bandit—his presence an affront to the rule of law. Funston gained approval from General Wheaton to offer a $600 reward for him, dead or alive. One of the flyers, in Spanish and Tagalog, reached a bounty hunter who needed the money, and he knew Fagan's whereabouts. He found him, decapitated him, and returned with his head for the bounty. Along with Fagan's head, he brought three Remington rifles, two revolvers, and the West Point ring taken from Lieutenant Alstaetter when he was captured. Problem solved.

Rumors of another bandit, this one white, were investigated by Funston's command. George Raymond was a former soldier discharged in the Philippines. Raymond was arrested, and convicted of murder, robbery and other crimes. Ten thousand Filipinos gathered in the public square to watch a white man die on the gallows. Justice served.

Then a big surprise! Doroteo del Rosario, the former insurgent who had been Lacuna's adjutant with a protective letter as a double agent, was proved to have ordered several murders. Del Rosario was brought before the commission, found guilty and hanged. Military commissions worked well to enforce the rule of law in wartime conditions.

§

Vice President Theodore Roosevelt wrote to Funston twice in the days after Aguinaldo was captured, while the military command was still in a period of counterinsurgency stability operations. The first letter of praise and caution on March 30th, 1901, said: "This is no perfunctory or formal letter of congratulations. I take pride in this crowning exploit of a career filled with feats of cool courage, iron endurance and gallant daring, because you have added your name to the honor roll of American worthies. If I thought there was any danger of your head being turned, as poor, gallant Dewey's head was turned, I should not write to you; but I think you have it in your nature a fund of solid common sense which will prevent you being misled by hero worship you are certain to receive."

His second letter was dated August 20th, 1901. In this one he said he had heard from Funston's friend William Allen White that he was thinking of leaving the army. Roosevelt "urgently" advised him not to, signaling more was in store. "I think you have it in you to rise to a very high civil position; I know that what you prize is the chance to do work worth doing, no matter how arduous; and I feel that from both of these standpoints it would be well for you to stay in the army at present." Eda agreed with the Vice-President and probably had the final vote on the matter, weighing in that the army was a better career for her husband than another risky civilian venture. Besides, it was time to think about a family and she was determined that when she brought children into the world, they should have some stability in their lives. Eda was already certain she was in the "family way."

When President McKinley was about to announce his selections to fill the only two vacancies for regular army brigadier general from a list of twenty-six senior colonels, his selection of Funston resulted in their being bypassed. Funston hadn't sought the promotion, although it was welcomed at a time he was still considering whether to stay in the army. Still, many officers, who had long endured career stagnation after the Civil War, resented someone so junior being promoted ahead of them. The army's Adjutant General was among them. Brigadier General Henry Corbin told Kansas Congressman Chester Long that he saw no basis for the promotion. "I am making lieutenants of better stuff every day. Funston is a Boss Scout—that's all."

Corbin knew the president could promote whomever he chose, but that wasn't the end of it. When the appointment came before the board, some disgruntled officers tried a campaign to discredit him. Thirty regular officers, who asked their names be anonymous, signed a petition charging he deserted from the Cuban Army, and asserting his capture of Aguinaldo was treacherous and recklessly irresponsible. But officers, who knew him best, including many he outranked, carried no animosity. Brigadier General Thomas Barry proclaimed Funston had the full support of "every man of the Regular Army whose opinion is worth anything." The board approved his appointment unanimously.

None of the debate in Washington influenced those in Manila who knew him. Regular officers there held an elaborate dinner to fete the man and his unparalleled accomplishments. MacArthur was unable to attend, but General Barry hosted as his representative. General Wheaton toasted Funston's health and welcomed him into the regular army ranks as a brave, able, and distinguished soldier. In his remarks, Funston spoke only of others, "who despite their gallant services ... are still unrecognized." He said, somewhat embarrassed, that promoting him over the others would make it "hard to look an old army colonel in the face."

§

On July 20, 1901, William Howard Taft succeeded MacArthur as governor general and Adna Chafee became military commander on July 4th. A farewell celebration was held at the Manila Club for MacArthur, but Taft wouldn't attend, and snubbed him again at the change of command. Prior to vacating Malacanang Palace, MacArthur hosted a party for over one thousand people including officers, their wives, and local officials, but didn't invite Taft. Bad blood between them didn't initially affect Funston, but eventually would. MacArthur returned to the states, fondly remembered by those he mentored, including Fred Funston.

While peace was the prevalent condition in Luzon, the insurgency didn't end entirely with Aguinaldo's capture. The military governor still controlled provinces not pacified, civil establishment controlled the others. As bandits were run to ground and more provinces transferred to civil authority the size of the army was cut in half and stations cut by more than half. On July 4th, 1902, President Roosevelt officially declared peace, granted amnesty to all who swore allegiance, and established civil control over most of the islands. But fighting wasn't over, as expeditions continued against a Moro uprising in 1903, 1905, and 1906.

While MacArthur and Taft were never cordial, Funston stayed clear. Taft thought highly of Funston, and reported to Secretary of War Elihu Root he had gained "the united respect of every regular army officer in the Island." He also categorized Funston and his fellow officer, Franklin Bell, as members of "the suicide club," those few who thrived on exposing themselves to danger. Taft found Funston modest, quiet, and strictly about business, and lobbied Root to retain him to help run the civil government, or perhaps the Filipino constabulary.

Taft emphasized civil policies to win over Filipinos with education, civil government, and benevolence. MacArthur, Chaffee and Funston stressed winning with tough responses to guerilla warfare, but leniency in punishing infractions. The combined "carrot and stick" approach to counterinsurgency eventually prevailed. On looking back within the entire Philippine counterinsurgency campaign, it was most effectively balanced in central Luzon, in Fred Funston's domain.

But while he commanded the 4th District in northern Luzon, he was struck down—not by a bullet but by appendicitis. This, added to his run-down physical condition, sent him to the 1st Reserve Hospital in Manila for the rest of the year. He was visited often by Generals Chaffee and Wheaton, helping him to pull through without Eda by his side. Eda returned to San Francisco in May. She was definitely pregnant. While Funston's surgery by Major H.P. Birmingham, was declared successful, the incision was slow to heal. In characteristic style, he wanted to return to duty, and did, but high fevers, vomiting, restlessness, and loss of appetite kept him confined to the ward for months.

Soon after he was discharged he was right back under the doctor's care. General Chaffee agreed with his surgeon that he must return to the states to recover as he was subject to fits of heavy sweating, inability to hold down food, and difficulty breathing. Finally, two days before Christmas in 1901, he was able to board the army hospital ship, *Warren*, and begin a quiet voyage for San Francisco, Kansas, and Eda.

Eda had returned to Oakland several weeks prior to Fred's attack of appendicitis. She was pregnant with their first child and wanted to give birth in California instead of the Philippines. Before she left Manila she wrote home to her mother that she was "dying for something German." She specifically asked to have cucumber salad and marinated herring when she arrived, along with good black bread and decent coffee. On her arrival the press intercepted her to comment about her husband's exploits in capturing Aguinaldo and promotion to brigadier general. Reporters sprung questions about criticisms by General Frederick Grant and Adjutant General Corbin denouncing the raid as sensational and foolhardy. Eda never condoned criticism of her husband quietly. She compared the negative reactions of "desk soldiers at Washington" with the spontaneous and unanimous responses of "regular officers" in Manila. Once started, she pressed harder, saying about Grant, "for some reason he resents the promotion of a man who won on his merits, although he has accepted a similar promotion for himself, though it was based wholly upon the distinction and services of his dead father!"

When Fred arrived in San Francisco on the *Warren* there were no civil committees or military formations, no carriages waiting at the wharf, no bands playing or streamers flying. But eight hundred soldiers aboard the ship raised a hearty cheer as the small man climbed down the ladder. He was uninformed about the birth of a child and when a reporter mentioned the baby, Funston asked, "When did it happen?" He was told it was three weeks before. "And Mrs. Funston?" He was assured she was doing magnificently and was shown a photograph published in the newspaper.

"Then it's a boy?"

Eda was living with her parents at a pretty red house at 1319 Twentieth Avenue in East Oakland with vines twisting around the columns and an American flag waving beside the entrance. She was there when the baby arrived at Letterman at The Presidio on December 18th, 1901. Fred's arrival had been delayed, but in time to argue with Eda about their first son's name. While Eda favored Fred, he wanted Arthur. He finally ended it with his clear rationale: "You, my dear, are a tall woman. The baby…will be a six-footer, and then I shall have the humiliating experience of having my son pointed out as 'Big Fred Funston,' while my old name of 'Little Fred' will stick to me. We'll get around it by calling him MacArthur."

§

The years after Fred Funston's return from his second tour of duty in the Philippines—Medal of Honor, capture of Aguinaldo, selection as a regular army brigadier general—would seem to be a time to enjoy the fruits of success for most people. For Funston, the period between early 1902 and 1914 were troublesome and included the dreariest days of his life. Although interspersed with opportunities to return to Cuba and the Philippines, shore up defenses in the territory of Hawaii against a possible attack, put down a gold miner's strike, and rescue San Francisco from the great 1906 earthquake and fire, many of these doleful years did not rise to Funston's expectations for excitement, challenge, and fulfillment. As a result, he was often out of step, locked in controversy, and bounced from one unfulfilling assignment to the next. The nation and the army needed Fred Funston out front in a war, but found him a difficult samurai to keep busy during the stagnant days of relative peace.

He always held friends and family close but during this period of transition he lost close family members, mentors, friends, and almost lost his way. While his courageous heart longed for adventure, he was expected to behave differently as a regular general officer than he had as a volunteer colonel, freelance adventurer, or lifelong maverick. He remained a "wild goose," and did not fare well when bounded by physical or societal norms. The years between 1902 and 1914 were important years, but not the happiest in the spirited lives of Fred and Eda Funston.

The period was marked by frequent changes of postings, including some of the happiest of times in San Francisco, despite the great disaster there in

1906. He also found his duty productive in a third tour in Luzon where he completed his book, *Memories of Two Wars*. And his good years at Fort Leavenworth in command of the army's service schools, where he was a caretaker commandant for policies in progress, not an innovator; he was able to reconnect with his Kansas roots. An opportunity to return to Cuba with William Howard Taft for the 2nd Cuban intervention, proved unsuccessful and disappointing. And worst of all, he lost his father, his first-born son, and his mentor Arthur MacArthur during these doleful years. Then he was rebuked by his mutual admirer, President Roosevelt. Although Roosevelt still appreciated his nonconformist ways, winning support from William Howard Taft and Woodrow Wilson came at a steep price—harnessing his true nature. Many of his problems stemmed from his tendency to speak his mind, take the initiative, and simply follow his natural tendencies—to be "Fighting Fred" Funston.

Although he had always been a man of action, he was also a man of words. He had read extensively in his youth from his father's vast library, taught school, worked as a reporter, published in major periodicals, lectured, memorized long passages of poetry, and when challenged, he fought back with fists and words with equal skill and vigor. A rebuke by the President silenced him—except, after a few drinks, when his temper came unhinged.

§

Funston's emergency surgery in Luzon for appendicitis in late 1901 resulted in hospitalization in the 1st Reserve Hospital in Manila for several months. However, the incision didn't heal properly in the tropics and became infected, requiring more surgery. His army surgeon concluded he wouldn't mend properly in the tropics and recommended returning to the United States to recover. As soon as he was well enough to travel, he left for San Francisco, arriving on January 9th, 1902. Notoriety from capturing Aguinaldo raised his profile in the press and he was dragged into interviews when he arrived.

He bragged on his men and their successes in bringing outlaws to justice, described changes in the insurgency, and discussed prospects for business and agriculture in the islands—hinting an entrepreneurial venture. He said he believed the Philippines were safe enough for soldiers, their wives and families to travel about Manila in groups and with caution, but occupation would likely continue for a long time. When asked about his own future, he replied following his recovery he hoped to be assigned somewhere in the west, possibly in California near Eda's home.

When he slipped the press, he headed for a reunion with Eda and little Arthur in Oakland where they were staying with her parents. But, after a few days he realized he needed to see another surgeon—infection could mean life or death and this time they must get it right. He telegraphed the Adjutant General requesting permission to see his personal physician, Dr. E.F. Robinson, in Kansas City, Missouri, instead of an unknown army doctor at The Presidio. The reply was disappointing—he could arrange his own treatment, but only at personal expense. He dallied a few days in Oakland, resting, writing letters, making some official visits, especially enjoying the company of Eda, baby Arthur, and her parents—postponing his decision. At the end of January, he notified the War Department of his impending address at the Midland Hotel in Kansas City, and then caught an eastbound train.

In Kansas City, Dr. Robinson first kept him under observation, and then decided another operation was necessary. A week later, he declared six weeks was needed for recovery. The doctor informed the War Department he should remain in the states long enough to heal. Funston wrote to the Adjutant General, for a leave extension and changed his address to Iola, where he intended to recover on the farm. His mother's cooking had brought him back once from Cuban wounds and undernourishment.

As he recuperated, he received hundreds of personal letters, fan mail, and over two hundred offers for lectures at Sunday Schools, Chautauqua assemblies, lecture bureaus, and schools, promising compensation between $25 and $1,000. One contract was offered for fifty lectures around eastern major cities for $50,000. He rejected them all, making clear he didn't intend to write or lecture, only to do his official duty as a brigadier general in the regular army.

But, he never intended to go into seclusion, and accepted personal invitations for the prominent Lotus Club in New York, and the Marquette Club in Chicago. He found his stride before leaving Kansas City by taking on Captain George A. Detchemendy, who claimed credit for Aguinaldo's capture. Detchemendy grabbed some publicity in *The New York Times* and other newspapers for his outrageous claim. First, he asserted to the War Department, then the press, that he was more instrumental in capturing Aguinaldo than anyone else, especially Funston. He demanded promotion to Brigadier General, and threatened resignation. Funston responded, "Captain Detchemendy had nothing to do with the capture of Aguinaldo. To Lieutenant J.D. Taylor of the 24th United States Infantry belongs the credit for capturing the correspondence that resulted in the capture of the rebel chief. Sometime after the capture made by Taylor, Detchemendy captured a member of Aguinaldo's body guard, but the information received from the captured man was of no material importance." He reiterated that Detchemendy was the subject of an investigation for domestic difficulties. Funston's backblast made clear he intended to strike back at improper criticism or attempts to ride his coattails. Detchemendy accepted the alternative and resigned.

On March 1st, Funston caught a passenger train from Kansas City to New York for his speech to the Lotus Club. He checked in at the Holland House and visited his old professor at the University of Kansas, James Canfield, now the librarian at Columbia University. Canfield asked about his future plans. He repeated the same line he had used with the press in San Francisco, that as a soldier he would do whatever he was ordered to do, but privately he preferred to go to the Department of Pacific in San Francisco. Canfield made note and later that day penned a letter to his friend, George Cortelyou, private secretary to President Roosevelt. Canfield expected Cortelyou to forward the letter to the War Department, but instead, he gave it to the president. Secretary of War Elihu Root received the presidential request and, eventually, made Funston's move to San Francisco reality.

His speech at the Lotus Club was "one of the most successful ever given at the club." Funston defended national policies in the Philippines and justified the actions of the army there. But he didn't stop there—he attacked the anti-imperialists, like Mark Twain, as "misguided dupes." Then he changed tact abruptly, saying he wanted to talk about those who died in defense of their country. Funston told the story of Sergeant O'Brien, who was in the hospital when he learned his company was going to the front. The doctor tried to restrain O'Brien, but he went anyway, and was killed in an ambush. After that story he told of a little Filipino boy who came to his house to learn English. He and Eda helped him learn until he was captured by insurgents, tortured for hours and killed for associating with Americans. At the end, the entire club stood and waved white napkins, proclaiming approval. The banquet hall seated more than three hundred members and guests of the club, including Funston's friends, Canfield, Charles Gleed, and other acquaintances and club leaders at the head table. The press was also in attendance and leaped at an opportunity to stir the debate between him and the anti-imperialists.

The brutality of the war had generated a strong base of protests at home. While Funston's actions proved him among the most humane and effective of American generals—he was also the most audacious. But, his words were often strident, salted with uncensored profanity, and, as a result, he was singled out as an easy target for those opposing the administration's imperialist policies as inhumane. Another target of his ire was the Dominican friars, who had proved corrupt, over-controlling of Filipinos, and in cahoots with the Spanish. American Catholics took exception and piled on with the old false allegations about looting the church at Caloocan. He returned fire in his personal style.

While he was popular in the press for his public disputes with disgruntled soldiers and anti-imperialists, he had detractors in the regular army as well. His promotion to brigadier general so young was based on merit and achievement, yet was opposed by officers of the old school who believed he should bide his time and be promoted the regular way—by longevity. Roosevelt and MacArthur had seen his potential, believed in promotions based on merit, and bumped him over hundreds of old line colonels. Prejudices about his youth continued until his untimely death.

While he made appearances before the media, reports seeped out of the Philippines about volunteers routinely shooting wounded or captured Filipino soldiers and civilians. Most incidents were supplemental to normal combat activity. During the attack on Caloocan, one Kansas soldier alleged five prisoners were shot and cited justification as there was no place to keep prisoners. Even more appalling, the letter writers insisted Funston had made clear that no quarter was to be given. An army investigation exonerated him and several witnesses recanted both the allegations of shootings and the orders.

Following his speech in New York, he went to Chicago to keep his engagement at the Lincoln Club in the clubhouse of the Marquette Club. He made much the same remarks there but declined a public reception due to his weakened physical condition. He rested in Chicago for a few days before going to Washington, where he had lunch with the president, met with senators on Capitol Hill, and with General Corbin at the War Department about his next assignment. Next day, an announcement was made that Funston would replace MacArthur as commander of the Department of Colorado.

In the Philippines, relations between the army and the press were sometimes supportive, mostly unbiased, and occasionally adversarial. Deployed soldiers were mostly amused by inaccurate reporting and opinions, but incensed by diatribes from the Anti-imperialist League, including Mark Twain. Most journalists overseas were respected but the press was generally considered enemy spies—aiding the enemy and keeping the insurgency alive. A decade after the war, Funston, the former correspondent, still fumed over libelous, unfounded accusations against him. But, much dissent in the U. S. was caused, not by reporters, but in letters from soldiers serving in the Philippines. Some were accurate, some less so, but yellow journalism was eagerly published in American national and local newspapers by editors who never left their cushioned chairs for the jungles, especially those in cahoots with anti-imperialists.

Mark Twain was vice-president of the Anti-imperialist League, opposed occupation of the Philippines and used his popularity and sharp satire against the administration's policies. The anti-imperialist clique included a long list of other notables, such as Grover Cleveland, Andrew Carnegie, Samuel Gompers, William Jennings Bryant, and a fair share of newspaper editors. Twain's essay, "To a Person Sitting in Darkness," published in the *North American Review* in February 1901, criticized United States policies toward the islands. Then he used a satirical essay in May 1902 as a blunt instrument comparing Frederick Funston to George Washington. He sarcastically titled the article "A Defense of General Funston." His lampoon "defended" Funston on the grounds that the characters of both men were influenced by their environment, therefore Funston should not be held accountable for his actions. Twain's principle grievance centered on Funston's raid to capture Aguinaldo using an elaborate deception to gain entry into his hideout. While he admitted all techniques used had been employed previously, and he excused those, he took exception to one—asking for food. Twain described that as an intolerable act and swung it as a club against Funston. Twain expressed fears that rising "Funstonianism" was taking hold, making him a dangerously flawed folk hero in military circles and in public schools.

Funston was stung by the criticism but he dispelled Twain's spoof simply as "very lady-like." His style was always direct attack and he had no use for the indirect satire of Mark Twain. However, Twain went as far as suggesting all evils of the world were tied to the same flaws that characterized "Funstoninism," including all the atrocities in the Philippines and Cuba, earthquakes around the world, even massacre's and crimes committed before Funston's birth. In the end, he suggested patriots turn away from the heroic example of Funston.

While Fred was travelling, his biggest fan received visitors in Oakland. One found the Blankart's parlor decked in Philippine rugs, candelabra, quaint Spanish pictures, brazed bells and odds and ends far removed from German trinkets from the Fatherland. She came down the stairs wearing a Philippine dress for the society page photographer. He wrote "not an atom of affectation spoils her sweet simplicity." And when she spoke of Fred, "it was to tell of some little act of personality that will not be writ in history's pages." In her words, "Fred and I are very different in some things," she said. "He is very impulsive and acts on the thought of the moment, while I was brought up on the motto, 'Little girls should think twice before they speak once.' ... Fred just goes ahead without weighing the pros and cons. But whatever he does turns out to be the right thing and done at exactly the right moment. When he makes up his mind to get a thing, he always gets it without wasting time." She continued, "Wherever Fred goes he makes warm friends, and he goes everywhere." The reporter mentioned she never spoke of him as "the general," but only as "Fred" or "my husband." Speaking of their time in the Philippines, she said, "Only a soldier's wife knows of the days of anguish—and sleepless nights. It is worse for the women than for the men; they have the excitement to buoy them up."

§

Funston's orders to San Francisco were delayed until there was an opening. Meanwhile, he was to command the Department of Colorado in Denver. Before he settled there, he again visited Washington where the appearance of a hero caused a flutter of excitement, especially among lady secretaries in the War Department. Curious department clerks posted a lookout and when Funston arrived a signal rippled down the corridors. The hallway to the secretary's office was flooded with breathless female admirers, and a rising hum of murmurs, chatter, and clapping broke out as he stepped off the elevator. A former soldier from the Philippines met him at the door to request an autograph on a blank card. Funston obliged, and after he departed, female clerks bid against each other for the soldier's prize. He refused to sell it. Someone tried to snip the page Funston signed in the visitors' book but a guard stopped him. Roosevelt had warned him not to "have his head turned" by hero worship. There was no chance of that.

While in Denver he resumed an acquaintance with General Irving Hale, commander of the Colorado Volunteer Regiment and a brigade in the Philippines. They'd fought alongside during the breakout from Manila. Hale discovered former troops from his old regiment were in deplorable economic and physical condition with virtually no medical or economic support provided to veterans. Funston lent his support to their cause. Colorado veterans from the Philippines eventually joined forces with Ohio veterans from Cuba and formed the Veterans of Foreign Wars.

In Denver, he was set up for his heaviest criticism yet in a speech to a banquet marking the Colorado Society for Sons of the Revolution. He spoke of his experiences in the Philippines along the expected lines, but once again laid blame for the prolonged war on outside influences, specifying newspaper editors and anti-imperialists. But he directed his strongest attack at certain members of Congress, singling out George Frisbie Hoar, an outspoken anti-Imperialist, but fellow Republican, for special attention. Funston expressed his sympathy for the senior senator from Massachusetts, for "suffering from an overheated conscience," and "playing peanut politics and gambling in the blood of their countrymen."

Senator Hoar was furious when the comments were published in a Washington, D.C. newspaper. President Roosevelt sided with his Republican colleague. Roosevelt called their mutual friend, William Allen White, asking him to advise Funston unofficially to keep his mouth shut.

He got the message and complied, going practically mute in public. However, Hoar was not satisfied and demanded a public rebuke. Roosevelt sent a personal memorandum to the Secretary of War, pointing out that while "I am in cordial sympathy with his general view on the Philippines...he expresses himself at times in a way that is very unfortunate." Roosevelt suggested the Secretary of War request Funston not make any more public speeches.

He'd already requested a leave of absence to attend a banquet at the Middlesex Club in Boston. His request was disapproved, and the Acting Secretary of War sent him a reinforcing letter. "Sir: I am directed by the President to instruct you that he wishes you to cease further public discussion of the situation in the Philippines, and also to express his regret that you should make a senator of the United States the object of public criticism or discussion. Very respectfully, William Cary Sanger." From that time, Roosevelt kept a safe distance from the explosive general, and the general kept his mouth shut.

The rebuke was bad, but worse, he was confined to his bed with recurring attacks of malaria contracted in Cuba. His temperature spiked to 104 degrees and confined him to quarters again under doctor's supervision.

§

The War Department moved him again, further west but not to San Francisco. This time to command the Department of Columbia headquartered at Vancouver Barracks in Washington State. This was a "briar patch" for the outdoorsman as he loved the Pacific Northwest, and his area included Alaska with opportunities to revisit his early adventures in the Yukon Territory. From a military perspective, he was especially interested in field exercises in the vast expanses of the region with inherent challenges of terrain and weather. Hunting and fishing was unrivaled in Washington, Oregon, and Alaska. Eda was also happy to be near home— she was pregnant again.

En route to Vancouver Barracks, across the Columbia River from Portland, Oregon, Funston stopped in Portland with Lieutenant Mitchell and a new member of his family—an English bird dog presented by a friend from Colorado. He told reporters he intended hunting with the dog when the season opened. The dog was so exquisite, he occupied the best quarters the Hotel Portland could offer. Funston spent the evening with his aide and two other Philippine veterans prior to meeting with General Randall, the officer he was replacing.

Old allegations from the Philippines that he had ordered prisoners killed soon surfaced again, raised by Herbert Walsh. Funston requested the Secretary of War convene a court of inquiry to allow Walsh to bring his witnesses to testify and put the matter to rest once and for all. Funston offered to resign if any of allegations were proven. The Judge Advocate General replied to both Funston and Walsh that the Secretary of War had reconsidered the allegations in light of the three previous investigations interviewing over two hundred witnesses. He had determined the charges were without foundation. The Secretary also expressed his satisfaction for Funston's willingness to have a complete and open hearing; all charges were dismissed. Case closed.

While the Funston's were in Washington State, Frederick II was born on September 23, 1903, giving Arthur a younger brother to pal with. Little Freddie was also born in Oakland, while Eda stayed with her parents to help care for two children. Fred took the train to Oakland to spend time with them before accompanying Eda and the boys to Vancouver Barracks.

A society reporter for the *Oregon Sunday Journal* visited the Funston's home at Vancouver Barracks to get a story. Eda quickly won him over and he gushed that the lovely Eda Funston had brought California sunshine to the cloudy region. Eda said she loved Vancouver and expected to always love army life. Young Arthur and younger Frederick had also made a home in the army. Arthur played with his toy gun and drum as they talked. He had been an enthusiastic participant in the field games the previous Saturday at the barracks, cheering on the sack races. The young soldier boy asked the reporter to take his picture for publication, although Arthur was already better known around the post than many officers. Arthur was frequently seen following his father around the golf links. He also accompanied his mother to concerts for the Army Relief Society at the barracks, where she played the violin along with musical contributions of other volunteers. During the summer, while Funston made his inspection tour of Alaska, they returned to Oakland to visit grandparents.

He submitted his annual report from the Department of Columbia, making a strong appeal to raise the pay for enlisted soldiers throughout the army. He reported, "The government cannot get something for nothing.... When there is considered the amount of work they are required to do and the degree of intelligence necessary for the proper performance of their duties, the pay of the enlisted men of the army is ridiculously small." He went further to mention that at Fort Egbert, near the Arctic Circle in Alaska, officers cultivated a garden to raise vegetables to supplement their diet. It was a trend that Funston continued through his military career—lobbying for increased pay and benefits for soldiers and officers while standing aside to allow peers to be promoted over him. This likely stemmed from a sympathetic condition passed down from his father, Edward Funston, the "farmer's friend" always battling in congress for improved conditions for farmers, ranchers, and hard-working Kansans in his district.

In the army, change is constant. Fred, Eda, and the boys left from the Hotel Portland, heading for Chicago on the night train in the private car of E.E. Calvin, general manager of the Harriman System. Funston recognized how important the Department of Columbia had become with forty-five hundred troops distributed among eighteen posts. Washington State had more troops than any other state at that time, with a thousand artillerymen manning ports of Puget Sound. Facilities were significantly improved during his short tenure. Future plans called for even more, with a cavalry regiment in Oregon, two mountain batteries, and infantry conversion to the improved Springfield rifles with clipped cartridges for rapid fire.

He had been ordered to command the great Department of the East in New York, but his orders were suddenly changed to Chicago, clearing the way for one of his detractors, General Grant. Chief of Staff Adna Chaffee offered to rescind the relocation orders to allow Funston to remain in Vancouver, but he declined and proceeded on to Chicago. Funston and Eda however, first visited Washington for a special luncheon with the Chaffee's and other friends.

§

An assignment from the west coast to Chicago and command of the Department of Lakes represented a low point during his doleful years of peace, especially having been outflanked for command of the more prestigious Eastern Command. For nearly a year, he was ensnarled in routine paperwork and formal social functions. While Eda enjoyed the social aspects of the posting, both were happier with smaller, more intimate entertainment with close friends. Funston found no opportunities for field exercises in the big city and certainly no battles to fight.

Chicago society editors quickly found Eda at the Virginia Hotel, even before they found a place to live. When she was unexpectedly telephoned from the parlor, she replied, "I'll be down in a minute," and breezed right down. The reporter was impressed that when she said a minute, she meant exactly a minute—a "true soldier's wife." But her manner was pure California, although she was born in Illinois. She stressed that the family wanted to get settled quickly for the children's sake and were considering a north side apartment although it was some distance away, a long commute. Asked if young Arthur would be a soldier like his father, she said, "No. Now he wants to be a doctor. He knows how to apply bandages, put in stitches, and do other surgical work." When Eda had a minor operation on her foot, Arthur watched closely. Eda and her two blue-eyed, fair-haired boys discovered Lincoln Park, enjoying the lions, tigers, and foxes. But they also missed the large playgrounds and open spaces of Vancouver.

Funston and Colonel Metcalf did encounter a fighter during a trip to Kansas City. Robert "Lanky Bob" Fitzsimmons, the former heavy-weight boxing champion, was staying in the same hotel as the officers. A mutual friend introduced them. While they were talking, Funston pointed out that the two hundred pound Metcalf had several bullet holes in his body. Fitzsimmons said, "I'm glad him's the one that's got 'em and not me. I'd rather face a right swing any day than the smallest cannon you ever seen."

Funston replied, "That's where we differ. I would rather stand in front of a whole regiment of soldiers than one of your left punches." Funston quickly covered his bases and said to the huge pugilist, "Bob, if I ever insult you, I'll apologize."

Although Chicago was too tame for him, things became exciting in Iola when Edward Funston was arrested. On July 10th, three saloons were blown up by dynamite during the evening and "Foghorn" Funston took to the stump, declaring the explosions would not have occurred if the local police had been doing their jobs. While the elder Funston was a teetotaler, he was no fan of Carrie Nation, who had been arrested thirty times between 1900 and 1910 for hacking up saloons with her famous hatchet. Nation was no stranger to Kansas either, and was hospitalized in Leavenworth in 1911.

However, an Iola patrolman, Officer Cannon, took exception to Edward Funston's public assertions and ordered the elder Funston to desist with his rabble-rousing, but to no avail. Funston resisted arrest and the giant man confronted the smaller policeman with gun drawn. Reinforcements wrestled him to the ground, strapped him unceremoniously into a buggy, and hauled him off to jail. Fortunately, only verbal shots were fired. When Edward was released he swore out a warrant for the policeman, that also to no avail. A judge found him guilty of disturbing the peace and carrying a concealed weapon, and was required to compensate for the torn police uniforms and pay fines totaling $31.55. Fred Funston wondered if he really was a smaller chip off the larger block—except that he loved his drinks, while his father was a teetotaler who defended saloons.

True to his warnings, Fred remained mute in public and tried not to make any new enemies in the War Department or the White House, while he freed Eda to speak her mind whenever she wanted. But he was miserable there, and Eda missed her home in San Francisco. Funston finally succeeded in getting new orders in April, 1905, and was finally reassigned to San Francisco. Then their lives really got interesting.

SEVENTEEN

As Fred Funston recovered from surgeries and hospital confinements, he contemplated his future—whether to stay on this course or find a new challenge. During the uncertainty of the turn of the century while stalled in the doldrums of peace, he was buffeted between a series of short, unsatisfying assignments—an adventurer stranded in a passionless purgatory, suffering through peacetime service and aches and pains from soldiering hard. Easy access to the press had stirred up more trouble until he was rebuked by the president—then he fell silent. After intervals in Colorado, Washington State, and Chicago, he finally settled as commander of the Department of California in April 1905.

On July 21st of that year, Funston was riding to work in a carriage with his two aides, Lieutenant Long and Lieutenant Mitchell, when suddenly an electric trolley collided with their horse-drawn carriage. The officers jumped clear, but Funston's left hand was badly bruised. Mitchell was banged up as well, but Long and the horse were unscathed. None of their injuries required hospitalization but the crash of new technology against old was a wakeup call—more crashes were coming.

§

By April 1906, Funston's family and professional life had settled down—Eda was happy near her parents and sisters, and with little Arthur and Fred, Junior, keeping them company at home. Home finally seemed like a real place and with Eda and the boys in San Francisco, he was content. This city by the bay was where they had fallen in love and married on the margin of war, and he still considered marrying Eda "the smartest thing he ever did." They found a large house at 1310 Washington Street at the corner of Jones, high on a hill with an exquisite view of the city. Army life now was considerably different from seven years of swimming rivers, dodging bullets, and chasing guerillas or being hunted as one. They had paid their dues in the tropics with few social amenities, strength-sapping weather, and a harsh and dangerous environment. He had served time in unrewarding commands around the country. Eda especially appreciated the communal status of her splendid city, while he spent quality time with her and his two handsome boys. But even at a leisurely pace, in a relaxing lifestyle and comforting luxuries of a genuine home, trouble always reached out to find Fred Funston—a dedicated family man destined to live at the point of greatest danger and controversy.

Eda was especially happy to be back in the bay area near family, music, and culture, but deep down she knew it couldn't last. Her experiences overseas shaped her as an unusual army wife, and officers and their wives, as well as San Francisco's social elite were fascinated by her beauty and refinement—flavored with thrilling stories of a bride at the frontlines. She held tea parties for wives of senior officers, made house calls on families of junior ranks, was available for advice to anyone, attentively listening with an understanding ear. Sometimes she nudged her husband to help with solutions. Social life revolved around home and The Presidio. She was matchmaker for many young bachelors as her local network enabled her to make introductions between soldiers and ladies eager to meet them—to capture what she had. Eda was a superb cook and those invited to her home anticipated her celebrated blueberry pie. Her gentle words frequently soothed feelings bruised by brusque and sharp-tongued rebukes of her husband. She loved this life, but never forgot she was married to Fred Funston … after all … how long could it last?

Their house on Nob Hill was a comfortable refuge from the outside world. Passers often paused on the sidewalk to listen to soothing violin strings drifting from the home of the former concert musician, or phony wars of happy boys playing soldier. Many passed through those doors, including friends, neighbors, and local citizens, cohorts from the military community, seeking good company or to complain about some grievance. But in the sanctity of her home, she tolerated no criticism of her husband and detested the distasteful politics of city hall as much as he did. She listened quietly to his fuming and tried to calm him, but she sometimes whispered, "If Fred ran the city, things would be different." Neither knew how close they were to finding out just how true that was. It was April, 1906, and San Francisco was about to find out.

§

The San Andreas Fault was only discovered by scientists thirteen years before. San Francisco sat on the topographic fault line marked by gradual, sometimes sudden, tilting and shifting. In 1865, while the gold rush was on, San Francisco's plank sidewalks rocked with two tremors that cracked city hall, tilted lamp posts, and broke gas lines and water mains. In 1867, the fault yawned and the earth opened twenty feet wide and forty miles long before snapping shut again. Three years later, the Hayward fault claimed the first five victims. Then, the city was roughly shaken again in 1890 and 1898. Yet San Francisco Mayor Eugene Schmirtz took no actions to protect the city or citizens. He was hardly qualified to lead the city anyway—a concert violinist and orchestra conductor elevated as a puppet of Union Labor Party organizer, Abraham Ruef. For Schmirtz and Ruef, San Francisco was a money pot. Schmirtz said, "People will never ask how you made it, only get it." Everyone, even President Roosevelt, knew the mayor was under investigation for graft by Fremont Older and former mayor James Phelan. Walls seemed to be caving in on the corrupt mayor.

Funston was always fond of San Francisco, his adopted home. He had brought his famous 20th Kansas Volunteer Regiment there before shipping out to the Philippines, met and married Eda there, and both of his boys were born at The Presidio. San Francisco was a natural fit. He lived a short walk from the financial district on Nob Hill and his headquarters was in the Phelan Building, but all too close to the seedy Barbary Coast. He believed City Hall could do something about the slums but refused. Funston had cleaned up dingier towns in the Philippines and saw no reason this one couldn't be fixed. He threatened to post military sentries to collect drunken soldiers and sailors wandering past his quarters returning to the ports and forts from drinking sprees and other sins. But the mayor was tainted by money and only interested in profits. Bold men would have to save the city and the people, and the mayor was not one.

One courageous man had been trying unsuccessfully for years to protect the city—Fire Chief Dennis Sullivan. Sullivan was a giant among firemen with a firm jaw and deep-set eyes beneath bushy eyebrows; he had been chief for thirteen years and a fireman for twenty-nine—a consummate professional. Sullivan waited impatiently for the results of a meeting in the Hall of Justice, convened at the suggestion of Major Schmirtz. Judge W.W. Morrow had gathered citizens and officials to discuss a fire safety report from the National Board of Fire Underwriters, complaining that San Francisco was violating all traditional fire safety precedents and should have burned down already. Only vigilance by the fire department had prevented it thus far. Sullivan's battle for funds brought him into direct conflict with Mayor Schmirtz. He needed a budget from City Hall to build firefighting facilities, a supplementary salt water system, cisterns beneath streets, and to purchase high explosives and train men to use them to check fires. The War Department agreed to have the corps of engineers secure the explosives at The Presidio and only asked the city to provide a brick vault to hold them. City Hall refused. This latest report concerned a fault in the water distribution pipes to fight a major fire. The mayor asked Judge Morrow to chair the meeting but didn't invite the outspoken fire chief.

Sullivan and Funston were kindred spirits, on equally acrimonious footing with the mayor. Funston considered the entire civil administration corrupt and ineffective—all but Sullivan's fire department. He'd pressured the War Department to approve Sullivan's plan for the dynamite squad, only to have the mayor stymie it. He found the mayor too slick—too self-assured to accept advice, too quick to smile and turn his back. Schmirtz failed the firm handshake test, the "word-as-bond" and "look-into-the-eyes" tests, sure indicators of character. But, Funston admired Sullivan's dedication, leadership, and solid friendship.

Sullivan was concerned about the potential for catastrophe and appealed to him to try to make the case again with Schmirtz. Funston declined his friend because when the mayor refused, as he certainly would, he couldn't trust himself to control his temper. He avoided all contact with the mayor for that reason. However, when Major General Adolphus Greely left for a family wedding and made Funston acting military commander of the Pacific Division, he was unable to avoid the mayor.

§

On the evening of April 17th, 1906, Fred and Eda sat down together for dinner instead of going to the Grand Opera to hear Enrico Caruso sing in *Carmen*. He had some War Department work to tend to and wanted to catch up on reading. He'd been perusing a report in the *San Francisco Examiner* about the temperamental volcano Mount Vesuvius acting up again, threatening Naples. Editorials questioned why people would continue to live on top of an active volcano. In another column, the mayor encouraged people of San Francisco to send contributions to aid their international neighbors—surely there was a profit angle there. But he was more concerned with the upcoming war games he'd control at the end of the month. A sequence of events needed to be scripted and he disliked detailed formalities. Eda encouraged him, gently reminding the games would be worth the preparation and more fun than paperwork or politics. The exercise was just training, but a diversion from his dislike of City Hall.

After dinner Eda sent the boys to bed and they retired to the drawing room; a maid served coffee. But, instead of the after-dinner quiet he expected, gunfire in the Barbary Coast district agitated him. It reminded him the mayor wouldn't clean up that festering cesspool. Eda heard it too, and read his thoughts and body language. She'd heard others say what she was thinking, so she made a stab. She asked him point-blank, "Fred, why don't you just resign your commission and run for mayor? You'd be elected in a landslide!"

He looked back at her as if she'd lost her mind. "Good God, woman, the army's my career! I would have left long ago, but you encouraged me to stay in, you and MacArthur and Roosevelt."

But Eda wouldn't be deterred so easily and stood taller than him to point out the obvious. "But you know you wanted to stay in the army. You know that! But you've been unhappy lately and San Francisco is our home, now! Arthur's and Freddie's, too. It always has been, really. The city is unsafe and those crooks in office will never clean it up. You can do that, you and Chief Sullivan. Strong men are needed to take charge. San Francisco needs you," she told him. "Just think about it. I'm going to bed now! Don't stay up too long!" She left with skirts swishing.

She left him with those thoughts and climbed the stairs to their bedroom. He worked late in his study, mulling his reply to a long War Department memorandum. The paper from Washington, containing details for the upcoming war games, arrived that afternoon at his headquarters. He had read it several times, but hadn't decided on his response. He finally relented at 0400 and climbed into bed beside Eda, who didn't stir.

Fate had intervened again in Fred Funston's life when General Greely left for his daughter's wedding, leaving him in charge of the army's Pacific Division. Headquarters was at Fort Mason, and for the Department of California in an office building in the city. Officers with duty in the Department of California lived nearby in the city, as did Funston; others lived at nearby army posts, including The Presidio and Fort Mason.

He knew the locations of all troops under his authority. Ten companies of coastal artillery were stationed at military installations near San Francisco, as was the 22nd Infantry Regiment, three troops of the 14th Cavalry, and a company of the hospital corps, totaling seventeen hundred men. That morning, two companies of the 22nd Infantry and all cavalry troops were at Point Bonita at the rifle ranges.

§

At 0512 on the morning of April 18th, 1906, the plate of earth along the San Andreas Fault shifted without warning. Fred and Eda were shaken awake shortly before they would normally get up. He checked his watch; it read 0516. A second shock wave sent Eda running to see about the children while he scrambled into civilian clothes.

Outside, chimney bricks fell and church bells clanged erratically in their steeples. He hurried to catch the streetcar into the city, but the entire trolley-line was at a standstill, so he made a fast, hobbling walk-run into the financial district to ascertain damage. From the elevation of Nob Hill, he saw several columns of smoke rising south of Market Street and fires raging in the banking district. People stood in the streets, disbelieving, stunned, scared, fully dressed or in nightclothes. He continued along California Street, where several fires blazed, but fire department hoses were dry, water mains shattered, water pouring underground.

He was struck seeing the entire city in jeopardy from fire, the transportation system and all city services disrupted. Not only was the fire department disabled, but city police would be unable to keep order and protect property. He saw panic in the eyes of people in the streets; they needed leadership and authority. He decided then to call out troops to respond to the emergency, but this wasn't easy as communications were down. Seismographs notified scientists around the world that San

Francisco was in trouble, but communications within the city were out. The city was powerless and reverted to basics for survival. As military instincts kicked in, he became the de facto military governor of San Francisco. Legal limits on military actions within the United States wouldn't impede him in a crisis. San Francisco was in danger and he was the only one with the wherewithal and gumption to do something about it.

He watched several new automobiles race by in a panic and tried to flag one down, but drivers ignored him in their rush out of the city. So he limped and ran on his painful hip to the army stables on Pine Street, over a mile away. When he reached the stables, winded, he directed his carriage driver to saddle his horse. While waiting, he scribbled a note to Colonel Charles Morris, garrison commander at The Presidio, and directed Lieutenant Long to use his horse to deliver it. The note ordered Colonel Morris to report to the chief of police at the Hall of Justice, with all the troops he could muster. He knew this was in violation of *posse comitatus*, the 1878 law limiting the use of military troops for law enforcement, but he'd never hesitated before and certainly wouldn't now with lives at stake.

When Long arrived with the message, Morris realized Funston didn't have constitutional authority to issue such an order. At first he refused to comply, infuriated by the presumptions. Morris told Long, "tell that newspaperman to look up his Army regulations, and there he will find that nobody but the President of the United States can order regular troops into any city." Lieutenant Long didn't want to report failure to Funston so took matters into his own hands—ordered the bugler to sound a call to arms. Within minutes, the entire garrison assembled and marched off under Long's command. Funston sent similar orders to Captain M. L. Walker, an engineer officer in command at Fort Mason. Then he collared an overwhelmed policeman and asked him to inform Police Chief Jeremiah Dinan that troops were coming to report to him.

Since he had loaned his horse to Lieutenant Long, Funston walked back to the summit of Nob Hill to check progress of fires and damage from the earthquake. Streets were still filled with people watching black smoke rising from densely populated areas south of Market. Silence of the city made a powerful statement—no sirens, no whistles, no clanging bells, no traffic, no talking. The sky was clear, except for dark smoke rising in columns with no sea breeze to swirl it. Funston turned and walked home, only four blocks away. Eda had already prepared coffee, and he sat to have a cup. While he sipped, he issued nonstop instructions to her about packing trunks and taking the boys to the safety of The Presidio.

She'd made such moves without complaint in Manila, but this was her home and their possessions. "I'm sure Washington Street is safe at this end," she said, hoping he'd relent, but seeing that uncompromising look in his eyes. He had studied the smoke with a trained eye—their house was in the path of fires and would soon be destroyed. "Nowhere is safe against the pestilence of fire," he told her. "You must go!" That was settled.

He left Eda and the boys to move to The Presidio alone as best they could. He made the short walk, also alone, to the Phelan Building, headquarters of the Department of California. Several officers from the Pacific Division and the Department of California were waiting for instructions. A few minutes before 0700, engineers from Fort Mason, arrived in complete combat regalia, cartridge belts filled and bayonets fixed. The crowd on Market Street greeted them heartily—the presence of armed troops reassuring. Captain Walker had them fan out along the main street with two men per block. The police chief instructed them to shoot anyone looting or committing other crimes—they meant to comply.

§

Fire Chief Sullivan, in his quarters on the third floor above a fire house, was asleep when the cupola of the California Hotel next door fell sixty feet, crashing through his roof and all floors to the basement. Sullivan snatched a mattress and ran to the next room to cover his wife from falling debris. Before he got there, her bed, with her in it, and all the furniture plunged three floors to the basement. She was spared by the bedding, but Sullivan fell to the bottom through the hole, landed next to a burst radiator and was scalded by steam and boiling water. He was moved unconscious by horse-drawn ambulance to Letterman Hospital at The Presidio. His wife lived, but he died along with his hopes to protect the city.

Mayor Schmirtz whipped his buggy toward City Hall until he learned the building was destroyed—the result of nature mixed with corrupt politics and faulty cement. Twenty years were required to build it, the pride of the California coast, but the first shock rocked the building and it swayed until it cracked. The interior collapsed first, and then fire broke out, setting off an alarm.

Schmirtz veered from City Hall to the Hall of Justice, badly damaged but still standing. He found Police Chief Dinan and the elderly acting fire chief, bushy mustachioed John Dougherty standing on the steps. The mayor followed them into the dark basement where an impromptu disaster center was established, lit only by candles. The first item for consideration was the problem of liquor stores and bars left unattended; secondly, fires raging without water to extinguish them. The glaring error of the mayor's refusal of Chief Sullivan's plans to prepare for this disaster went unspoken.

Funston entered the bunker, bringing him face-to-face with his arch-rival. He had just sent a telegram from his headquarters next to the Pacific Cable Company to the War Department, describing the actions he had taken and requesting approval. He made clear to the mayor that army troops would remain under military command. But he assured him all military actions would be in consultation with civil authorities, and the first troops had already been deployed according to the police chief's instructions. Both Funston and Schmirtz knew their positions were indefensible without working together although they despised each other. The mayor requested more troops—common ground was found. Funston immediately requested all troops within a hundred miles be dispatched to the city. Mayor Schmirtz contacted California Governor Pardee and Mayor Frank Mott of Oakland for all the help they could send.

Communications problems came early in the first hours. Someone reminded Funston the commercial Pacific Cable Company was in the Grant Building next door to his headquarters. Since Pacific Cable was created by the federal government and leased to the company, he federalized it. His first telegram to Washington read: "We are doing all possible to aid residents of San Francisco in present terrible calamity. Many thousands were instantly homeless. I shall do everything in my power to render assistance, and trust to War Department to authorize any action I might have to take. ... We need tents and rations for twenty thousand people." The urgent message wasn't read by Secretary of War Taft for some time, as it was routed circuitously through Hawaii, the Philippines, Japan, Russia, and Europe before finally reaching Washington. The next day Taft notified him that enabling orders had passed the House of Representatives and would breeze through the Senate the following day. He was told to do everything possible to assist and keep order. The issue of constitutionality was on course to be resolved, so he had high-level cover to manage the crisis.

He saw how widely troops were dispersed and wanted the 22nd Infantry from Angel Island right away. Telegraphic communications were out so he sent the large army tug, *Slocum,* to deliver verbal orders to Colonel Alfred Reynolds. The tug was to return with troops aboard and they were to march directly to the Phelan Building. While awaiting additional troops, clerks who normally worked there reported. Funston instructed them to save the records and they began loading files in a wagon for transportation to Fort Mason for safekeeping. Then at 0800, an aftershock rattled buildings and nerves. He ended their work saving papers and evacuated the building.

Troops from The Presidio began arriving with cavalry and coastal artillery equipped as infantry, field artillerymen were mounted on battery horses. The police chief had plenty of assignments for the troops, with fires eating at the heart of the city, streets crammed with tens of thousands of people suddenly homeless, petty thieves and looters running wild. Homeowners had to be pushed away from their burning homes by strong-willed, well-armed soldiers. Before 1000 hours, soldiers from Forts McDowell and Miley arrived, bringing the troop strength to seventeen hundred regulars. California National Guard troops were on the way.

Troops acted under direct orders of their assigned officers, carrying out missions set by the police and fire chiefs. They protected citizens and guarded property, secured the sub-treasury and mint, patrolled streets to thwart looting, maintained fire lines, pulled hoses when there was water pressure, and any other duties assigned. The army also confined prisoners when jails were destroyed; one hundred seventy-six were taken to the military prisons at Fort Mason and Alcatraz.

Funston needed transportation to get about rapidly. He hired a Pope-Toledo with driver for $100 per day from William Levy of Levy Bag Company. The price was exorbitant, but under the circumstances, necessary. A "U.S." sign was placed on both back doors to announce its official status. At noon, he had lunch with former mayor James Phelan at the exclusive Pacific Union Club at Union Square—a stark contrast to the fires raging only blocks away. Their conversation concerned efforts to save important buildings, as Phelan headed Mayor Schmirtz' committee to develop an emergency organization to save San Francisco.

§

Schmirtz consulted with his friend and lawyer, Garrett McEnerney, and composed a proclamation backing up the police chief. "The Federal Troops, the members of the Regular Police Force, and all Special Police Officers have been authorized by me to KILL any and all persons found engaged in Looting or in the Commission of Any Other Crime.... E.E. Schmitz, Mayor." He ordered five thousand copies made and distributed, then greeted the first of those named to help run the city in emergency, the Committee of Fifty. Funston was a member but was not there when the meeting began—he was already running the crisis with an iron hand, while the mayor and his fifty-man committee argued about it.

No one took minutes of the meeting, which comprised the mayor's worst enemies, including Phelan and the attorney designated to eventually prosecute him. They deliberated in closed session for several hours until Funston walked in—eyes red from smoke, face grimy with soot—a commander from the frontlines of battle, situation map in hand. He cut off introductions when he spread his map over a crate used as a desk.

His first words stunned them, "Dynamite is the only answer!" he said. He knew Fire Chief Sullivan, had he lived, would agree blasting was the only way to stop fires without water. Blowing up parts of the city to create fire breaks was the only way to spare other sections. His plan was sketched out on his battle map. He assured them he could get supplies from military garrisons and railroad yards around the state and said he'd already ordered some districts evacuated to prepare for destruction, and ordered troops to guard parts of the city not scheduled for demolition. He paused, allowing them time to grasp the implications. Then he said the mayor's proclamation concerning looters—waving a copy before them—would be strictly enforced. Silence filled the room. He stared at the politicians and business leaders and they stared vacantly in disbelief. Mayor Schmitz finally conceded, "Very well." With that, he left.

The committee continued organizing after he'd gone, forming subcommittees to consider the numerous problems facing the city. Before they adjourned they agreed to resume in eighteen hours. But for all practical purposes, Funston and the military were already running the show. While no one wanted to admit this, it was perfectly clear to the mayor and everyone else in town. By their third meeting, shifting locations to avoid fires, the committeemen still shuffled papers while Funston exercised uncontested authority.

§

Funston shook his head at fires burning with no water to fight them. There was also none for drinking—a major problem for his troops and other emergency crews and parched citizens. The only running water was in Golden Gate Park. He ordered military and civil engineers to develop a backup water system, working with the Spring Valley Water Company. Meanwhile, the navy hauled in water from ships as an emergency measure, along with milk and other liquids for dehydrated refugees.

Early on the morning of the earthquake, the fire department had already sent a messenger to The Presidio requesting all available explosives. Army engineer Captain LeVert Coleman escorted him to Colonel Morris, who told Coleman to assist. Coleman rounded up forty-eight barrels of gun powder and loaded them onto field artillery caissons under control of Lieutenant Raymond Briggs, and directed him to deliver the explosives as requested. He then found two larger wagons and loaded the rest of the powder plus three hundred pounds of dynamite. Coleman accompanied these demolitions into the city, reporting to Colonel Morris, who was already on the scene at the Hall of Justice. The chief fire engineer, John Dougherty, designated blocks to be destroyed.

Coleman joined Briggs, who had acquired another large quantity of dynamite from John Bermingham of California Powder Works. The mayor agreed with Funston that Captain Coleman was the best person to oversee control and handling of demolitions and directed Bermingham report to Coleman. But Coleman found Bermingham was drunk and ordered him to stay clear of explosives. Lieutenant Briggs and a fire captain began setting explosives and dynamiting select buildings along Montgomery Street.

City authorities only permitted buildings in close proximity to the fire to be destroyed, but the fire repeatedly outflanked the clearing operation. Dynamiting continued for three days, with Captain Coleman and Lieutenant Briggs doing almost all the work with three enlisted assistants. Delays getting committee approvals for specific demolitions allowed the fire to spread, so on the second day, Colonel Morris authorized Coleman to just use his best judgment—not wait for the committee. With this authority, he designated a perimeter along Broadway, Franklin, and Gough Streets, enough ahead of the fire to create an effective fire break. Unfortunately, demolitions sometimes propelled burning debris into other areas, setting off new fires. A horrific fire started in the tinderbox of Chinatown shacks that sent rats scurrying all over town.

Coleman's duties were distasteful. His small team made risk assessments, broke into basements of public and private buildings, set charges, cleared buildings, ran electrical conductors to detonators, fused charges, handled and safeguarded dynamite, and set off explosives. The work was dirty and dangerous. Sometimes charges were laid in buildings already burning; other times electrical wires were stripped from poles to use as conductors. Worst was when civilians resisted evacuation of their homes or offices. Coleman and his team considered threats to them and the city, confiscated property, and destroyed it. It was treacherous and thankless work that saved half the city from fires while destroying the other half with dynamite.

Late the first day, troops of the California National Guard arrived to take up positions. Lack of communications left them initially uncontrolled by their commanding officers, Adjutant General Joseph Lauck and Brigadier General John Koster. They set up a headquarters initially at the Occidental Hotel, but moved to the Pacific Union Building when fire threatened, then vacated again to the Fairmont, then to North End Police Station on Washington, and finally all the way out to Oakland. Since the National Guard belonged to the governor, Funston didn't control them, and lack of firm control by authorities led to allegations of abuse.

During the first few days, the Navy's Pacific Squadron landed several hundred sailors and marines to assist with firefighting, but nearly every hotel, bank, large store and warehouse in the city was destroyed. Some docks and freight sheds along the waterfront simply slid into the bay. Deep fissures opened on reclaimed land near shore, and the Union Ferry station was badly damaged. It was impossible to reach city center directly from the bay without skirting far around the burning district.

§

Three-hundred thousand people were homeless, thousands more with no means of support. Rations, tents, and blankets from army posts around the city were distributed with no accounting. Within two days, relief supplies from neighboring states and cities began arriving. Schmitz and Funston agreed the army was best suited as a clearing house for those supplies. The army quartermaster, Major Devol, and his deputy, Major Krauthoff, were put in charge of supplies. The Red Cross agreed with these distribution procedures. Simultaneously, the Hearst Relief Corps set up several well equipped emergency hospitals with physicians and nurses from Los Angeles to accept overflow from army hospitals, already filled to capacity.

On April 21st, Mayor Schmirtz was alarmed by the progress of the fires and feared how his actions, or inactions, would be perceived. He wanted to swear in a thousand special police, untrained but under his authority. He requested rifles from the army for his private army. Funston refused, but informed Secretary Taft of the request. Taft approved the issue of weapons to civilians and instructed him to provide non-commissioned officers to show them how to use them. Schmirtz was joyous over the small victory over Funston, whom he called the "little dictator."

On April 22nd, Funston issued General Orders Number 12, organizing the city into six military districts, defining boundaries, locations of headquarters, naming commanders of each district and assigning troops. He also directed communications be established by the signal corps between each district and the Pacific Division headquarters. Included were his written agreements with the mayor—no seizure of vehicles for transportation, lights-out after 10 p.m., fires prohibited in houses without a special permit, and only suspicious persons could be stopped by sentries. Funston stressed restraint in dealing with unfortunate citizens of the devastated city.

He placed Lieutenant Colonel George Torney of the army medical department in charge of city sanitation with concurrence of Mayor Schmitz and the San Francisco Health Commission. Diseases, from impure drinking water or spread by Chinatown rats, were serious concerns. Captain James Kennedy was placed in charge of the military general hospital, while the hospital company was deployed into the city and to refugee camps to treat the sick and injured. A large circus tent was erected in an accessible location for storage and issue of general medical supplies.

As soon as communications was established on the second day, a telegram was sent to the medical supply office in St. Louis, requesting supplies for sixty thousand people, enough for four months. Two days later, five railroad cars departed under escort of an officer ordered to stay with the supplies until handed over. A week later, all nineteen carloads had been shipped. All medical personnel temporarily in the city or in transit were held over to assist. Another hospital company was deployed from Washington Barracks in the nation's capital to set up a field hospital in Golden Gate Park, one ward for maternity cases, the other for contagious diseases. A second civilian contagious disease hospital was set up in Harbor View Park, with Dr. McKenzie of Portland, Oregon, in charge.

Funston had experienced difficulties with the breakdown of communications when he used his horse and a messenger to deliver his first orders and later his rented automobile. However, the signal corps responded quickly and Captain Leonard Wildman needed no orders to get started. By 1000 hours on the first day, the signal corps had strung wire from The Presidio to the edges of the burning city. They kept one line open to Washington until 1500 hours, which was critical since all city lines were down. This enabled Funston to stay in touch with subordinate commanders and Washington. When he established six military districts, the signalers connected all the headquarters within three hours. When the earthquake struck, there'd been only a dozen signal corps officers and men to do everything, but they ramped up over time to one hundred seventy-eight officers and men. Signalers operated eighty-seven telegraph stations, fifty-six of them newly established, and put civilian stations back into use over telephone lines. They ran one hundred fifty miles of insulated wire and loaned material to the Western Union and Postal Telegraph, obtaining approval of the Secretary of War over the single Washington line.

The direct line to Washington failed on the afternoon of the first day, but the signal corps opened a new line to the San Francisco Ferry, where

Western Union kept an office connected with the Oakland cable. They cut non-functioning electric light wires to make part of the run, spliced with any other wires they could find on the streets. By the following day, Funston was talking to the Secretary of War over the patchwork connection. On April 23rd, he requested two thousand, five hundred additional troops. Two days later the Secretary of War requested he reconsider the numbers and ensure they came through civilian political channels, as "there is no law for such use of the army." Two days later, California Governor George Pardee telegraphed the president confirming more troops were needed for an undetermined stay, and emphasized troops were working in close coordination with civil authorities.

Signalers worked hard to ensure the "commander's voice" was heard. Captain Wildman had confiscated the only government automobile in San Francisco to personally run orders between Funston and his commanders until wire communications were reestablished. When flames threatened or burned communication lines, signalers rerouted the lines. A Western Union man was amazed by the rapid response and continuous high level of signal activity. He asked, "Where did you get these men? That sergeant has been at his instrument for three days." Over two weeks operators handled two thousand messages a day on lines strung over ruins.

Soldiers were all over the city, responding to solve the problems they found before them, often without any directions. Privates McGurty, Ziegler, and Johnson organized a relief expedition on their own. They impressed wagons to use, their only authority the Krag-Jorgensen rifles they carried. They used the wagons to transport supplies to North Beach and build two relief camps to house two thousand people, showed them how to set up tents and had them set up the others. On the fourth day, a lieutenant colonel from the 22nd Infantry found them there and questioned what they were doing. When they explained, he granted permission to continue and they received permission from the mayor to set up a food station near Fisherman's Wharf. They kept up their good work for ten days, fed and housed all the people there, issued two thousand sets of blankets, fifteen hundred pair of men's shoes, and twelve hundred pair of women and children's shoes before being relieved by the Red Cross. The *San Francisco Chronicle* editorialized: "The military power of the United States lies in the fact that the American regular soldier can be a machine when a machine is needed, but when a command is so separated that each man acts on his own initiative, Mr. Private Soldier uses his brains as well as his eyes...."

§

A controversy resulted from an Associated Press report that General Funston and Mayor Schmitz were in heated dispute over jurisdiction of police matters. It was widely known they were not on good terms, so reporters were especially tuned to their strained relationship during the crisis. The incident reported by the AP stemmed from an episode between National Guard troops and firemen over dynamiting on Van Ness. Colonel Morris had been given authority by the Mayor and Funston to make final decisions and he did so in this case, but not before a heated discussion was overheard and reported. The report reached Secretary of War Taft, and he cabled Funston reaffirming Mayor Schmitz's ultimate authority and requesting his response. The response to Taft the next day came from the mayor, declaring the AP report untruthful and emphasizing cooperation and harmonious relations with the military at all levels. However, their disputes actually continued and erupted again over control of militia, arming the mayor's private army, and other matters.

When monetary claims started coming in, some took time to settle. On April 19th, Colonel Morris had passed a message to Funston over the signal corps land line asking permission to destroy liquor to maintain law and order. Funston approved, believing Morris was referring only to liquor on the streets or being served in saloons. But based on verbal approval without detailed discussion, Morris issued a general order directing all liquor, except beer, be seized and poured into gutters or on the ground. Officers led details of troops to break into closed or damaged saloons and warehouses to destroy the stocks.

When claims poured in, Funston was surprised to discover closed saloons and warehouses had been broken into to seize liquor. While he considered the destruction wrong, he and General Greely contended that Morris acted in good faith; therefore the claims should be paid. Lieutenant General Arthur MacArthur replaced Greely late in 1906 and tried to bring closure to charges against all involved, stressing the critical role the army played during the catastrophe. The War Department wouldn't agree to pay claims based on an illegal order but agreed that any liquor claims could be paid from excess recovery funds. Congress stepped in to overrule that, denying all claims for destruction of liquor.

Additional claims followed from storeowners and complaints from individuals, charging looting during rescue efforts. Unquestionably, looting occurred by soldiers and civilians but charges of indiscipline were taken seriously by the army. The first response came from Captain Orrin Wolfe of the 22nd Infantry, who was responsible for property on the city blocks affected. Although his mission was to protect the custom house and post office, the warehouse was not guarded due to lack of manpower and higher priorities. Greely dismissed the charges but the owner hired a law firm to write to Secretary Taft for compensation. Hearings by the inspector general continued into 1907 but were inconclusive. This claim was denied.

A number of articles appeared in the *San Francisco Examiner* relating accounts of soldiers or marines shooting thugs or lawless people under the mayor's dictum. Most articles were favorable to soldiers, saying criminals deserved what they got. Some reports were accurate, others flawed. General Greely's investigation accounted for only nine deaths by violence. Two of the victims were killed by the California National Guard, one by a citizen vigilante committee, one by a police officer, one by a policeman and a marine in cooperation, and the other four were in areas not occupied by military forces. The final report was closed. However, there were abundant opportunities to cover up crimes in the fires and destruction.

In July, 1906, *Cosmopolitan Magazine* published General Funston's account of "How the Army Worked to Save San Francisco." His modest recounting, on four pages, was a straight forward narrative of all the military actions taken. However, a Mr. Lafler disputed Funston's account in a counterpoint article submitted to *The Argonaut*. The magazine editor rejected the manuscript, not due to content, but because of length, asking it be shortened. Lafler had prepared an extensive narrative based on interviews with many people upset about the dynamiting of their homes, and looting. His most prevalent complaint was that people had worked to save their homes from the fire, only to have soldiers force their evacuation to dynamite them. In other cases, burning debris from the explosions started new fires. In some cases he contended houses in the burned district were looted by soldiers. A judge advocate report of inquiry confirmed some looting had occurred in a report on April 28th, 1906. The JAG determined that from fifteen to twenty members of the California National Guard had been arrested by sentries for looting in the burned district.

§

While her husband was busy managing the crisis, Eda had taken their children and portable valuables out of the fiery streets into The Presidio. The undaunted lady worked tirelessly with Colonel Torney, the commander of Letterman, and Dora Thompson, the head nurse, to assist civilian victims of the earthquake in the military hospital. Eda led Torney on a scouting mission into a forgotten and darkened basement storeroom of the hospital. She stood tall as ever, dressed for the mission in a black blouse with long skirt. In storage beneath the wards, she found hundreds of forgotten blankets neatly folded and stacked. She quietly issued orders. "At a blanket each, there should be enough for two thousand. Mothers with babies and children first." Torney nodded in agreement as he had been doing all afternoon since her arrival. After eight years of marriage to Fred Funston, much of it in a war zone, she spoke with authority. She knew what she wanted and how to get it. Her suggestions were direct and forceful. He would agree with her every move, and been very proud.

As Eda made the earlier journey of thirty-six blocks to The Presidio from her Washington Street home on foot, bags and children in tow, she scouted the city she knew so well. She saw the injured, helpless and homeless with her own eyes and intended, as did her husband, to use every available army asset to help. She knew then that only the army was functioning and had the material and leadership to control a bad situation. She saw how it was done in the Philippines and was prepared when leadership was needed. She approved the swift and decisive actions of her husband at every turn and would bear no criticism of him. The Presidio was mobilized to help, including cookhouses to make bread, stew and large cauldrons of hot, black coffee. Urgently requested supplies from the commissaries at Portland, Seattle and Los Angeles soon began arriving and Eda Funston saw that they were put to good use.

Having worked those problems, she made her way back to Letterman Hospital—a welcomed sight to Colonel Torney and Dora Thompson. Her calm self-control was a model for the officers and medical personnel overwhelmed with crisis. Yet, her continual presence there also confirmed their fears that the situation was worse than they imagined. She worked straight through for twelve hours, seeming to appear everywhere at once. Major Devol, the garrison quartermaster recalled, "She was quite determined that anything she thought would be useful was done—and things like army regulations didn't apply here and now."

Refugees streamed in all day, all night, and the next day; troops kept setting up camps between the rows of army huts and tents. In one day, thirty thousand were encamped there on the grounds under Eda Funston's watchful eye. Many were panicked, crying, searching for lost children or spouses. Fred Hewitt, a reporter for the *San Francisco Examiner*, saw Eda leading a group of women and children gathered around a camp fire late at night. Presbyterian Eda Blankhart Funston was reciting the 23rd Psalm, a timeless charm of comfort to help them through their "valley of death."

§

Days were unending and wore heavily on everyone. Fred was exhausted, as were police, firefighters and soldiers battling fires and rats, trying to keep order and feed refugees. His authority as military governor came into question as Mayor Schmitz began to use his Committee of Fifty more effectively. Questions also came from Washington asking how long he intended to keep control. Shootings, accidents and looting piled up and decisions came with increasing difficulty. He approved once more blasting with artillery charges to block the fire; the noise signaled the situation was still tenuous. Tempers flared. Fires still raged.

Finally, seventy-four hours after the conflagration began, the fires flickered out. At precisely 1915 hours on April 22nd, after seventy-two hours of fiery rage, rain fell on the remnants of the city by the bay, too late to help fighting fires but dampening the last embers, while creating new misfortunes for the unsheltered homeless. Buglers on horseback raced through the streets announcing the fire was extinguished and the army band marched, playing martial music, and refugees wept.

Hours after the fire was out, Schmirtz journeyed to Fort Mason to free himself of another problem—looting and killing by his private militia and the uncontrolled National Guard. He requested Funston assume control of them. He refused, saying he had no authority over them. The Committee of Fifty instead approved a resolution requesting the governor withdraw the militia. However, political maneuvering between the governor and mayor continued while the civilian militia persisted in abuses.

Years later, President Woodrow Wilson wrote of Funston's actions: "His genius and manhood brought order out of confusion, confidence out of fear and much comfort in distress." Fred Funston had thrown himself into the breach once more on that Wednesday, April 18th, 1906, and he remained on duty without relief until Sunday, April 22nd when General Greely returned. Funston had charged straight ahead for five endless days with little rest and was nearing exhaustion. His efforts to gain control of a catastrophic situation while civil authorities were out of action was recognized and praised by the mayor, governor, fire chief, and many ordinary citizens of San Francisco. His place in the city's history was secured while his own home was being destroyed. Funston had always been a man of action, never deterred by danger or controversy, was proved once again in the great San Francisco drama of earthquake and fire.

Months later, Mayor Schmirtz and labor leader Abraham Ruef were convicted for graft and bribery. Schmirtz got a suspended sentence, Ruef did not. General Greely returned to complete the army's mission until his retirement in June 1906. After that, Funston stepped up as commander of the Pacific Division until Lieutenant General Arthur MacArthur arrived. The war games were canceled. Funston withdrew with Eda and the boys for a while, aloof from the city and from Washington. However, his insatiable appetite for action was unshaken.

EIGHTEEN

Fred, Eda, and their two boys, Arthur and Frederick, had been very happy at their spacious San Francisco home on Washington Street—until it was destroyed in the great earthquake and fire. They had lived near Eda's family in Oakland and the social and cultural activities she loved.

After the San Francisco catastrophe, Fred was established in the minds of many as the army's "trouble-shooter-in-chief," the "go-to" man to take on problems too hot to handle, except by an audacious adventurer who hungered for it. Between 1906 and 1914, Funston would be called on to quell problems in Cuba, Nevada's Gold mines, in Hawaii, laying a foundation at the Leavenworth schools, and back in Luzon to construct and field test an army capable of fighting major wars.

§

The first intervention in Cuba, the Spanish-American War, had resulted in a free Cuba—*Cuba Libra*. But by 1902, Cuba was independent in name only. The new president of the Cuban republic, Thomas Estrada Palma, the same man who had given Funston his start as an *insurrecto*, was now determined to undo everything American in Cuba. This conflicted with American interests in developing the island economically. The United States wanted to use Havana, Santiago, and Guantanamo as naval bases, but eventually settled with only Guantanamo as the least offensive to Cubans. Roosevelt grew increasingly frustrated with the political breakdown in Cuban politics and sporadic violence breaking out after the 1904 Cuban elections. The island's Presidential elections in 1906 became contentious and a fresh outbreak of civil war appeared imminent. Roosevelt reluctantly decided to move bluejackets and marines on the *Marietta* and *Denver* to Havana, with a delegation under Secretary of War William Howard Taft and Secretary of State Robert Bacon.

In mid-July, Funston was at American Lake, Washington, for a two-month long annual encampment and field exercises for regular army and National

Guard units. He and his aides, Lieutenants Mitchell and Long, had stopped in Portland, Oregon, to visit at Vancouver Barracks. In an interview, he corrected reporters calling the maneuvers a "sham battle," emphasizing his headquarters would be in the field for two months for "field practice" where "thousands of blank cartridges" would be used in much the same way as in actual warfare. But, field practice was cut short for him by the real thing—another crisis.

On September 15th, 1906, Funston received orders to proceed to Washington D.C. without delay. With his family still in San Francisco, he proceeded directly from American Lake to Washington, D.C. without a clear purpose. Since the battleships *Louisiana* and *Virginia* were joining the *New Jersey*, cruisers *Minneapolis* and *Newark*, and marines were en route to Cuba, it seemed logical that he would return to Cuba as well. He was delayed in Washington until Taft established contact with Cuban President Palma. The overweight Taft arrived in Cuba on September 19, 1906, not happy with his second assignment in the tropics. His initial analysis was discouraging—Palma's Rural Guard was woefully inadequate to protect the government or American interests against an insurgent army eight times larger. Taft met with disgruntled insurgent generals and decided they were essentially lawless characters. He told Roosevelt he needed to have more troops and Roosevelt approved.

Meanwhile, Funston met with his friend Major General Franklin Bell at the War Department to discuss the Cuban situation and readiness of the army to react. Funston's experience in Cuba had been primarily on the eastern side of the island; the activity now was in the west, around Havana. But he'd served with General Menocal—now heading the Cuban veterans department—in the fight at Las Tunas. The General Staff was planning for moving troops from all across the United States into deployment posts and ports, while the ordnance corps planned for weapons and ammunition from depots at Rock Island and Frankfurt. More marines landed in Cuba on the *Dixie* as requests for protection poured in from plantation owners in Cuba.

Taft's early reports confirmed differences between Palma's government and the new insurgents. Trade was dead as business interests demanded troops for protection of tobacco and sugar crops. Cuban government troops were much better armed and organized, but the gangs of insurgents greatly outnumbered them. Armed intervention seemed imminent—the War

Department considered a force of one hundred thousand for a second Cuban intervention. General Bell sent a message to Taft informing him Funston and Lieutenant Mitchell were headed his way and asked their proper destination. Taft requested they report to Havana at the earliest opportunity, apparently to intercede with insurgent chiefs. An open insurgency was most feared by officers who had served in the Philippines and by almost everyone in positions of authority.

Palma insisted rebels lay down arms as a precondition for him to stay as caretaker executive until a replacement was named. Suddenly, Palma resigned with his entire cabinet, leaving his country without a legal government. Roosevelt and Taft, who wanted to avoid a full scale intervention and war, assumed responsibility for law and order. Taft appointed proconsuls from among experienced military officers while he assumed full powers as governor. Charles Magoon was designated to run the civil administration and had fortunately brought army officers with strong experience in Cuba and the Philippines to help. Cubans had respected the tough General Leonard Wood as military governor in 1900, but in 1906 they didn't like Magoon. Under those conditions Fred Funston sailed for Havana, returning to Cuban battlefields still haunted by many old soldiers he had fought beside in his salad days.

Two thousand more marines had landed—the second full Cuban intervention. Pacification began by disarming rebels, and no one was better at that than Funston. He spoke adequate Spanish, knew and understood many of the old rebels, and had negotiated disarmament in the Philippines. He took over the disarmament commission, responsible for collecting the weapons of the insurgents. Other members of the commission appointed to assist him included Major E.F. Ladd and Lieutenant Mitchell of the army and General Mario Menocal, General Sanchez Agramonte and Colonel Charles Hernandez of the Cuban army. Disarming began immediately and went smoothly at first as Funston sent a military commissioner to each insurgent division to assemble and collect weapons. No cash payments were made for arms, only transportation home and subsistence.

All disarmaments didn't go smoothly. In one case Funston traveled by automobile to Guines to settle a dispute between the disarmament commissioner, the mayor, and the insurgent army commander. He threatened to bring marines to enforce law and order, making clear bloodshed might result. However, en route back to Havana, his automobile was stopped by insurgents who threatened to shoot them. But as soon as they learned it was Funston, they profusely apologized and allowed them to pass. News spread ahead of him and as his car passed through towns Cuban women along the route tossed flowers over his car. As everywhere, he was both loved and hated.

Fresh trouble erupted in Guines three days later. Insurgents had faked complete disarmament and kept one-third of their arms. As soon as Funston found out he telegraphed Marine Captain Feland at Guines to send out patrols, look for signs of trouble, and ensure disarmament was completed. While his mission was successful, one insurgent commander, General Del Castillo, wanted a Cuban solution without American involvement. But when Funston arrived, he was placated enough to raise a toast to President Roosevelt and the United States.

Thornier problems cropped up concerning twenty thousand horses confiscated by insurgents but never paid for. Taft wanted all the horses returned to their owners, influential plantation owners and businessmen. He was willing to allow rebels to retain stolen mounts only until legal ownership could be verified. But during negotiations, whether by translation error or misunderstanding, Funston left rebels with an erroneous impression they could keep the horses and the United States would reimburse owners. Horse owners were unhappy with that arrangement—Taft was outraged! Suspicions grew that the quandary was created by cunning Cuban insurgents from Funston's days and who still believed he'd deserted from Cuba. It was possible they set him up for failure but that was never proven. Whatever the cause, it reflected poorly on Funston, and Taft made him the target of his abiding wrath. Taft relieved him and ordered him back to the United States. However, he diplomatically cloaked his dismissal of a general very popular within the War Department and across the country, protecting his presidential aspirations.

The War Department believed Funston had been undermined by disgruntled insurrectionists because he'd protested killing Spanish prisoners. General Bell was on a coordination tour in Havana and took temporary control while Funston stood silently behind the perception he'd been set up. When they departed Cuba, Secretary of War Taft sailed on the *Louisiana*, while Funston sailed on the *Virginia*. Their personal relations remained stained and strained, adversely affecting Funston's future promotions and assignments.

Before he left Havana, he was guest of honor at a banquet thrown by old comrades of the Cuban revolution, casting doubts on conspiracy theories. Political differences couldn't blemish strong bonds between battle veterans. General Carlos Garcia, the Cuban minister to the United States, was toastmaster. Eighty-one former insurgent officers attended, along with Thomas Estrada Palma. Funston was surrounded by sixty-five close comrades from the Department of the Oriente, as former artillery commander in many battles. He recalled: "It was hard to realize that those well-groomed men in evening dress were the worn and wasted men who had led the Cubans at Cascorra, at La Machuca, and many another good fight, and had stormed the ridge at Jiguani and led their men through wire entanglements at Victoria de las Tunas; or were the same comrades, always kindly and considerate, who in the grim days of hunger always saw that the American mambis got their share when food strayed into camp. That one evening of reminiscence and good-fellowship was pay enough for it all."

§

Following his unsettling experience in the second Cuban intervention, Funston took command of the Southwestern Division in St. Louis for less than a year. This was only slightly less painful than his detention in Chicago. In 1906, Funston's mentor Arthur MacArthur had been finally promoted to Lieutenant General, the system still based on longevity instead of merit, and rotated surviving Civil War generals though the highest rank as the Chief of the General Staff until mandatory retirement. MacArthur, the youngest of the Civil War generals, was last in line. When his number came up, old problems with Taft in the Philippines caught up. As MacArthur and Funston learned, Taft held long grudges and used his influence for revenge. MacArthur was only promoted to avoid a flare up within the War Department, but assigned to lesser positions until he reached mandatory retirement. Both MacArthur and Funston languished on Taft's list of disfavored generals—too popular for direct attack, so inflicted with a measured demise. In 1909, MacArthur finally retired, embittered, and returned to his home in Milwaukee to live out his days with Pinky.

Eda Funston was undaunted by politics and moved again from Oakland to St. Louis with the boys and was immediately absorbed in setting up residence. They selected a large, old-fashioned house on a hill surrounded by a mammoth forest. A spacious grassy lawn sloped away from the house on all sides, a stable, chicken yard and vegetable garden in the rear. Eda laughed when talking about it with another society reporter from St Louis. "The general thinks he is going to cultivate vegetables and raise chickens next summer." The army post is visible in the distance through the trees and the Mississippi River curves languidly around the property. "I feel like the river is an old friend of mine, and I am glad to be close to it," she said. "I was born in Quincy, Illinois, and although my parents removed from there when I was only a few weeks old, I retain a feeling of fondness for the dear old river."

She digressed under questioning about army life. "One has an opportunity of living in many different places. Why, we have moved seven times in the past five years! I have serious objections to packing up, but like everything else, one meets some disadvantages, and this is one of them. I enjoy every pleasure of my home, whatever it may be, to the fullest and don't worry about another move until the time comes."

She spoke of her fondness for mahogany furniture, but avoided owning expensive pieces for fear they would be damaged in shipping. However, she realized life is short and decided to have as many nice things as possible while young enough to enjoy them. She reflected back to her two prized mahogany chairs in San Francisco when the earthquake and fire devastated the city. After she scurried to The Presidio with the children and only what she could carry, two soldiers took a supply wagon at midnight to salvage what they could. The chairs were broken and badly scratched, but saved. Most of their cherished pictures and furniture had been burnt like those of other unfortunate residents.

Eda reproduced the color scheme from San Francisco in her St. Louis home on the river, using shades of greens on the walls and oriental rugs over hardwood floors. But she contended, "One of the pleasant phases of my life as an officer's wife is that I meet so many people who are worth knowing." She reveled in the music, dances, dinner and parties on post and in the community.

Arthur and Frederick ambled into the room wearing stocking caps. They were not used to wearing caps in California and considered these new toys, wearing them everywhere until they were eventually lost. When the reporter asked five-year-old Arthur a question, he said, "You need not ask me to talk, because I won't say anything more." Young Frederick was no more responsive. "I have met all the strangers I care to see." They had learned from their father the danger of unguarded comments to the press.

Funston's support from Roosevelt, Taft, and MacArthur had been cut off, although his friend Franklin Bell still held sway over the army. Some lobbying with the War Department finally paid off and he was able to return to San Francisco, where he remained with Eda and the boys for over a year. Funston contemplated a gentile future, but even in a benign, semi-retirement, the army's trouble-shooter could not side-step trouble.

§

Fred, Eda, young Arthur and Fred Junior, were back in another house in San Francisco, their previous spacious house on Washington Street destroyed in the great earthquake and fire the year before. Eda's family was still nearby in Oakland and the proud grandparents visited often. While they were there, Barbara Eda Funston was born in July 1908. Eda again wrapped herself in culture and beauty of the city while Fred threw himself into his work as commander of the Department of California. She wondered if he would ever be able to ease into a quieter life, instead of constantly serving as the point man for the army on every crisis.

Shortly after arrival in San Francisco, Secretary of War Taft passed over him for promotion to major general even as the army's senior brigadier general. His supporters, especially Kansas Congressmen and old friends, protested. General Bell, as Chief of Staff, released excerpts to the press from Funston's letter saying he had no objection to General McCaskey's promotion ahead of him because of the man's character as a soldier and his Civil War record. He'd have made the announcement himself, but believed the timing should rest with the War Department. He discouraged well-meaning supporters from lobbying on his behalf.

Yet, trouble reared in a troubled community at Goldfield, Nevada, a mining town one hundred seventy miles southeast of Carson City—a boomtown after discovery of gold in 1902. By 1904, Goldfield had produced eight hundred tons of ore, valued at over two million dollars, one third of the state's entire production for the year. Population reached thirty thousand miners, families, and supporting businesses. During boom years miners organized a local branch of the Western Federation of Miners, but disputes over wages broke out between miners and owners in December, 1906. Tempers boiled.

By April 1907, while the Funstons were still settling into new quarters, it was clear to mine owners in Goldfield miners were "high-grading," stealing high-value ore concealed in their clothing. Owners implemented a shakedown policy, requiring clothing be changed when entering and exiting the mines. Trouble between miners and unions smoldered until Governor Sparks appealed to President Roosevelt for federal troops for mine security. Destruction of property and loss of life seemed imminent. The Nevada governor reported state militia was inadequate to confront the union-owner issues, or more likely to sidestep state and local politics.

On December 4th, 1907, Roosevelt directed the War Department send federal troops from San Francisco to Goldfield, and gave Funston wide discretion in how to use them. He contracted special trains of the Southern Pacific Railway with right-of-way to rush nine companies of the 22nd Infantry from Oakland and San Francisco to Goldfield. The contingent included two hundred sixty-four men, fully armed and equipped, including machineguns. Military bands from Angel Island and The Presidio played at trackside amid cheering soldiers left behind. Troops left in four Pullmans and two baggage cars under the command of Colonel Alfred Reynolds. Another special train under control of Captain Curtis followed from The Presidio with another one hundred men, but a train wreck near Davisville delayed both trains.

Funston remained initially at headquarters coordinating the movement of troop trains, monitoring the situation in Goldfield, consulting with the War Department about expectations and rules of engagement, and preparing to go if the situation became more serious. Wild rumors made the rounds—miners were prepared to fight off soldiers with five hundred rifles, vast quantities of stolen dynamite, tunnels undermined main buildings with explosives. A winter storm in the Sierras restricted wire communications, but no violence was reported. Funston met with a mine operator from

Goldfield, who confirmed there were thirty-two hundred miners—a thousand with shotguns and rifles. He knew three hundred miners were trouble makers who instigated disruptions in Colorado and Idaho, and the sheriff was a member of a union that favored miners.

General Bell and President Roosevelt monitored the situation closely, relying primarily on Funston's reports. Roosevelt made clear more troops would be sent if he recommended, but sent cabinet representatives from labor, commerce, and business to Goldfield for an independent analysis—and to institute visible civilian control. Recent military interventions in San Francisco's earthquake, the St. Louis balloon races, and another mining dispute in Coeur d'Alene, Idaho, had raised a chorus of complaints about using the military within United States' borders despite the *posse comitatus* act. Roosevelt emphasized federal troops were not to take sides, but only prevent riots, violence, and disorder.

Curious crowds gathered in Goldfield on December 12th for the arrival of Funston. Governor Sparks met them and declared the troops arrived in time to avert serious trouble, but recommended against martial law. Funston assured the governor, the public, and the miners, that martial law would be imposed at the first sign of violence and guaranteed he'd be on site until calm was assured. They kept a tight lid on violence and the Mohawk mine reopened without bloodshed, but members of the American Federation of Labor met with Funston, complaining they felt so threatened by the miners' union they had carried arms everywhere for months—the mines virtually armed camps.

With the situation stabilized, Funston planned to depart Goldfield on December 17th, but power and telecommunications were inexplicably cut the night before. Expecting trouble, he cancelled his departure and deployed armed guards and patrols at all mines and critical installations. The breakdown was eventually found in Palmetto, another mining town twenty-one miles southwest of Goldfield, the cause unclear. Next day power was restored. Roosevelt requested separate reports from all parties—his commission, union leaders, mine owners, and Funston.

Funston and Governor Sparks believed the federal troops had arrived in the nick of time to prevent major violence in Goldfield. But, Roosevelt believed the governor's request for federal troops wasn't justified, so he ordered Funston to withdraw. The Governor believed it was too soon, so Nevada's legislature authorized mobilizing state police to handle mining labor issues and they maintained order through the winter. Funston departed, having steered clear of political disputes, sticking to straight soldiering. He rode with the troops into festively colored decorations and lights of the bay cities—home for Christmas.

§

The following year, Fred was assigned as Commandant of the Army Service Schools and Commander of Fort Leavenworth, Kansas, from mid-1908 until early 1911. That posting seemed unusual as he was a pure operator and, while well-read, he was never fond of formal academics. Roosevelt was still president but maintained a discrete distance from him for political reasons. William Howard Taft was still Secretary of War but their experience in Cuba in 1906 had not ended well. Major General Franklin Bell was Chief of the General Staff, had served with Funston in the Philippines, sometimes fighting side-by-side, remained a close friend, and had a strong interest in the Leavenworth schools. Bell was prominent in leading development of Fort Leavenworth as the premier military center for thought and doctrine, with international recognition. Bell wanted him there to burnish the image and prestige of the school with his stellar record, while verifying the curriculum against his field experience.

Fred never graduated from a civilian or military college, although his intellectual interests were many and varied. He was diligently self-schooled in military arts and sciences, yet remained a maverick, well outside mainstream traditions of the army. Still, he was famous in his home state, an achiever who surpassed his peers in tactics and operations, solid in practical applications, a pragmatic thinker, therefore imminently qualified to lead the army schools. Exposure to the Leavenworth curriculum was also excellent preparation for higher command. Funston's presence was good for the army service schools, and good for him.

Fort Leavenworth's schools had advanced from "kindergarten" remedial training of its early years to a superior military institution, perhaps the most advanced in the world, although it had not yet reached university-level prominence. Between 1902 and 1910, Army Service Schools expanded to include four schools for junior officers. The former Infantry and Cavalry School of Application were reestablished as a one-year course in 1902, then as the School of the Line in 1907. The other schools included the Signal, Field Engineer, and Correspondence School for Medical Officers. Top students in the School of Application were selected for a second year of study at the Army Staff College.

Funston arrived at Fort Leavenworth with his aides to an eleven-gun salute followed by a formal reception. Their arrival was typically unusual. They traveled from Lawrence on the only Union Pacific train available—a freight train. When he settled in as commandant, he couldn't resist writing to his close college fraternity friend, William Allen White, a Pulitzer Prize winning newspaper editor. As Funston had been a mediocre student at the University of Kansas, never completing degree requirements, he wrote with a sense of humor:

> *Dear Bill:*
> *I am a College President.*
> *Break it gently to the boys in the fraternity.*
> *Me a College President—my God!*

Fred moved his growing family into the large quarters of the commandant on 1 Scott Avenue, a stone's throw from the Missouri River. The commandant's quarters had been built in 1861 on the former site of an enlisted soldiers burial ground, using locally produced red brick at a cost of $14,000. However, a year after his arrival, Funston took two months leave with his family during the summer to return to California. While there, he purchased a farm near Haywards, in Alameda County, near Eda's family home. Thinking of the future, he planned to take his furloughs there and eventually make the farm his permanent home. But he insisted he didn't intend to shift his suffrage to California, but remain always a Kansan. "I am a citizen of Kansas and I always have been since I was old enough to be anything—I always expect to remain a citizen of Kansas."

Trouble followed him from San Francisco to Fort Leavenworth. Eda was with the children visiting her family in Oakland when a Mr. Dunawald, a former army private, discovered his address and called unexpectedly. Dunawald had received a court martial from him, resulting in hard time in Alcatraz Prison in San Francisco's bay. Once released from jail he sought revenge. Dunawald entered his quarters and hid in a closet, waiting, intending to shoot him while he slept. But Funston stayed up late as usual and then lay awake in bed for an hour, turning over details of the day in his mind. He saw the intruder step from the shadows with pistol in hand. Dunawald also saw Funston stir and fired into the dark, missed, the round embedded in the mattress. Funston snatched his pistol from under his pillow and sent three rounds into the shadows before he switched the light on. Dunawald ran for his life. Both had missed at close range, but Dunawald's misses qualified him for more hard time.

Despite his many exploits, Funston was never a good shot or athletic. Limping from old injuries, he tripped on an uneven sidewalk and fell on his right shoulder. X-rays showed it was fractured, foreshadowing more miseries. Lieutenant Mitchell notified Eda, still in Oakland with the children and she made immediate plans to return to Leavenworth. Young Arthur was ill and was left with his grandparents, while Eda traveled east with young Fred and Barbara by train. When they reached Kansas City, Fred Junior was running a high fever with pneumonia. Eda checked into the Hotel Baltimore and phoned for Dr. Robinson. Fred sent Lieutenant and Mrs. Mitchell to Kansas City to assist her and the children travel on to Leavenworth while he waited in pain. Then on October 30th, Fred and Eda received a dreadful telegram from Otto Blankart in Oakland—eight-year old Arthur had died suddenly of whooping cough. Due to his fractured shoulder and Fred Junior's pneumonia, neither grieving parent could attend the burial of their first born son.

As soon as Fred was on his feet, Eda returned to Oakland. Then in June, 1910, he called doctors from the post hospital to his quarters, complaining of severe chest pains and was restricted to quarters under constant care of physicians and nurses. The diagnosis was angina pectoris, likely brought on by oppressive summer heat. Eda was notified again in California, and with the children, immediately returned to Leavenworth to be by his side.

Fred was already well known all over Kansas, but he made news at the end of September 1910 by standing firm on principle. He'd gone to the Hotel Baltimore in Kansas City for dinner, but paid his bill and stormed out without finishing. Before leaving he complained to management that he would never stop at any hotel which "attired its head bell-boy in the uniform of a United States Army captain." When questioned by reporters who watched his every move, he said, "I was probably a little hasty, yet I think I was right." Army officers in Washington applauded his action since the War Department sought, unsuccessfully, legislation to end wide spread practice of civilians wearing military uniforms. Funston, the conscience of the army in the field, again put into action policies Congress and the War Department couldn't settle.

Major changes in officer education were institutionalized before Funston's arrival. He'd met Colonel Arthur Wagner in Tampa during the Spanish-American War, and the transformed school remained very much under Wagner's influence. Another officer overseeing improved education between 1906 and 1912 was Major John Morrison, who reorganized the curriculum for teaching tactics and staff procedures. During this period Leavenworth students included such notables as George Marshall, Billy Mitchell, and Douglas MacArthur. For six years at the School of the Line and the Army Staff College, Morrison served as an assistant instructor in military art, department chairman, assistant commandant, and acting commandant. He was a brilliant teacher and tactician and years later, his students would proudly declare: "I was a Morrison man." General George Marshall, one of Morrison's students at Leavenworth, proclaimed "he taught me all I had ever known of tactics."

John Morrison was Assistant Commandant under Funston. He was responsible for modernizing the curriculum and published his book, *Studies in Minor Tactics* in 1908, which served as a principle text for students using seventeen tactical problems for study. George Marshall graduated in 1910 and was a tactics instructor under Morrison, also while Funston was commandant. Funston guided along set paths, adding prestige to the school and contributing his experience to field exercises and staff rides—there was little to change.

The post was a humming, vibrant, spirited, and contagious center of thought and action, becoming one of the finest posts to serve in the western United States. Between 1904 and 1916, Leavenworth became the postgraduate military institution that prepared well-qualified officers for general staff duties and positions of high command. During that time, the first official army doctrine appeared as Field Service Regulations of 1905 and 1910, inculcating the works of Wagner, Swift, and Morrison into the frame of reference for army officers and the organization and functions of the army—a bible for tactics and operations in the field.

Funston was involved in curriculum and doctrine development, but more in its practical application. During his tenure, the War Department General Staff was preparing contingency war plans. Students were not involved in actual war planning, but solved problems of mobilization, concentration, and movements of large bodies of troops and supplies over great distances using internal lines of communications. These tested student problem-solving abilities while validating general staff plans. One map exercise tackled by the class of 1910-1911 resulted in a fifteen-page plan to move thirteen divisions from scattered posts and stations to ports in Seattle and San Francisco as quickly as possible. The solution resulted in a time-phased force deployment plan, including the order of movement for troops, equipment and supplies, and the trains, routes, and schedules to move them. That plan was developed over two days.

Between 1904 and 1916, military art and science consumed more time than engineering, law, languages, or care of troops. But, those were also significant. Care of troops included field sanitation; something Funston experienced in Cuba, the Philippines, and San Francisco. He was involved in controlling civil disturbances and confronting legal issues in San Francisco, in Goldfield, and in counterinsurgency in Luzon—all integrated into classroom studies and field exercises. Although over six hundred thousand new patents were issued between 1865 and 1900, the most significant shortcoming of the Leavenworth curriculum was failure to recognize the full impact of technology, including aeronautics, automotives, machineguns, and artillery.

Officers on the War Department General Staff sought advice and guidance from students and instructors at Leavenworth for the staff study: "Organization of the Land Forces of the United States," intended to shape defense legislation and organization and geographic disposition of land forces. This started discussions about the relationship between the Regular Army and the National Guard. But, the enduring contribution to the pre-World War I army were Field Service Regulations, first prepared in 1905 by Captain Joseph T. Dickman on the General Staff. Dickman began work on the first army doctrine while a tactics instructor at Fort Leavenworth.

Fort Leavenworth schools were the unifying influence on the army, leading line officers to learn the importance of staff work, and the general staff to recognize problems of the line. Infantry, cavalry, and artillery were thrown together to solve tactical problems. The fact of being a Leavenworth man engendered a corporate sense of pride to graduates and those exposed to disciplined thought about military matters. During Funston's tenure as commandant between 1908 and 1910, he was responsible for schooling one hundred seven officers of the line and sixty-six in the Staff College, many rising to become key future army leaders.

Arthur Wagner stated in the preface to his volume on *Organization and Tactics*, published in 1865, that "The best school for acquiring a knowledge of organization and tactics is that furnished by actual experience in war." His book was widely read by junior and senior officers. He surmised "if an officer would prepare himself to be of service to his country, he must attentively consider the recorded experience of those who have learned war from actual reality, and must accumulate by reading and reflection a fund of military knowledge based on the experience of others." While Wagner emphasized study of history, he considered the doctrinal manuals only a basis for learning the art and science of war, as "no two battles are fought in the same way and the most carefully matured plans have to be quickly altered to meet new and unforeseen circumstances." Fred Funston couldn't have said it better.

Funston was a custodian of doctrine and training development. He brought realism and experience directly from the field to the institution, blending training and tactics with developing thought about the shape of the future army. While he didn't shape the institution, he was the litmus test, the doer and implementer, adding experience to doctrine, education, and training. Funston absorbed Leavenworth's lessons, acquiring better tools to do more important things for the army and the nation.

§

Fred Funston had a difficult, though educational tour of duty at Fort Leavenworth, but was ordered back to the Philippines to command the Department of Luzon. Eda and the children waited in Oakland until he moved into residence in Manila at the former home of Don Valeriano Weyler, the ruthless Spaniard called the "Butcher." Weyler was nearly

Funston's executioner when he was captured in Cuba. Nine years after Cuba, he completed his book, *Memories of Two Wars*, while residing in Weyler's former house. Many of his experiences in Cuba and the Philippines were already published as articles in leading magazines. He dedicated the finished work to his first-born son, Arthur, whose death in 1909 still weighed heavily.

The *New York Times* published a review soon after it was published. "...There is a warmth of feeling and a genial enjoyment of the life Funston lived that leaves one with the pleasantest of impressions about the character and personality of the cheerful warrior. ... He had a perfectly boyish interest in everything he does. But it is a detached and impersonal interest, without an ounce of vanity. No vain or egotistical man could announce his own blunders and criticize his own deeds in the relentless fashion in which Funston does." Then in concluding, the reviewer looked to the future: "We part from him with regret. Isn't there some way to get him into a larger war?"

This was a poignant period for Funston, while his losses burdened him. He had lost Arthur only two years before and while he was still pained by that, his father died of heart disease in Iola at the age of 76. His mentor, Arthur MacArthur, had left the army bitter and lived in Milwaukee with his wife Pinky. There MacArthur died in 1912 while speaking to survivors of his old Civil War 24th Wisconsin Regiment. Taft, now as president, again ensured Funston was passed over for major general. Funston had never opposed more senior officers catching up with him but he was saddened by the animosity and again considered his future.

While he was in Luzon this third time, fighting was essentially over except for a few bandits roaming the countryside. He turned his attention to large field exercises for training, maintaining readiness, and war planning, and applying lessons from Leavenworth and new doctrine. He conceived and prepared a large field exercise in the plains of central Luzon shortly after assuming command of the department. He used the Field Service Regulations as the standard for evaluating tactics and support for the deployed troops. He selected twenty observer-controllers from divisional troops for safety, and to keep the free-flowing practice battle under control. Inspectors general made their independent evaluations, focused on standards established in regulations.

The exercise progressed through three general situations over eight days in the field, finally combining both task forces into one large division formation and final push. Each phase was critiqued, efficiencies and deficiencies recorded, then reported to the commanders for praise or corrections through intensive training. Funston concluded in his official report that the exercise was not designed for "writing a report, but to test a machine to the end that in effects and defects made manifest, it could be tinkered with to attain higher efficiency."

As his third tour of duty in Luzon came to a close, another crisis emerged in nearby archipelagos—Hawaii and Japan. The army's reliable troubleshooter was called to once again interject a fighter into the midst of trouble, to keep the peace but prepare for war—and if war came, to fight.

§

Following the death of Emperor Meiji of Japan in 1912, Crown Prince Yoshihito ascended to the Chrysanthemum Throne. Final years of Emperor Meiji's rule saw high government spending for overseas investments and defense, with little credit or reserves to cover it. When the prime minister cut defense spending, the army minister resigned in protest. The constitution required the army minister be an active-duty general, but none were willing to serve. Unable to form a cabinet, the prime minister resigned in December 1912. Popular protests spread and by February 1913, thousands rioted in Tokyo, threatening government buildings, setting fires and vandalizing pro-government newspaper offices.

In the United States, the threat of instability and rise of Japanese military power raised fears of war with Japan, especially an invasion of Hawaii. Washington tamped war fever with public reassurances, while simultaneously improving military readiness of Hawaii and the Pacific flank. Funston was ordered to leave Luzon for Honolulu to take command of Hawaiian territorial forces.

He arrived on a transport at Honolulu, flanked by Eda, Freddie, and Barbara. Eda was received at a dressy formal ladies reception, but he ordered service uniforms for his reception to save time—he got into high gear quickly. He intended to clear the office work to visit Schofield Barracks, Castner, and all the posts of Oahu as soon as possible.

No military department had been established in the islands, but increased troop levels raised Hawaiian territory to a higher standing. He was named territorial commander of defense forces in the region. He redesigned the defenses of Oahu, including Honolulu and Pearl Harbor, and developed defense plans in the event of an invasion of the islands.

After his initial assessment of readiness and defense preparations, he cracked down on indiscipline. It was known before his arrival that he was a stickler for military appearance, courtesy, and discipline. He was not impressed with what he saw. One of his first acts was to impose a "good conduct pass" system, administered by commanders of companies and batteries. The best one-third of troops in military courtesy, dress, and without bad conduct reports, were authorized a "good conduct pass" allowing them to come and go freely. The middle group was authorized passes on a case-by-case basis. The lower third were restricted to post. Drunkenness or disorderly conduct of any kind resulted in loss of privileges. Funston disliked corporal punishment, so used this as a reward system to reduce punishments while improving discipline. He advocated such a system army-wide.

The crisis in Japan soon passed and the War Department considered a departmental organization for long-term security of the Hawaiian Islands. Funston warned Japan would remain a threat for some time to come. Crisis management was finished there and he continued with his family to take command of the 5th Brigade, Second Division, in Galveston and Texas City, … and into a new emergency.

NINETEEN

In 1910, war clouds gathered over Europe as brawny, standing European armies flexed, threatened, and brandished arms. Reports of war spread to conference rooms and kitchen tables and defense-minded people in Washington lost sleep over resources and commitments to transform a cumbersome national defense establishment into fighting form. The U. S. Army more resembled the dispersed camps, posts, and forts of the Indian wars than a conventional army—more a collection of regiments and militia than a military machine. Fred Funston, wondered how the army could go from where it was to where it needed to be. Think-tanks needed an operator on the frontlines to slam it together and make it work.

Funston had always been proximate to trouble. Muddy boots fit him perfectly in Cuba and the Philippines, but fame and failures at political correctness made his general officer shoes binding. The old wanderlust returned. He was still very much a public figure following his raid to capture Aguinaldo and the dramatic rescue of San Francisco, but silenced by Teddy Roosevelt, then stymied and passed over by William Howard Taft as Secretary of War and President. Yet, Funston was the first name mentioned when a trouble started.

Secretary of War Elihu Root created a General Staff in 1903, but Funston was a field commander and not cut out for staff—too blunt for Washington circles, boots too muddy, too restless to sit behind a desk. But change comes slowly to an army without a crisis and ideas spawned at the War Department, Carlisle Barracks, and Leavenworth remained untested. Major General Leonard Wood, a physician and Rough Rider, was appointed Chief of Staff in 1910. Wood sensed the urgency of creating an army to defend the nation, and knew how long it takes to transform a large tradition-bound establishment. He argued his vision on Capitol Hill where it met deaf ears, blind eyes, and empty pockets. Yet, he spurred the General Staff to proceed with organizational planning and war preparations within constrained resources. Wood knew a crisis would soon move strategic planning to execution.

While strategic plans were worked out, a sound tactical organization for command and control was also needed. The General Staff developed one to organize the Regular Army and National Guard into a cohesive field army of divisions with three brigades each. Tables of organization were drawn up and argued, but until Congress came up with funds to test, it remained a paper tiger.

While major war threatened Europe and the United States, there was trouble closer to home—revolution in Mexico. While the Mexican problem was a recurring internal issue, it threatened to spill over the border. Texas Governor Colquitt wanted to attack first with Texas Rangers, but President Wilson threatened with Federal troops to stop incursions in either direction. The situation was viewed seriously within the United States, with two thousand miles of open common border and significant financial investments and business interests deep inside old Mexico.

§

Chaos in Mexico was a perfect excuse to test an organization to defend the southern border. General Wood convinced President Taft to order an assembly of troops to protect the hard won, yet still disputed border. This provided an opportunity to field-test the conceptual organization and support system, while training the army on a large scale. Numerous mobilization orders were sent out by telegraph to posts scattered about the country beginning on the night of March 6th, 1911.

Within hours soldiers began loading material while those on pass were recalled. Troops began arriving at their designated southwest destinations over the next four to ten days. Brigades designed the year before were discarded and new ones drawn up for the existing situation, some even during deployment moves. Thirty-six companies of coastal artillery were re-designated infantry and formed into three provisional regiments near Galveston, Texas; two regular infantry regiments were assembled at San Diego, California. The most significant new organization was the provisional division concentrated at San Antonio, Texas, along with a separate cavalry brigade. Major General William Harding Carter, the designated division commander, gathered and organized his staff on the train to Texas. All units were heavily reinforced with new volunteers.

The mobilization drill exposed glaring deficiencies, not only noted by the army and Congress, but by German axis observers in Mexico. Units were delayed reaching their destinations as railroads couldn't furnish enough cars to move masses of troops on short notice, then transportation at destinations was inadequate. Division and brigade headquarters were created from scratch and lacked staff cohesion or procedures. Infantry units were deficient in marching, shooting, and communicating, and needed more training. All military branches and units lacked uniformity of equipment, complicating supply and interoperability. The most appalling deficiency was insufficient numbers of trained and equipped troops to meet a national emergency. General Wood declared the exercise demonstrated the need for more troops within regiments, and a national reserve force. Supply depots were needed to support mobilization. In short, the nation needed a proper military organization and a higher state of preparedness.

Fred Funston, a firm believer in field trials, missed the test of the maneuver division in 1911 although he was involved in discussions of those policies and procedures while commanding the Army Service Schools at Fort Leavenworth. He was already on his way to command the Department of Luzon when mobilization occurred, but he used the same concept of field testing in his Philippine command. Yet, even as he missed the mobilization test along the border, it set the stage for his own next tests.

§

Revolutionary zeal in Mexico pressured the anti-war president, Woodrow Wilson, to do something. When Huerta took control in Mexico, relations with the United States worsened. Few American troops patrolled the long border but trouble erupted when a naval supply party was detained in Tampico. Mexico refused an American admiral's demand for a public apology. President Wilson's response to the newly-elected Mexican president was uncharacteristically strong when several U.S. marines were taken prisoner in Vera Cruz, Mexico's chief port of entry—he would seize Vera Cruz!

The decision to occupy Vera Cruz was not difficult, even for the idealistic and anti-war Wilson. He was less interested in the minor incident in Tampico than a German ship filled with Remington arms from the U. S. headed there. From his perspective it was simple—cut off arms supplies and drive Huerta from power. He expected little resistance to landing troops or a brief occupation. While Congress was tied in knots, he acted. He ordered Rear Admiral Frank Fletcher and the navy to punish the Mexican government by taking Vera Cruz, which offered a strategic possibility—an overland attack on the capitol at Mexico City. He committed troops without reservations, initially the United States Navy and Marine Corps. By the time Congress approved, it was fait accompli. American troops were on Mexican soil, but Wilson was only partly correct in his estimate of the situation.

Admiral Fletcher expected to only make a show of force, and was surprised when the War Department ordered him to occupy Vera Cruz, prevent arms shipments into the port, and seize the customs house. At his disposal were marine contingents aboard the *Prairie, Utah,* and *Florida,* plus a battalion of seamen on the *Florida*. In all, he had seven hundred eighty-seven men in the initial landing party, just over five hundred of them marines under Navy Captain William Rush, the *Florida's* commanding officer. *Utah* remained outside the harbor to intercept the German ship *Ypiranga* and prevent the delivery of arms and ammunition.

The American consul in Vera Cruz, William Canada, was informed in advance and chartered two passenger ships to evacuate Americans. Some took advantage of the offer, most did not. On the morning of April 21st, the *Prairie* entered the harbor and prepared to land troops, ordered to occupy only the docks, harbor facilities, railroad station and the custom house. As the landing party shoved off, Canada notified the Mexican commander, General Gustavo Maass, Americans were occupying the city. The harbor fort at San Juan de Ulua was warned large guns of the battleships were trained on it. The German *Ypiranga* was expected soon as three empty trains sat at the station awaiting the arms.

§

Arrival of American troops on Mexican soil surprised and overwhelmed the small detachment of Mexican soldiers, who scrambled for the safety of sand hills outside the city, but General Maass left tenacious snipers behind. The Mexican 18th and 19th Regiments were under-strength but capable of armed resistance. Maass maneuvered them through familiar streets while distributing Mausers and Winchesters with ammunition from the military arsenal to willing citizens of Vera Cruz and to prisoners released from the fort. He had no time to develop a battle plan so he left resistance up to small unit leaders and individuals while curious Mexicans and Americans flocked to the pier to watch the landing. No shots were fired, but as Mexicans realized this was actually an occupation they faded away, closed shops, shuttered windows, and kept careful watch from a safer distance.

General Maass hurried to reach the train station before Americans. When sailors arrived empty trains had departed and were beyond reach, but bluejackets found the station's Terminal Hotel useful as a headquarters and occupied it. From the rooftop, signalers wig-wagged flags to send reports to ships in the harbor, and received instructions the same way. Sailors and marines took over the custom warehouses, post office, cablegram station, and power station. There was still no sign of trouble, as Wilson expected.

But Mexican soldiers, armed citizens and prisoners set up on rooftops, in windows, and behind street barricades. As marines approached the main custom clearing house, the first shot broke the eerie silence, followed by a fusillade from all directions. One navy flagman on the roof of the Terminal Hotel fell dead—the first casualty of Vera Cruz. Sailors and marines were caught by surprise. They returned fire but had no plans to deal with street fighting. On the first day, four Americans were killed and twenty wounded—might have been worse. At nightfall, Maass and most Mexican soldiers completed their withdrawal to the sandy hills, leaving defense of the city to naval cadets, citizens, and armed prisoners.

Although regular Mexican forces evacuated ten miles out, armed prisoners, joined by militia units and civilian volunteers, made up an unorganized guerilla force. They continually sniped for three days, requiring marines to clear house-to-house. Naval gunfire silenced more remote targets, but Mexican naval cadets joined guerillas in the Naval Academy building until naval guns firing three-inch and six-inch shells neutralized them. In those early days, Americans lost seventeen killed and sixty-three wounded.

Three reinforcing regiments of marines with an artillery battalion joined those under Colonel L.W.T. Waller, freeing the original landing parties to re-embark ships. But managing the situation was difficult, and Admiral Fletcher believed he needed army troops to relieve marines.

Flies covered corpses left in streets and buildings and sanitation, already a serious concern, became worse as bodies were collected into piles, doused with petroleum and set afire. American consul Canada requested the mayor get businesses reopened; some proprietors complied, mostly cantinas. Admiral Fletcher proclaimed that occupation was temporary, trying once more to get city government functioning, but without success. Finally, he declared martial law when the city failed to function.

§

Fred Funston had just returned from his mission to Hawaii and the administration was pleased with how he shored up the defenses of the island territory against the possibility of war with Japan. He knew intimately the southwest United States and Mexico, spoke passable Spanish, and had wartime experience with civil governance. He was also available, and already on the minds of those who needed a trouble-shooter—once more enroute to a rendezvous with fate.

President Wilson's decision to occupy Vera Cruz was the first true combat test of army division deployment readiness. Marines proved their preparedness with the initial insertion and follow-on forces. On April 19th, 1914, the 5th Brigade of the Second Division was in Houston to train and participate in exercises to commemorate the Battle of San Jacinto. Just before midnight, the brigade commander received a warning order of trouble in Tampico and to prepare to respond. Less than an hour later, he received orders to return by rail to Galveston and prepare for embarkation.

On April 21st, the brigade was notified it would be reinforced. Orders called for the reinforced brigade to sail on April 24th with five days rations. Regimental trains and tents would be left in Galveston. Enough mules would accompany the regiments to transport machineguns and pull medical wagons. The brigade staff was too lean to control an independent force that large abroad with the additional units assigned, so the staff of the Second Division was designated to control the expeditionary force. The total force was to embark and sail to arrive in Vera Cruz on April 27th.

Command of the reinforced brigade on such a sensitive mission was an issue for highest-level consideration. The current brigade commander was in poor health. The Second Division Commander relieved him with

Washington's approval, and the Secretary of War ordered Fred Funston to take the reinforced brigade, with the Second Division staff to command and control the expedition, to Vera Cruz. The feisty, red-headed Funston was still the youngest brigadier general in the army at forty-nine, already at that rank for twenty-three years. Despite his experience in such matters, he was considered a risky political choice.

Funston and his aide from Hawaii, Captain William Ball, stopped in Kansas City on February 6th, and Funston met with his former surgeon and friend Dr. Robinson at the University Club before departing by train later that evening for Galveston. They arrived on February 8th and registered at the Galvez Hotel before proceeding next day to Texas City to sign an order assuming command of the 5th Brigade, and 2nd Division staff, and to meet subordinate commanders. Eda, who was very much pregnant again, stayed behind in Oakland with the children to get help from her sisters.

Soldiers and sailors involved in deployment were busy—Funston busiest of all. He was stalked all day by war correspondents looking for a story. "I am too busy to be interviewed today," he said. Late that afternoon he received the press, including Jack London, but told them, "I really have nothing of interest to give out. You know as much as I do about the probabilities and possibilities," he said, "and you also know the last orders that I received—to embark. When we land at Vera Cruz I expect additional orders, but not much before then."

Units worked through the night preparing for embarkation on the *Sumner, Kilpatrick, Meade*, and *McClellan*. Every able bodied man was tired but expected rest on the way to Mexico. Three long, shrill blasts of ship's whistles, twenty thousand cheering people on the wharves, and a band aboard each vessel signaled their departure from Galveston. When the transports set sail, they were accompanied by the battleship *Louisiana* and four destroyers until the naval convoy arrived off Vera Cruz near midnight on April 28th. On the same day, two detachments of AB-3 Curtiss flying boats arrived in Vera Cruz, the first U.S. military naval air support on a mission outside the continental United States. Troops remained on board ships for two additional days while Washington wrangled over transferring control of marines to the army, and Funston and Fletcher worked out transfer of command authority.

While he was steaming from Galveston, snipers were active in Vera Cruz, concealed within hotels, shops, and houses. Marines and sailors returned fire and bystanders and innocent civilians sometimes were casualties. Although Mexican soldiers had left, more troops were needed to counter snipers and establish control. Admiral Fletcher committed the battalion from the *Utah* and edged three launches with one-pound guns into the harbor. After the Mexican Naval School was cleared, Fletcher and Consul Canada searched for Maass to negotiate a cease-fire, but he had no intention of returning. Finally, they found the mayor hiding in his residence but he pleaded no jurisdiction, and suggested the police chief might help. But police had deserted and there was no one to negotiate with.

By nightfall, armed convicts roamed the streets, firing indiscriminately, but criminals were more occupied with looting than shooting. Americans returned fire with rifles and naval guns whenever a suitable target was identified under lit streetlights or a ship's searchlight illuminating shadows. During the night the *San Francisco, Chester, Minnesota,* and *Hancock* arrived from Tampico and the fleet commander sent landing parties of more marines and bluejackets ashore. Admiral Badger, commanding the fleet, also arrived with the ships but directed Fletcher to retain control of operations ashore until the army arrived.

By then, marines had organized for house-to-house fighting and began systematically clearing block-by-block while sailors controlled the waterfront. Outposts were positioned to protect main streets cleared of snipers, so people could move safely. But streets were littered with debris, shattered buildings, and dead bodies—in tropical heat decay began fast.

While Funston and his brigade task force were enroute from Galveston to Vera Cruz, Fletcher had his hands full restoring order without a functioning government. A military government was called for. When Funston arrived the two worked out a plan for transfer of control to the army and a temporary municipal government. Naval personnel ashore would be released from shore duty, minus the marine brigade, which would come under Funston's command. He went ashore with army troops on April 30th. The total force numbered around seven thousand.

While Fred was aboard ship preparing to go ashore at Vera Cruz, Eda was at Letterman General Hospital at The Presidio in San Francisco. News was telegraphed to gulf ports and flashed by wireless radio, hoping to catch up with him. He celebrated the good news, "It's a girl!" he shouted and sent a telegram in reply, "Love to all, including baby. Fred." Eda replied, "Mother and child doing well." It would be a while before Funston would see his youngest daughter, another born while he was deployed.

Funston and Fletcher were informed a civilian governor should be named for control of Vera Cruz. Without consulting Washington, they settled on Robert Kerr, an impressive lawyer who was available. However, Kerr was also a staunch critic of Wilson's policies toward Mexico. Wilson rejected him and decided if the Mexicans couldn't self-govern, the military would do it—that is, Funston would.

The original governance plan called for legislative, executive, and judicial functions vested in an American civil governor who would report to the military commander. The military would tend to other essential functions of security and keeping the city operating. Funston would now have to install a military government similar to the one used in the Philippines. The following day he issued that proclamation and installed the first officers to keep the city operating. Additional administrative personnel arrived within two weeks to run public works and sanitation, port operations, customs and taxes, and some judicial matters.

Funston considered his brigade task force and divisional staff insufficient for the entire job. He needed more troops. Funston and Fletcher spent two days in discussions with the War Department and Navy about establishing a unified command. A cabinet decision was required to approve putting marines under the army. Eventually, three thousand marines already ashore under the command of Colonel John Lejeune, were detached from the Atlantic Fleet and placed under Funston's command. On April 30th, Funston's army brigade marched ashore to join the marines.

News of American occupation of Vera Cruz spread like wildfire throughout Mexico, portrayed in the press as "naked and unbridled American aggression." Mobs, riots, and angry protests erupted all over the country, especially Mexico City. Huerta broke off diplomatic relations and expelled the American ambassador. Wilson was shaken by the unexpected casualties and turn of events in Vera Cruz, where he expected a cake-walk. He attended a funeral for casualties evacuated to the Brooklyn Navy Yard, and told the press, "We have gone down to Mexico to serve mankind, if we can find out the way." In Vera Cruz, the wait for diplomats to find the way was long and hot. Funston made his own way.

On April 30th, 1914, Fletcher's and Funston's commands formed in ranks on the waterfront for a formal change of command ceremony. In all his campaigns, Funston carried a .45 caliber pistol that extended from his waist to his knees. When he went ashore, Admirals Fletcher and Badger and their staffs were drawn up in lines of dress whites, swords shining, and with all accruements to receive him. The army general wore olive-drab battle dress, no blouse, and the enormous pistol slung low along his leg. The British consul, in attendance, mistook him for a "little Chinaman." As long as he was at the front, Funston proudly wore the same khaki and olive uniforms, laundered over and over until the color was gone.

The hand-over ceremony turned out to be a "family affair," a Sunday picnic with plenty of good will and high spirits. Soldiers, sailors, and marines all passed in review then began shouting when a captain jumped on a bench and led a cheer for the navy. Bluejackets reciprocated. The band played *Auld Lang Syne* while Mexicans saluted what they mistook for the American national anthem. Then, girls from the bordellos recognized their favorite clients among the sailors boarding ships and rushed out for farewell hugs, kisses, and embarrassing laughter.

In Vera Cruz, sickness and death were as accepted as dirt, disorder, flies, and filthy water. For every thousand people, fifty died each month, mostly infants, with dysentery, malaria, tuberculosis, meningitis, or small pox. One of Funston's first tasks was to reduce conditions that led to such a high rate of disease and death, protecting his soldiers as well as Mexican residents. No one in Washington anticipated a massive cleanup just to make it habitable. Many called for the limited invasion to be turned loose, allowing Funston to march all the way to Mexico City as Winfield Scott had done. Funston favored that. But Wilson didn't want a wider war and knew if he released him he'd certainly have one. So Wilson concentrated on getting Vera Cruz running efficiently, keeping Funston on a short leash.

The army force Funston led ashore on April 30th included 183 officers, 3,147 soldiers, 11 civilian employees, 155 mules, 27 wagons, four ambulances, three buckboards—and four newspaper correspondents.

Funston hadn't fared well with reporters on his speaking tour after his fame in the Philippines. He believed he'd endured quite enough from newspapers and would've gladly left them behind, but his orders explicitly permitted embedded reporters.

Consistent with his mission, he had authority to appoint provost courts to try Mexican offenders. Mexican courts ceased to function, so one of his first official acts as military governor was to reestablish courts. With one stroke, practically all law and order functions fell under his provost marshal. As military governor, he retained authority over the Mexican general treasury in Vera Cruz, customs and lighthouse services, civil courts, and all Mexican and U.S. mail services.

Active combat ended before the brigade's arrival, but the possibility of a major counterattack couldn't be ignored. Funston wanted to press on to Mexico City, but was tightly reined in by orders not to extend out of Vera Cruz while national negotiations were underway. But an American traveling physician arrived with news of five crowded troop trains and fifteen flatbed cars loaded with machineguns and artillery parked between Mexico City and Vera Cruz, ready to roll. Funston passed that report to Washington with assurances he could hold the city while hoping something would happen to liven up the occupation.

A few days later, on May 2nd, five hundred Mexican soldiers appeared at the pipeline pumping station at El Tejar, nine miles away. A Mexican officer under a white flag approached the outpost and demanded they surrender within ten minutes. The commander, Marine Major John Russell, wired an urgent message to Funston, who replied with rules of engagement—do not, under any circumstances, fire the first shot, but self-defense is fully expected. Within minutes, Funston dispatched a thousand men, army troops under Colonel Robert Van Vliet and marines under Colonel John Lejeune. When they arrived, Mexicans vanished.

Funston became restless and frustrated in Vera Cruz. Passivity cut across his grain but he remained under tight orders from the president and secretary of war. Funston had arrived with his reinforced brigade, added marines, whipped them into fighting shape, expecting war to be declared and limitations eventually removed. Instead, he was restrained and put in charge of a cleanup operation. He pushed his scouts out as far as allowed and reported every threat, but to no avail. He protested to Washington, warning Mexicans had taken the initiative, still stinging from their recent humiliation. He tried again, stressing occupation of Mexico City was necessary to protect against the threat of a massacre by Zapata. Secretary of War Garrison also rattled his saber, as did most American newspapers, members of the Republican Party, and American and British citizens living in Mexico. However, peace-keepers and anti-imperialists held sway.

Funston kept his troops in fighting form, even while cleaning up and policing the city. Artillery target ranges were established and constantly improved. Daily combat drills and exercises kept men from getting lazy and maintained their focus on their real purpose as fighters. Discipline and training honed a fighting edge while demonstrating combat power to Mexican citizens, soldiers, and spies. Drills and governing duties notwithstanding, the expeditionary force was marking time during the hot and sultry summer of 1914. During off duty hours, boredom set in and popular diversions included bullfights, grade B motion pictures, and large quantities of Mexican beer in cantinas. However, Funston's strict sanitary demands, strenuous exercise, hard work, and nourishing food kept the expedition healthy under the vigilant eyes of a keen medical staff. Yet everyone on the expedition prayed for trouble, especially Funston.

On the evening of May 6th, Private Parks of the 28th Infantry rode a horse at a rapid gait along the railroad line out of Vera Cruz. He was allowed to pass, headed toward the pumping station but he left the rail trail and stumbled into a Mexican outpost. A Cuban bookseller in the area witnessed his execution by firing squad, his body doused with oil and set aflame. General Aguilar allowed Funston to send a detachment to recover the remains and send them to his mother in Indiana.

Lines of communication between Vera Cruz and Galveston stretched across the Gulf of Mexico. The navy ran weekly transports for supplies, mail, and other necessities between the two ports. Funston set up a rest and recuperation program, with War Department approval, allowing ten officers and twenty enlisted men to go to Galveston on each transport run to spend a few hours with their families, back on the return voyage.

Vera Cruz changed under American occupation. Not only was it cleaned up, but troops brought new business to cantinas and other enterprises.

When the bugler played "First Call" in the mornings, the city woke up, breakfast came earlier, shops opened on time, gambling was reduced, and cockfighting and bull fighting were banished. Mexico boasted *federales* were coming to rescue Vera Cruz but they never did. Troops remained ready, daring them to come. Funston still hoped for orders to take Mexico City and peppered his dispatches to the secretary of war with warnings of the danger to his small contingent if the Mexican army mobilized and moved in force. But Wilson wanted a peaceful way out.

As military governor, everything fell under Funston's direction or approval, especially sanitation and public health. Refuge, trash, stagnant water, mosquitoes, and venereal disease, all were threats to the task force. He kept troops engaged solving those problems. A thousand soldiers and marines gathered filth and hauled it to the public dump to soak in oil and burn, while fighting off rats, flies, and vultures. He kept Americans fully occupied but Mexicans needed constant prodding to clean their own city.

The market was more unsanitary than the dump. Fresh blood dripped onto the boardwalks and soil, flies covered exposed meat, and worthless scraps were tossed under tables for dogs, meat counters were filthy and maggots cleaned up the scraps. Fruit and vegetables rotted in the streets along with dog and bird droppings and feces of burros. A thousand Mexicans were hired to clean up the market and collect trash daily. Large cans were distributed for refuge and litter—violations merited a stiff fine. Military inspectors enforced sanitary food preparation everywhere there was cooking, including Mexican restaurants. Vultures circling the carcass of Vera Cruz finally left for easier pickings elsewhere.

A problem in summer heat was disease prevention with malaria, tuberculosis, meningitis rampant. Sewage and garbage disposal were unknown and civilians suffered from endemic dysentery from contaminated water and food. Repairs followed cleanup. Funston put half the contingent to clean and repair the city and marketplace with Mexican workers hired to help. Doors were hung on hinges, roofs sealed, walls patched and concrete laid. Soldiers covered merchant stalls and added flytraps. Windows were screened against mosquitoes and the marketplace and streets were hosed daily with sea water. Fines were levied for improper handling of garbage. They drained ponds and stagnant water and spread crude oil to stop insect breeding. Medics administered forty-six thousand small pox vaccinations and inspected prostitution for contagious diseases. The death rate among Mexicans fell twenty-five per cent in seven months.

Mexicans were pleased to see Americans working hard on their behalf but hardly understood why—they were accustomed to the flies, trash, and vultures. They knew when Americans left, they'd return to former ways but were amused watching as sewage, clean water, lighting, and bridges were restored. The prison was itself a crime. Funston ordered the population reduced by releasing all political prisoners and keeping only felons. Everything inside the thick walls was hosed, scraped, patched, and twelve hundred pounds of Sulphur burned to sanitize it.

Soon the port was functioning and the customs house collecting taxes. By September, a postal service was reestablished and public schools were opened. Mexican police were completely dysfunctional and the military provost marshal brought public safety and security under military governance, but a local Mexican notary handled legal transactions between Mexicans. The city operated more efficiently than it ever had.

Children were on the general's mind—birth of his unseen daughter, and loss of his first son—and he attended the commencement for Manuel Herrera Girls' Public School, took a seat on the front row and delighted throughout the lengthy program all in Spanish. A ten-year old Mexican girl gave a fiery patriotic oration and Funston praised her loudly, "Well done!" Little Lillian Henry, the only American girl in the class was privileged to hold the general's hat during the ceremony.

While Funston was in Vera Cruz, World War I broke out between Germany and France. Captain Ball entered in his diary, "Europe is involved in the most gigantic war the world has ever seen. Interest is very tense. News meager." A German light cruiser, *Dresden*, lay in the harbor and a brawl erupted between the German crew and those of French merchant ships. Funston ordered the *Dresden* out to sea and held back the French as well as British Navy cruisers, *Berwick*, *Bristol*, and *Suffolk* to avoid an international incident at sea. Wilson was proud of these accomplishments since the initial scrapes in taking over the city.

§

Huerta resigned and skirted to Jamaica as Carranza occupied Mexico City, bringing the opposing side of the revolution to the table. But political wrangling continued between Washington and Mexico to transfer Vera Cruz back to Mexican authority, while Mexico still verged on civil war. The general assembly finally issued a proclamation giving Wilson enough political cover to order a military departure. He directed Funston to negotiate with Mexicans in Vera Cruz to take over there. But no Mexicans had assisted in managing the city under American occupation so Funston needed four more weeks to emplace a local government for a handover. Integral to handing over the city was guaranteed protection for those who had worked with Americans. Carranza delayed such guarantees for nearly two months. Funston had worked hard to get the city running and didn't want to walk away and see it fail again.

When news spread Americans were leaving, transit offices overflowed with those wanting out before the *federales* returned. Despite Funston's offer to work with the new government, the *federales* were not interested—only imposing double duties against citizens, and punishing those who cooperated. Wilson pressed for safety guarantees but they didn't come, so he directed Funston to warn citizens they wouldn't have protection after he departed. City government began shutting down again as Mexicans walked away, knowing they would be held accountable when *federales* came. Panic struck local citizens and Funston chartered several private vessels to evacuate many who had helped.

He was ready to go on November 20th, 1914, when he got his warning order to evacuate within three days. He had held marines, sailors, and soldiers packed and loaded for departure while waiting for high level negotiations. Offices were already cleaned, inventoried, and prepared to hand over, although there was uncertainty who would receive the keys. On the morning of November 23rd, troops stood ready for evacuation, government offices vacated and security pulled in to the port for boarding. The entire contingent of seven thousand marched to the waterfront to music of a military band and walked up the gangplanks of naval vessels. The city was ghostly quiet although some women wailed as troops marched aboard ships.

At the end of the Vera Cruz occupation, the last U.S. troop ship, fittingly the *Kansas*, steamed out of the harbor. Mexican cavalry made a last gasp to save face and claim credit for the American retreat. They charged to the docks on horseback, flying a large Mexican flag, shooting and shouting—but after it was safe. Funston watched and told his aide, "If they are firing at us we will go back. But, so far they are just firing in the air."

Funston took the last ship out of Vera Cruz, the *Cristobal*. The naval convoy arrived at Galveston through the mist on a rainy Thanksgiving Day, the flag ship flying the two-starred banner of a major general. From a military perspective the landing and occupation of the city and the subsequent military government was flawless, in fact a model for civil affairs. But American influence and efficiency didn't stick—Mexicans quickly resumed their old ways. The *federales* took over and within a short time the city of Vera Cruz looked and functioned much as it had for centuries before Funston's occupation.

On November 28th, he wired the War Department the expedition had arrived in Galveston, the last journal entry made, and the Vera Cruz Expedition ended.

§

Throughout the occupation, his role had been delicate, a political-military tight-rope with sensitivity to the Mexican culture while keeping his troops safe. Orders prohibited occupation of more territory, yet his forces occupied a city virtually surrounded by Mexicans, a city filled with spiteful former prisoners, guerilas, and disgruntled citizens. He harnessed his volatile temper when tested by Mexican bellicosity, hurling insults at his troops, and taking pot shots at army and marine outposts. When a Mexican general warned "he could not hold his troops back," Funston replied, "If you cannot hold your troops back, I can!" He welcomed the opportunity.

During the expedition, Captain Douglas MacArthur, son of Funston's mentor in the Philippines, arrived unannounced, but not as a member of his command. He was an observer reporting directly to Washington. MacArthur undertook a secret and reckless reconnaissance deep into Mexican territory on his own, without Funston's knowledge or approval. Had he been compromised, captured, or killed, Funston's position as commander and administrator would have been jeopardized. He was offended by Douglas MacArthur's discourtesy but owed too much to

Arthur MacArthur to turn it into an embarrassing incident. Funston only found out about his excursion when one of Douglas MacArthur's friends submitted a recommendation for the Medal of Honor. Funston's endorsement acknowledged the exploit was probably worthy of the award, but made clear he had no knowledge of any of the facts or any authority over it. Two boards considered the award and disapproved it.

Funston was able to keep peace for seven months of occupation and establish a model military government. Yet he left embittered by a compromise of principle, having to withdraw without proper transition and firm guarantees for the safety of those who worked for the military government, and without taking the fight to the enemy. But, when time to leave, he dutifully boarded the ships with his troops. His civilian superiors in Washington were pleased with his performance and restraint. The week prior, Chief of Staff of the Army, Major General Wotherspoon, reached mandatory retirement age and Major General Hugh Scott was named to succeed him, leaving one vacancy for a new major general.

Funston was finally promoted to major general on November 17th, 1914, a week before Vera Cruz was evacuated. Funston left holding the highest rank the U. S. Army could bestow at the time, finally past Taft's vindictiveness.

Some friendly members of Congress pressed to promote him to lieutenant general, but he discouraged them. He'd lost interest in promotions after so many years. Senator William Thompson of Kansas pressed him to accept even this promotion. Funston replied, "I suppose my principle crime is my youth.... I used to be young, but have been getting over it at the rate of 365 days a year." President Wilson had ensured his promotion based on his handling the occupation of Vera Cruz--but he had more in store.

§

While the removal of Huerta was promising, Carranza was unable to stop cross-border raids into United States' territory. Funston's next role would bring expanded dimensions of responsibility. Rather than a tactical field commander, he would now control an entire theater of operations, a complex effort demanding higher degrees of management and administrative skills. The new division structure put in place by General

Leonard Wood and exercised by General Carter became the forerunner for the mass armies that would fight wars in the future. Funston was needed to test it for real and fix its deficiencies.

The year 1914 held great promise for Fred Funston's family. Fort Sam Houston in south Texas was a pleasant place to raise a family in old San Antonio. Eda had given birth to their youngest daughter, Eleanor Elizabeth, little Betsy, on April 14th, 1914. She was the third of Funston's children born while he was away on duty. But after completing his official report for the War Department at Galveston, he had one stop to make before going to see Eda and his new daughter for the first time. Aboard a train skimming across Kansas' fertile plains, he gazed from the window. "Wish I had had enough sense to stay on a Kansas farm," he said idly. "I was reared on a farm and I like the feel of the soil. It's good to hoe potatoes and plow corn." When Funston, still deeply tanned from the Mexican sun, stepped off the train at Carlyle, Kansas, he scanned the crowd of townsfolk and farmers gathered to welcome him. He smiled at friends and neighbors but then spotted the small woman still wearing black for her departed husband. "Mother!" he called out before gathering her in his arms.

His next assignment was not merely reward for his successful expedition in Vera Cruz, but a herald of more hard times ahead. After two months leave in Kansas and California, the new major general returned to Fort Sam Houston to take command of United States troops massing along the Mexican border with Texas, New Mexico, and Arizona. As always with Funston, trouble loomed large. Vera Cruz was only preparation for a larger mission, the largest of his still-young life.

TWENTY

Fred Funston's promotion to major general came with the posting as commander of the Southern Department. Following two months leave to visit his mother in Kansas, and then Eda and the children and in-laws in California, he reported for duty at Fort Sam Houston, Texas, on February 14th, 1915 and assumed command from General Tasker Bliss the following day. War had broken out in Europe while he was still in Vera Cruz, yet the United States debated whether it should become involved in another foreign war. German meddling in Mexico's turmoil and threats to American shipping implied the inevitable. But, trouble was closer to home.

Chaos churned south of the border for decades. General Diaz seized power in a coup d'état in1876, ruling as a dictator until 1911. Madero was elected to replace him but General Huerta had him assassinated and imposed a new dictatorship. Huerta was forced out by the trouble at Vera Cruz and Carraza became the "First Chief." Villa and Zapata turned against him leading to a wider civil war and more violence. This was the situation waiting for Funston—Mexico in turmoil.

President Wilson watched trouble developing in Mexico and Europe while trying to remain neutral on both fronts, thereby offending Europeans and arousing Mexicans. Instability in Mexico prompted the War Department to expand its military posture in San Antonio and Galveston, Texas, and around San Diego, California. Prior to Vera Cruz, the War Department reorganized the continental military structure. The vast Southern Department at Fort Sam Houston in San Antonio included all of Texas, New Mexico, and Arizona along the border, plus Louisiana, Arkansas, and Oklahoma. After the maneuver division was mobilized and tested in exercises around San Antonio, some troops stayed to patrol the unsettled border, but it was thinly picketed.

That border extended from the Gulf of Mexico near Brownsville, Texas, along the Rio Grande River to El Paso. From there, it shriveled to a line in the sand, marked sometimes by barbed wire extending across the

Chihuahua and Sonora deserts for nearly a thousand miles through New Mexico, Arizona and California to the Pacific Ocean. Prior to the Mexican revolution, the border was lightly policed by an army organized around small western outposts and forts to maintain law and order by protecting settlers, miners, ranchers, and farmers. Americans and Mexicans had strong interests on both sides of the border as families, cultures, and businesses were intertwined. In addition to cross-border trade, Americans purchased seventy-five per cent of Mexican exports, owned three-quarters of their mines and half their oil fields, mostly in three northern Mexican states. American dollars developed Mexican railroad lines, mining operations, and cattle ranches.

Funston settled with Eda and their three children at Fort Sam Houston in San Antonio, home of the famous Alamo. His youngest daughter, Elizabeth, was born that year, joining Barbara and Fred junior. He was delighted with his children, although his heart still ached with the loss Arthur. His lifetime friend, Charles Gleed, had written in *Cosmopolitan* fifteen years before, "It is likely that when he is no longer wanted as a soldier ... he will select some settled business and, for a change, try the charms of a quiet life." Although he'd purchased a farm in Alameda County in California and longed for his Kansas farming roots, there wouldn't be that opportunity.

By November, 1914, Eda was already organizing ladies of Fort Sam Houston and San Antonio to support the grand military ball at the civic auditorium as a benefit for the Army Relief Society. Simultaneously, she was leading the establishment of the Fort Sam Houston branch of the San Antonio chapter of the American Red Cross. She was interviewed with other ladies in a spare room over the officer's mess while rolling bandages and other surgical dressings and sewing hospital pajamas for men sick or wounded in the border conflicts. Afterwards, they planned a luncheon at San Antonio's St. Anthony Hotel to explain their purpose to gentlemen and ladies of San Antonio, raising funds for supplies, and more volunteers.

Even challenges were mixed with good times on the pleasant frontier post. Dwight D. "Ike" Eisenhower recalled his duty assignment at Fort Sam Houston in 1915, while Funston commanded there. The fort was a showcase for the army, a plum assignment for a soldier made more intriguing with trouble stirring at border flashpoints. Eisenhower drilled and trained men to standards but with time left for hunting, poker, and parties. Funston knew his fellow Kansans' reputation as a football player at the military academy and when Ike declined an opportunity to coach at a local academy Funston convinced him do it, saying, "It would please me and it would be good for the army...." Ike was a successful coach and added to his reputation and publicity from his teams' wins. Then he stepped up to St. Louis College and turned a loser into another winner. But, Ike was restless and later applied to join Pershing's expedition. Instead, the War Department assigned him to train National Guard troops. He began then thinking of the army's highest headquarters as "that nebulous region where incomprehensible decisions are made."

Funston watched Eisenhower's performance in training, leading, and coaching, and encouraged him. He and Eda were also aware of a growing relationship between Ike and Miss Mamie Doud of Denver, Colorado. The Douds sometimes visited the post while staying over in San Antonio during the warmer winter months, and Eda never missed an opportunity to give romance a boost. When the time was right, Funston bent army rules enough to allow Ike to travel to Denver to marry Mamie.

The unsettled border demanded constant attention at Funston's headquarters. He became important there, easily recognized in his crisp, neatly cut uniforms, and well-groomed Van Dyke beard. In town, he was frequently seen at the old Menger Hotel, relaxing with permanent guests and late afternoon juleps. His exploits in Alaska and Death Valley, Cuba, the Philippines, San Francisco, and Vera Cruz were well known, and he enjoyed telling tales. His friend, Charles Gleed, had said Funston made "...little use of the pronoun 'I'...." in his writing or telling of tales. Gleed firmly believed he never sought the limelight for himself and insisted, "I know him well enough to know that he wishes he could divide equally among his fellow soldiers the thanks and applause which his countrymen have given him."

Unarmed Americans living or working in Mexico were struck by the increasingly hostile environment, and border incursions became belligerent. The situation near Brownsville, Texas, was worrisome as Carranza and Villa struggled for regional control. Francisco "Pancho" Villa was a flagrant outlaw, tormenting border towns and ranches with his raiding parties. Villa's raids escalated, citizen uprisings in Matamoros flared, and shots from the Mexican side peppered Texas and endangered Americans. Texas Governor Oscar Colquitt sent state guardsmen to Brownsville while pressuring Washington for federal troops along the Rio Grande. The governor's temperament raised concerns in Washington that a local incident could lead to an international conflict. More wary of the governor's actions than Funston's, the War Department ordered him to cooperate with the governor. That calmed the situation for a short time.

§

In January 1915, some Mexicans and Mexican-Americans devised the "Plan of San Diego" to reclaim the southwestern United States for Mexico by killing every North American over the age of sixteen, except old men, women, and children. The plan instigated a race war, drawing Indians, blacks, and foreigners into the Hispanic coalition to establish an independent republic. Two American citizens from Brownsville, Texas, Luis del la Rosa and Aniceto Pizana, crossed into Mexico to recruit troops for their cause during the summer and organized them into platoons and companies to carry out the plan.

Funston first believed these were bandits and the responsibility of local law enforcement, not the military. But the Mexican government under Carranza barely controlled the northeast sector, Villa firmly controlled the northwest. Instability of the entire border region was ripe for exploitation and it was not clear where trouble originated.

Raids increased after the hostile organizations were created, attacks targeting symbols of change, such as railroads, telegraphs, automobiles, and irrigation systems, and reprisals on Mexicans who worked for Americans. On Independence Day, forty Mexican bandits struck a ranch near Lyford, Texas, and a few days later the foreman of another large ranch was killed in a separate attack. Another youth was killed in Raymondville before a posse caught up with the band and shot it out. Raiders burned bridges and robbed a store of firearms. Another band performed ritual executions. Troopers of the 12th Cavalry fought a running clash with bandits north of Brownsville, but seventy raiders returned to hit another ranch nearby. This one was defended by ranchers and a small detachment of the 12th Cavalry who fought off the raiders. But a seventy-five-year old man was captured and forced as a guide for more attacks.

Local detachment commanders and civilian officials recognized the threat had changed by late summer and Mexican newspapers reported the raids had popular support. Funston was constantly on the go as raids increased, visiting El Paso, Brownsville and other trouble spots to make his own assessment. He realized two critical issues—raids were staged from Mexico, and raiders had sanctuary over the border. He knew only the army could stop them and informed the War Department of his intention to pursue and capture bandits. Yet his outposts had too few troops to be effective—the cavalry brigade at San Antonio covered nine hundred miles with three regiments in sixteen scattered posts and thirty smaller camps.

With troops far-flung along the border, they only waited for reports of attacks and reacted as fast as possible. Bandits had initiative, informants, sanctuary, and choice of time and place; they concentrated at will with the upper hand in weapons, men, and horses. Funston was frustrated and warned the War Department insufficient troops would lead to murder of defenseless people, destruction of property, and loss of national prestige. He wanted troops to prevent that and avoid an international crisis in any border town. He warned the "time for economy had passed; more troops should be supplied regardless of expense."

Raids caused hysteria in hard hit areas. Officially, Texas Rangers and local law enforcement were responsible, but most private citizens were armed for self-defense, and vigilante groups were active, including hanging or shooting "suspicious" Mexicans. Funston estimated three hundred Mexicans might have been killed in reprisals. Approximately half the residents of the lower Rio Grande fled violence, moving north or south. Control by law enforcement was failing—only the army could confront vigilantes and stop cross-border raids. The Rio Grande was a shallow, meandering stream—no obstacle to raiders who crossed at will, making commanders anxious and helpless to perpetual threats. The job wasn't easy as rugged terrain made tracking raiders difficult. Wilson made it impossible by forbidding hot pursuit.

Telegraph keys rattled at Southern Department headquarters with reports from outposts and soldiers coming under attack—even new Signal Corps aeroplanes drew fire from the Mexican side, while their military facilitated raids. Funston finally got more troops. By September, thin mobile patrol units between Brownsville and Laredo were beefed up, yet attacks increased with more targets. A raid of eighty Mexicans against Progresso was repulsed after a heated firefight but an American soldier, Private Richard Johnson, was captured and killed, his ears and his head cut off, and his head left on a pike in view of his comrades.

After a quiet spell, de la Rosa made a spectacular attack at Tandy Station, north of Brownsville on the St. Louis-Brownsville-Mexico Railroad. First, his men removed rail spikes, enabling them to yank the tracks apart as the locomotive approached. The engine flipped and the engineer was killed. De la Rosa and his men boarded the train, looted it, and shot three soldiers and a civilian. Again, they fled before the army could react, but struck again at a Signal Corps detachment at Ojo de Aqua. Three Americans and five raiders died there.

Funston rattled off another telegram requesting authorization to cross the river in pursuit. Residents had reached their limits and the only way to stop this was certain death as a consequence. The War Department again denied his request. Even with thousands of troops his hands were tied. Raids continued, and then slowed due to political wrangling inside Mexico. President Wilson was relieved and shifted attention to the war in Europe.

With the border problem reduced, Wilson recognized Carranza as "First Chief," hoping to settle their difficulties. But in late October, raiders struck again near Tandy Station. Funston was dismayed. He still wasn't allowed to cross the border in pursuit of bandits, nor control reactions of local authorities or vigilantes. The presence of troops didn't stop raiders from hitting at will, but made troops sitting ducks. His department had only twenty thousand men to protect a two thousand mile border—ten men per mile. As raids decreased in Texas, they spread to other border states.

§

Francisco "Pancho" Villa, was born in 1877. He killed his first man at the age of sixteen and never looked back. During his life, he was a ruthless killer, notorious bandit, and a revolutionary, unafraid of gringos north of the border or the Mexican government. Villa printed his own script, accepted by some banks in the U.S. as equivalent to the peso. His followers were called Villistas. Despite his character he was revered as a friend of the poor, an avenger of wrongs, and he robbed trains and seized hacienda lands for poor soldiers and peasants—a regular Mexican Robin Hood.

He despised Huerta and sought American support as a folk hero—a flamboyant rogue and a Hollywood movie star. He starred as himself in four American films between 1912 and 1916. When Wilson recognized Carranza as president, Villa was furious and swore revenge by drawing the U. S. into another intervention. He increased raids into west Texas, New Mexico, and Arizona. John J. "Black Jack" Pershing was dispatched with his 8th Infantry Brigade to Fort Bliss, Texas, to guard against those.

On January 11th, 1916, Villa's bandits stopped a train near Santa Ysabel. The train carried seventeen Texas miners and twenty Mexicans of the Cusi Mining Company. They removed the mining engineers and robbed Mexican passengers, then forced them to watch as they shot the miners in cold blood—all but one killed. The survivor feigned death, rolled down a bank, hid, and escaped when raiders left. El Paso was in frenzy so Pershing imposed martial law to stop an armed citizen's raid into Juarez.

Still, rules of engagement were not changed, military pursuit into Mexico prohibited despite Funston's and Pershing's entreaties. Villa, having failed to create an invasion, watched and waited, then struck again, this time with murderous blows at American and Mexican towns.

§

Despite losses, Villa had a substantial raiding force. Carranzistas denied access to sea ports and most border crossings except Juarez, and *federales* held Agua Prieta, the crossing opposite Douglas, Arizona. But Villa isolated the town, intending to seize it and open another crossing. He pushed his ten to fifteen thousand men further west, but the Carranzistas did not sit idle.

When Wilson recognized Carranza, he allowed the *federales* at Agua Prieta to reinforce through Douglas. Trains hauling soldiers, arms, munitions, supplies and building materials poured through Douglas into the Mexican garrison. Defenders built trenches, aprons of barbed wire, machinegun emplacements, and constructed an elevated platform for a large searchlight. When Villa's men arrived, Agua Prieta was a fortress.

Funston saw trouble and reinforced troops in Douglas to three regiments of infantry, one of field artillery, and several cavalry troops. They constructed defensive positions on low hills in the north with supporting strong points, barbed wire, and machinegun positions. When Villa arrived opposite Slaughter's ranch, he was furious Wilson had recognized Carranza. The situation was dangerous and politically sensitive, threatening to encompass Douglas. Funston moved his advanced command post there and assumed direct control from the camp of the 9th Cavalry.

Americans in Douglas could see Villistas crossing open plains to the east. Despite Funston's warning of danger from stray rounds, townspeople turned this into a social event and flocked to the railroad tracks. Some stood on boxcars with binoculars in hand; others crowded the roofs of buildings, some on the highest natural elevations with a clear view of the developing battle. At noon, artillery from the Mexican garrison opened fire and Villa's artillery responded, starting an artillery duel but little damage was done to either side while townspeople were entertained.

During a pause, Villa went to the quarantine house on the border and requested a meeting with Funston. He took General Davis and his aide with him. Villa was cordial and shook hands through the barbed-wire fence. Spectators gathered to watch while Villa complained about agreements broken by the *federales*. Funston refused to debate and said, "As a soldier I will obey orders."

Villa requested he move his troops away, so he could attack Agua Prieta without unintended consequences. This was embarrassing—he'd had already decided to do that, but he refused Villa's request so not to encourage an attack. Villa asked if the U. S. permitted Carranzistas to pass through and Funston confirmed it. They glared at each other through the wire. Villa stressed that Carranza was more "un-American" than he was. Funston interrupted, insisting he wouldn't discuss governmental policy. After the meeting, Funston directed Davis to make adjustments to his lines along the boundary for defense of his troops against unintended fire, but retain tactical flexibility in case fighting crossed the line.

Villa launched another ground assault in darkness on November 1st. The *federales'* searchlight was switched on and exposed them in the open. Villa learned a hard lesson when his troops were cut down in waves.

Erratic fire raked over Douglas and its citizenry, and the troops. Funston was authorized by the War Department to return fire if they fired into sovereign territory, but he restrained as they were not under attack and he couldn't fire on one group without engaging both. Sergeant Mays and Private Mitchell were wounded in the trenches before Funston moved the troops out of danger on the border. Private Harry Jones was standing guard on a supply wagon well back when a round hit him in the stomach, killing him. Funston moved civilians out of dwellings near the border, but six of them were wounded anyway. He personally patrolled the border on horseback and on foot with General Davis as bullets kicked up dust.

Two American doctors, Thigpen and Miller, ventured onto the battlefield with medical dressings to aid Villa's wounded. The doctors, their automobiles and chauffeurs were captured. Villa twice ordered them shot and they were twice lined up for execution, saved only by the intervention of one of Villa's officers whom Dr. Miller had once treated. Villa finally told them they were the "last Americans who would ever leave alive the country controlled by him." They were force-marched fifty miles without food and left on their own to get back to the border, eighteen miles away. Villa kept their automobiles.

He broke off his assault on Agua Prieta and Douglas, then hit Hermosillo in daylight, but with a worse outcome. They were ready for him there. His shattered band staggered toward Nogales, ravaging, looting, and murdering along the way. But Villa, instead of inciting an invasion, now wanted revenge on Americans.

Before leaving Douglas for San Antonio, Funston had meetings with General Obregon, overall commander of Mexican federal troops across the border, which he reported to General Scott. He arranged to meet the one-armed Obregon in a parlor at the Gadsden Hotel in Douglas. They discussed Villa's expected next moves and in parting, Obregon emphasized his strong favorability of the United States and desire to work in harmony. Next day, Funston received a telegram that Villa was threatening Nogales and was in an ugly mood. He returned to the Gadsden Hotel, and arranged a second meeting, including Colonel Slocum.

Obregon said if Villa occupied Nogales on his side, his troops would evacuate and not stand and fight, instead linking up with a stronger force in

Hermosillo. He laid out his own campaign plan against Villa, and then expressed concerns that Mr. George Carothers, a special agent for the State Department, had a business relationship with Villa and could not be trusted. Colonels Slocum confirmed that so Funston passed the information to General Scott for discussions between the War Department and State.

Funston left for Nogales by train immediately after that meeting. He found an anti-American movement stewing just over the border, with inflammatory handbills being circulated there. Since Villa was unable to launch an offensive for at least ten days, he returned to Fort Sam Houston.

§

Collection, analysis, and processing of intelligence about Villa proved difficult when patrols were not permitted across the border. On March 5th, Funston sent a report to Colonel Slocum, commanding the 13th Cavalry at Columbus that Villa intended to cross the border to raid border towns. Slocum added this to reports from cowboys who narrowly escaped a large band of armed men while driving a herd to a ranch along the Casas Grandes River. Slocum hired a Mexican scout to cross, ask questions, and report back, but he was unable to gather much more information.

Though warned, Slocum was blind to the situation developing on the other side. Yet, he was concerned for all his border outposts along sixty-five miles of border, with only twenty-one officers and five hundred thirty-two troopers—one for every six hundred fifty feet of border. He read Funston's warning again and drove his Ford to the barbed-wire fence at Palomas to question the Mexican commander, but found him hostile. Slocum saw Mexican soldiers behind barriers, aiming towards gringos instead of bandits. He beefed up his outposts and ordered more patrols. When he returned to his headquarters the night was pitch-black, street lamps off.

Americans in Columbus, New Mexico, knew Villa was nearby, but were unprepared for a surprise attack. In the early darkness of March 9th, 1916, Villa led four hundred eighty-five raiders across the border in two columns. One hit the center of the sleeping town, attacking the Commercial Hotel and killing five guests, then robbed and sacked the town, setting fires as they went. The second column hit the military tent encampment called Fort Furlong. Only cooks were awake at 0300, beginning breakfast. They defended themselves with shotguns kept for hunting quail and rabbit, tossed boiling water at intruders, and brandished carving knives, holding out until cavalrymen came to fight them off. One man, guarding the stables, killed a raider with a baseball bat.

Two under-strength cavalry troops under Major Frank Tompkins rallied fifty men on horses to pursue them twelve miles into Mexico, firing from their saddles as they chased them. When they caught up with their rear guard, they killed over thirty men and horses, searching out stragglers for eight more hours until their ammunition was exhausted. Tompkins knew hot-pursuit violated orders from Washington, but passions took control. When the cavalrymen returned, they found eighteen comrades dead in tent city, and several dead civilians in the city; over a hundred dead raiders were scattered in the streets.

Troopers collected bodies of raiders and piled them on a pyre for cremation. Before it was lit, the bodies were searched and two large packets were recovered with papers linking the raiders to Villa, along with further plans to violate U. S. territory. Among the papers were letters to Zapata, encouraging him to send people into cities to incite the populace against Americans. Translations were wired to Funston and Washington.

General Scott directed Funston send his Inspector General to Columbus to investigate the tragedy. While Washington wanted a scapegoat, the inspector, Pershing, and Funston all exonerated Colonel Slocum of any failings. Tompkins' pursuit was authorized by Slocum and Funston fully supported that in a telegram as well: "Under circumstances I believe Colonel Slocum entirely justified in violating War Department's order relative to sending troops across border and am of the opinion that had he not done so Villa might immediately have returned to attack after being joined by his men left south of the line. Funston."

Funston, pure soldier, was respected by subordinates and superiors, and in Washington his words were carefully considered. Women and children slept inside army posts, or in camp hospitals or adobe shacks under army blankets and pillows. Some clustered in schoolhouses in town with military guards.

While the odor of burning flesh mingled with embers of a burning town, the population of Columbus was in a state of hysteria. Wilson finally called out fifteen thousand militia to reinforce Funston's troops. Everyone was heartened to see troop trains arriving with New Mexican guardsmen from Deming, and Texans from El Paso. Nogales was reinforced by troops from Fort Huachuca, Arizona. Militia strengthened the border outposts and patrols so an expedition could be mustered for a deep strike. Then Wilson informed Carranza of his intention to hunt down Villa.

§

While diplomats exchanged notes, Funston, Pershing, and soldiers along the Mexican border prepared for action. Funston encouraged Washington in his strongest terms to act: "Unless Villa is relentlessly pursued and his forces scattered he will continue raids.... Troops of the Mexican government are accomplishing nothing and as he consequently can make his preparations and concentrations without being disturbed, he can strike at any point on the border, we being unable to obtain advance information as to his whereabouts. If we fritter away the whole command guarding towns, ranches and railroads, it will accomplish nothing if he can find safe refuge across the line after every raid."

The new Secretary of War, Newton Baker, informed Army Chief Hugh Scott that an expedition should be launched to capture Villa. Scott remembered Funston's words—"pursued and his forces scattered"—and convinced Baker that a more realistic objective would be breaking up Villa's band, reducing the threat. Funston reached that conclusion knowing actually catching the bandit was nearly impossible. But, they must take the offensive to stop raids. Funston's background made him ideal to lead such an expedition.

War Department orders directed him to organize to cross the border in pursuit of bandits that attacked Columbus with an objective to "break up Villa's band," although public perception was "capture or kill him." Funston was glad the gloves were off, but furious that orders specified "Black Jack" Pershing to lead the expedition. Leading such a deep raid was tailor-made for Funston's experience and abilities, but his penchant for independent actions, strong words, and aggressiveness were drawbacks. He'd chomped at the bit for months in Vera Cruz, imploring Wilson to let him go to Mexico City. In fact, Columbus, New Mexico, was in Pershing's district and he also had enough experience to do the job. Pershing was diplomatic, sensitive to international considerations, and willing to be constrained. Funston would orchestrate as theater army commander, leading almost the entire continental army in the field along an extended, endangered border, while simultaneously controlling the deep penetration.

Funston was unhappy with the way the order was received—a higher headquarters designating subordinate tasks and missions preempted his authority. Pershing knew Funston was unhappy with his appointment as expedition commander when his first order stressed his appointment came directly from Washington, and made clear his intention to control all aspects of the operation. He did ask Pershing for recommendations, implying he was not angry at him—only at the way it was handled.

Then Funston received new rules of engagement—authority to use stronger defensive tactics, hot pursuit of raiders, even preventive attacks across the border. Troops and supplies poured into the base at Columbus and filled out posts along the line.

He acted fast to assign units, missions, and initial concept of operation for the expedition. Pershing was to lead two columns, one directly from Columbus and the other from Hachita near Culbertson Ranch. The eastern column consisted of all but one troop of the 13th Cavalry, the regiment that pursued Villa after the Columbus raid, plus two infantry regiments, reinforced artillery, plus eight areoplanes of the Signal Corps' 1st Aero Squadron. These included six Curtiss JN-2 "Jennies," generally considered unstable deathtraps—when flown by inexperienced pilots. The western column had two cavalry regiments and a battery of artillery. The entire expedition was five thousand men. Units reached the lines of departure on horses, trucks, and trains for a pincer against Villa.

Funston distributed signal assets for communications between his headquarters in San Antonio and Pershing on the move or at a forward operation base; and more to enable Pershing to coordinate with his subordinate brigades and the two columns while moving. He emphasized using ciphers for secrecy and required Pershing stay in contact—promptly reporting combat actions or deaths. Strict rules of engagements forbid engaging *federales*. Then the War Department delivered bad news—

Mexican railroads could not be used to move troops and supplies, complicating logistics going forward.

Pershing issued orders creating a provisional division designated "The Punitive Expedition," organized into three brigades, and designated key staff and commanders. One of Pershing's aides was absent when the orders to move arrived. Lieutenant George Patton appealed to him to go as his second aide. Pershing hesitated but then agreed to take him.

Before they crossed the border the Mexican officer in charge of the outpost at Palomas informed them he was ordered to stop any military crossing into Mexico. Pershing sought guidance from Funston, who in turn queried the War Department. The prospect of a small fight didn't worry Funston and he gave Pershing permission to delay only until noon the following day, then to proceed. Funston informed Washington that unless he was ordered otherwise, he would send Pershing across. While Washington deliberated, Pershing notified the border officer he intended to cross in force, with or without consent. While Washington deliberated, the Mexican border guards vanished.

As the punitive expedition entered Mexico, General Scott passed additional rules of engagement to Funston and Pershing—to cooperate with Mexican government troops and show no hostility, but if threatened, defend, and if attacked, fight. Under no circumstances should they initiate an attack on *federales*.

Northern Mexico at the border was a giant wasteland with few towns, cut through by the dominating and rugged Sierra Madre Mountains. Peaks reached to twelve thousand feet, sliced by deep canyons. Roads were little more than dirt trails, dusty but turning to mud in the rain. This was home to Villa's men, unfamiliar and mostly unmapped for the Americans. Pershing was forced to rely on Mexican and Indian guides, their loyalty and reliability often questionable. Many of his soldiers were raw recruits.

Pershing's western column began a forced mounted march on March 14th to the vicinity of Culbertson's Ranch, the line of departure. Pershing had decided to lead this column, but an automobile accident delayed him. He finally arrived on horseback to cross the border during the night of March 15th. They marched hard for twenty-five miles the first night, thirty miles the next afternoon and another thirty miles the following day, arriving at Colonia Dublan, Pershing's forward operating base, on the third evening.

The eastern column moved slower as infantry marched on foot over a longer distance. Conditions were tough for both columns, temperatures frigid enough to freeze water in canteens at night, the sun blazing hot during the day. Trails were rough, narrow, dusty, and rutted. Dead bodies and ruined structures from the mayhem of revolution were scattered along the way. But by March 20th, both columns reached the forward base.

Colonia Dublan was a sparsely populated area and one hundred thirty miles south of Columbus, New Mexico, one of several Mormon colonies established in Mexico late in the 19th century. Mormons developed the land into a prosperous farming region, but it declined during the revolution. Unarmed Mormons were overjoyed to see columns of troops with Villistas nearby. There, Pershing developed plans for the second phase of the operation. Three independent cavalry columns would move south on parallel routes between the eastern slopes of the mountains and the Santa Maria River. Columns were mutually supporting and intended to squeeze Villa's raiders between them.

Pershing's main supply base was at Columbus, but getting supplies to Colonia Dublan was challenging without the railroad—cavalry columns relied on local purchases and foraging. Mexicans were reluctant to accept receipts, basically I.O.U.s, as it took months to file and receive payments. Worse, most inhabitants on Villa's home turf were sympathetic with him and his cause. They barely tolerated American presence.

Pershing had problems finding reliable guides. The best were Americans living in the south, employed by American-owned mining, ranching, or agricultural businesses. Apache scouts were politically neutral, highly skilled, and generally reliable. Mexican guides were most knowledgeable but couldn't be trusted. Funston authorized using Americans or Apaches for the duration of the expedition to avoid long-term contract pay issues.

§

Colonel Dodd, commanding the 7th Cavalry, discovered Villa was in Guerrero and reacted quickly. He led troopers toward the small town nestled in a river valley, unsure the report was reliable. When his scouts reported seeing Villistas there, he positioned a squadron to cover from high hills, while running another up the valley. The mounted column received fire, dismounted, and returned it. Shooters covered Villa's escape as he rode in the opposite direction under a deceptive Mexican flag. Most escaped but those covering were not so lucky—thirty killed, including a general. Dodd learned from interrogations that Villa suffered from a leg wound before riding out with one hundred fifty men.

The operation was partially successful because Dodd acted promptly and wisely. During that engagement the 10th Cavalry, Buffalo Soldiers, hurried toward Guerrero to support the 7th. When they drew fire from Aguas Calienta, Major Charles Young raised his saber and led a cavalry charge at the enemy. The ambush party fled before they reached them and again Villa escaped, but more of his men were killed. The message was clear—cavalry was there and pressure was on.

§

Scout-and-disrupt operations continued as Pershing and Funston concentrated on logistics. Without Mexican railroads, motor transport was essential for bulk supplies. Funston wired Washington about it and over six hundred trucks were purchased for resupply. Trucks required maintenance, and a large facility was set up in Columbus, New Mexico, but in the field, mechanics and drivers maintained in sun and dust. Truck convoys were strained by the number of trucks, distance, volume of supplies, and conditions of roads, while unused railroad tracks were idle.

The fledgling air service raised high hopes in Washington, but disappointed on the expedition. Captain Benjamin Foulois brought the small air section of eight areoplanes from San Antonio to Columbus, but they were older and less capable than those in Europe or even Mexico. Foulois was a student under Orville Wright and was aware of the deficiencies. The operational flight leg for the JN-3 Jennies was only fifty miles, and these were so dilapidated Fuolois and Funston decided to disassemble them and truck them five hundred twenty miles, a distance too unsafe to fly. When reassembled and deployed none made it to their initial destination on time—one crashed, one developed engine trouble, and the others made it only part way before landing or turning back.

Aeroplanes also disappointed in their reconnaissance role. The first mission called for two Jennies to pinpoint cavalry moving south, following the railroad tracks of the Mexican Northwestern. While trying to cross Cumbre Pass, the ninety-horsepower planes were driven down to treetops by down drafts, forcing them back to base. Foulois prepared a lengthy justification for totally re-equipping the squadron with two planes each from Martin, Curtiss, Sturtevant, and Thomas and Sloane, with stronger engines and spare parts. Those would be used for mission-related field tests to determine the most effective machines. Pershing forwarded the request to Funston, who approved it and forwarded it with his endorsement to Washington. Meanwhile, pilots spoke to correspondent Bryon Utecht of the *New York World*. His published account exposed the risk to pilot's lives with inadequate equipment. That article landed hard in Washington and precipitated a letter from Secretary of War Baker to Funston. Pershing's inspector general dug into Fuolois' details. The report was not discredited for accuracy, but because it wasn't cleared by censors. Utecht was thrown out of Mexico, but that didn't change the facts. Another report by Frank Elser of the *New York Times* reconfirmed it.

Yet it didn't end there. Pershing informed Funston several planes were grounded for mechanical problems, others too underpowered to cross high mountains. Two planes crashed. Serviceable aeroplanes were only used to drop written messages from Pershing to his cavalry commanders.

Funston needed aeroplanes to patrol the long Mexican border as those troops were thinned by the expedition. First Lieutenants T. Dewmilling, Byron Jones and eight enlisted men with an aeroplane from the army aviation school in San Diego were ordered to Brownsville for aerial patrolling. They took to the air and regularly drew fire from across the border. Funston called for more planes and by March of 1916, the Aero Club of America placed nineteen aviators, trained at their expense, at the disposal of the War Department.

As Pershing's troops huddled in their base camp at Colonia Dublan a strong gale swept over the camp. Frank Elser wrote, "doughboys are lying flat on their bellies in their dog tents. They are seeking shelter from the sand driven before a north wind of 60-miles-an-hour. It is mingled with snow now, and it cuts like a knife, filling the eyes and hair and mouth, filtering through the clothing and into boots and shoes. Even the horses are suffering.... Pershing's headquarters, a snarl of brown tents and wagons and horses and dirty men, under the cottonwoods which line the river's bank. Every man who has goggles...is wearing them, and over the mouth he had tied a handkerchief, after the manner of a cowboy. ... Any and everybody is covered with sand and grit. The food is full of it. Yet everybody is happy. Their only complaint...is that Colonel Dodd's men will kill or capture Villa before they have a go at him."

With communications strained, cavalry units were exhausted and without support. Pershing decided to replace them with fresh troops. The telegraph was unreliable in the field and aeroplanes ineffective, so he established a forward command post at San Geronimo and traveled by automobile to personally issue orders to them. He traveled with a convoy of three automobiles, his aide George Patton, and armed security guards.

Railroads were still needed to keep Pershing's force supplied. Arrangements were finally made for safe passage on the Mexico-Northwestern and clearances arranged. Funston held up the first shipment for a conference between Brigadier General George Bell, commander at El Paso, with Mexican General Gabriel Gavira in Juarez and Andreas Garcia, Mexican Consul at El Paso. Funston wanted to use the rails, but wanted to avoid a trap and loss of supplies and lives. He continued rolling the trucks while a test-run was formulated for the trains. Taylor Brothers, a local commission shipper, loaded seven cars with supplies marked for Mormon merchants in Colonia Dublan. The train arrived without problems and the disguised goods were welcomed by Pershing's troops. Subsequent runs were then organized, heavy with oats, corn, and alfalfa to feed horses that were feeding on prairie grass for fodder.

Supply problems were worrisome and train runs went a long way to solving that. Now payrolls for American troops and Mexican silver for Pershing to make local purchases got through safely, along with fresh bread from field bakeries, candy, tobacco, and other staples, including mail from home. Funston reported another success—aviators made a three hundred fifty miles sustained flight from Columbus, New Mexico, to Pershing's forward flight strip near Colonia Dublan.

By now, all but seven United States-based regiments were committed to Funston's missions; the nation had no strategic reserves left.

§

Pershing sent Major Tompkins and the 13th Cavalry forward, protected by the 10th Cavalry, and shifted his forward headquarters to Satevo, three hundred miles into Mexico. Major Tompkins met a Carranzista captain who offered to have a guide lead his troops into Parral, a town of twenty thousand, where they hoped to obtain provisions from General Lozano. Things started wrong when the guide failed to show. Tompkins rode into town and found Lozano, who was not cooperative. Meanwhile, an unruly crowd gathered in the streets, shouting insults until Lozano insisted he lead Tompkins' troops to a place outside of town to wait for provisions. Tompkins didn't like the site—surrounded by hills and indefensible. He ordered his troops to higher ground—too late! Mexican regulars already occupied surrounding elevations, boxing in the cavalrymen while the angry mob from town followed and began shooting at the rear of the column.

Tompkins ordered his troops to positions protected from civilians firing, but Mexican regulars in the hills began sniping—shooting fish in a barrel. The cavalrymen took casualties, one killed instantly. Tompkins shouted to mount for a breakout. Mexican cavalry shadowed them, so he dropped off twenty cavalrymen for an ambush. Forty Mexicans were killed within minutes, the others routed. They defended until the 10th Cavalry arrived to reinforce, followed by the 11th and 7th Cavalry, spoiling to fight. They had side-stepped Mexicans for far too long and were eager to engage.

Federales were now involved and couldn't be trusted. Communications were so unreliable that word of this incident didn't reach Pershing for two days, prompting him to move his command post to Santa Cruz, leaving Colonel Cabell, in Colonia Dublan to retain contact with Funston.

Funston received no new instructions from the War Department but had authority to use judgment in any situation, even committing nineteen thousand troops along the border. Yet he couldn't leave the border unprotected. He telegraphed Washington about the Parral fight, concluding Carranza's *federales* were hostile. He was convinced Dodd and the 7th Cavalry would have captured Villa at Guerrero except for deceit. He then warned *federales* were moving north to cut off Pershing—already at outer limits of supply and reinforcements. Pershing wanted to seize all of Chihuahua and all railroads. Funston agreed. General Scott passed this to

Secretary Baker and President Wilson, adding the entire National Guard should be mobilized.

§

Wilson and Baker were shocked, believing this meant all-out war with Mexico. Wilson suggested a meeting of Scott and Funston in San Antonio to straighten this out. Scott packed bags and rode the rails to the torpid climate of Fort Sam Houston, happy to leave the rarified atmosphere of Washington. He arrived on a night train and was met by Funston; the two adjourned immediately to Fort Sam Houston to confer. On neutral ground between Pershing's tactical expedition and Washington's highly charged political machinations, Scott and Funston calmly reviewed what had transpired, current intelligence, and the future. Scott telegraphed his conclusions to Secretary of War Baker with three options. First was to turn Pershing loose to take over the railroads, but acknowledged this wouldn't result in the capture of Villa. Second was concentrate Pershing's forces further north, nearer water and forage, and protect the Mormons at Colonia Dublan. Last was to withdraw altogether. He recommended the second option—concentrate further north.

While they talked, Scott complained about waiting until 0300 for Funston's report on the Parral incident. Funston wasn't sympathetic: "I stayed up all night, too; not one night, but many. I called for soldiers and I got only men, thousands and thousands of them, but not armies. They had to be put into brigades and divisions and regiments one day, and unscrambled and put together on paper the next day as a new batch came in equipped and trained, and some of them had to be petted, but we didn't do much of that. I didn't stay up to hear the news. I stayed up with a tremendous job of getting armies down where something would happen to them; or with luck, where something would happen to the other side."

While the telegram about Parral was on the wires, Dodd's 7th Cavalry was engaged with Villistas again, on the far side of the Sierras near the squalid town of Tomochic in a battle that left two troopers and thirty Villistas killed, twenty-five wounded. Meanwhile in Washington, a meeting was arranged between the Mexican Minister of War, General Obregon, with Scott and Funston, seeking a solution short of all-out war.

TWENTY ONE

Eda Funston was beside her husband in San Antonio from the beginning and had organized two thousand women as American Red Cross volunteers making bandages and clothing for soldiers involved in the intervention in Mexico and along the southern border. She also started other branches across the southwest. She was absorbed with all this and the children when she received a telegram in April of 1916 that her father had been hit by an automobile in Oakland and was seriously injured. The seventy-year old professor of music suffered from a fractured right hip and shoulder and was confined to the hospital for some time. She started making plans to go to him and her mother, taking the children with her.

Meanwhile, Funston had Pershing pull back to Colonia Dublan to patrol while waiting for a diplomatic solution. Pershing's forward camp was an enormous military facility, a railhead with supplies coming in by trains and motor convoys. Local cantinas were open all night serving Mexican beer, restaurants served meals, and Villa's spies intermingled with the population while enjoying western cowboy movies with Pershing's soldiers. Officially sanctioned bordellos were inspected for cleanliness and disease prevention, and participants required to take contraceptives, keeping infectious disease rate low. Pershing kept troops busy with training and sports, as well as routine security patrols and other duties. Meanwhile, Colonel Dodd kept the 7th Cavalry constantly prowling and ran into serious engagements with Villa's bands.

While Pershing consolidated in Mexico's interior, Funston kept vigil over border security. Efforts continued in Washington to convince Carranza to agree to a meeting between General Scott and Minister of Defense Obregon. Carranza didn't want this meeting, but permitted Obregon to travel to Juarez-El Paso for the first conference. Obregon sent word to the American consulate that he was available to meet with General Scott at the Hotel Aguana.

§

Scott and Funston were still conferring in San Antonio when word of the first meeting with Obregon reached them at Funston's headquarters. They left together by train for El Paso and asked Obregon to arrange the meeting. He set it for that afternoon in a dreary, gray concrete customs building at the Mexican end of the bridge connecting El Paso and Juarez. Wilson agreed Funston should also attend, as Obregon would bring an ensemble of officers and Juan Amador from the Mexican foreign affairs ministry—all trailed by the Mexican press. Wilson provided Scott with several diplomatic talking points but any request to completely withdraw American forces was to be referred to Washington—Wilson's only bargaining chip with Carranza.

Obregon followed his talking points and demanded a date for withdrawal. Funston exploded! His reaction came with salty profanity. Mexican reporters clustered nearby and watched and heard through windows as Funston cursed, waving his fist near the chin of the one-armed Obregon. He finally settled down and ordered lemonade brought in so the rest of the meeting went more smoothly. But reporter's interpretations of Obregon's demand and Funston's reaction were broadcast throughout Mexico. The agenda was mired, so Scott invited Obregon to dine in Funston's train car parked on a side track in the El Paso train yard. By crossing the border, they escaped the hovering press and talked until late. Funston, however, realized he shouldn't attend these diplomatic exchanges. Later, when he was chided for threatening the one-armed general, he smiled and said: "I didn't take advantage of Senõr Obregon. I shook only one fist!"

Despite his outburst, or because of it, the dinner meeting between Scott and Obregon ended amicably, although deadlocked and needing fresh political instructions. Before Scott and Obregon parted, they agreed to meet again after instructions were received from capitals. Wilson instructed Scott to tell Obregon forces would be withdrawn only with assured safety on the border. This was subject to interpretation, affording wiggle room.

While Scott waited for Obregon to signal another meeting, Funston received a disturbing report from Colonel W.S. Scott in Douglas, Arizona. An informant from Sonora had relayed that the Mexican army near Agua Prieta was preparing to cut Pershing's line of communications and isolate his troops for an attack at the end of the Obregon-Scott conference if Americans weren't withdrawn. Scott received another report ordering

Mexicans to "crush" American forces. Pershing forwarded a third report to Funston detailing several collective field summaries of Mexican intentions to disrupt his expedition. Funston and Scott took these reports seriously.

Pershing was still angry about double-dealing by the Mexicans and the precarious situation of his scattered cavalry detachments and Funston also worried about them and others on the border. Pershing had moved north but cavalry columns patrolled further south. Cavalry units were mutually supportive, but if exposed lines of communications between Columbus and Colonia Dublan were threatened the entire expedition would be isolated and Pershing would have to fight his way out—or Funston would initiate an invasion to rescue them.

Scott wired Wilson that he expected another ultimatum about withdrawal at the next meeting with Obregon. Wilson replied that the U. S. would not unilaterally withdraw, but advised him to inform Obregon that Pershing would pull farther north to an unspecified place to protect the border and his troops until the danger of raids diminished. Wilson insisted Scott give no excuse for a Mexican attack, wrecking hopes for a peaceful resolution. Obregon signaled Scott that another meeting could be set in El Paso.

Scott knew Mr. A.J. McQuatters, vice president of the Alvarado Mining Company in Mexico near Parral. McQuatters had a vested business interest in the success of Scott's meeting with Obregon, so he rented a large room at the Paso del Norte Hotel and arranged for them to meet there. Funston was busy with measures to protect his and Pershing's forces, a good excuse not to attend. Obregon left his officers behind and managed to shake the Mexican press on the American side. But American correspondents caught wind of the meeting and swarmed the city. Scott exited his train car and sauntered away from the hotel, gazing into store windows as he walked casually then jumped into a laundry truck that delivered him to the hotel. Yet, twenty-seven reporters beat him there and he elbowed past to get in.

They met behind closed doors for twelve hours with one interpreter. Scott used the informality of lunch to privately warn Obregon—if they didn't find agreement at this meeting, and if there was any aggression toward Pershing's expedition, he should expect a full-scale invasion! With such incentive, they found common ground by midnight. Scott agreed to begin a gradual withdrawal immediately—in fact, already begun by Pershing's consolidation further north. Obregon agreed to end preparations to cut Pershing's lines and actively pursue bandits threatening the border. Wilson agreed with this but Carranza was unwilling without a set date for withdrawal. The generals' agreement never reached a diplomatic solution but did end military confrontation.

Funston still called for more troops at the border, but Wilson was reluctant to send them, fearing war. Scott argued the opposite—failure to reinforce the border would tempt Mexicans to send more troops, exposing border towns to more raids. Wilson conceded. Initial reinforcements came from local militia in border states. With difficulty, enough men were rounded up by house-to-house door-knocking to place fifty thousand more at Nogales, Arizona, and another fifty thousand at El Paso and Brownsville, Texas. Their appearance quieted citizens' calls for invasion.

Scott saw that Funston and his staff were overextended in distance, time, communications, and span of control for one hundred fifty thousand troops. Funston was swamped with far more details than he could manage in the twenty-hour days he was working. Particulars of organizing, equipping, moving, emplacing, training, maintaining, and fighting the largest army the United States had fielded since the Civil War was enormous. Every commander and staff, the War Department, and civil authority operated on one rule—"Put it up to Fred"—and almost every decision was put before him for resolution--every task fell back on his small, but strong, shoulders.

§

An active threat along the Rio Grande reemerged when eighty Mexican raiders crossed at Glen Springs, Texas. They attacked a small detachment of the 14th Cavalry and rode into town to steal supplies, kidnapping the store owner and his young son, and then vanished across the river, leaving dead and wounded Americans behind. It took two full days for the news to reach Funston in El Paso. Funston immediately ordered troops from the 8th and 14th Cavalry, under Major George Langhorne, to pursue the perpetrators. Two more days were required for Langhorne's mini-punitive expedition to reach Glen Springs and pick up the trail. Langhorne led the way driving his personal Cadillac ahead of the horse cavalry. He was joined by another column under Frederick Sibley to travel one hundred miles deep into Mexico. Langhorne used the same tactics with fast-moving cavalry patrols to sweep the area for two weeks. They ran down many of the raiders, recovered some stolen goods, and safely rescued the captives.

Pershing's dispatches to Funston reflected hostile activity from along the border and deep within Mexican territory every day. When quizzed by reporters about the trouble, Funston said Pershing could take care of himself—"not to worry." But Funston was worried for the scattered cavalry detachments. The supply line was still fragile, and patrols could be picked off one at a time. Mexican *federales* were increasing in the area. Funston instructed Pershing to consolidate at Colonia Dublan. Pershing protested. They compromised by keeping a headquarters at Namiquipa and active patrolling continued.

Funston advised Scott if anything started, he wanted "those cusses to be indisputably in the wrong," because if fighting breaks out between Pershing's force and Carranza troops "the fat is in the fire." He believed they were in "more imminent danger of a rupture…than since the turmoil began." He reined in General James Parker in Brownsville, who was anxious to strike. He told him to forget about offensive operations and "keep in mind the job already laid out which God knows is big enough." Logistics and troops available would not support such operations even if the political will was there. He advised him those were the "meanest and worst" in the country. He admitted he was only pretending to patrol the border with so few available. Be content with what we know we can do.

Funston knew Carranza was at fault for the unsettled situation and stressed to Washington that more troops were needed to deal with it. Funston and Scott sent a joint telegram saying they expected more attacks, their lines were too thin and weak, and they needed one hundred fifty thousand additional troops, including the militias of Texas, New Mexico, and Arizona. This time Wilson called up the National Guard, ordering forty-five hundred from border states and another four thousand regulars to reinforce Funston's efforts. But raids continued. Finally, Wilson federalized the entire National Guard and dispatched them to the border.

Funston prepared to receive the new troops and train them. Some would be used on the border, but he was also ordered to train new regiments, including four new regiments of infantry, two of cavalry, two of engineers, and two of field artillery—regular army units to meet requirements of the national defense act. Three infantry regiments, one of artillery, and three of engineers were for overseas service in the Philippines, Hawaii, and the Canal Zone. The others would remain with him on the border.

Funston recommended using increased troops to push across the border and establish a buffer zone. Washington again prohibited anything beyond hot pursuit. Concentrations north of the border, Pershing's operations deep in Mexico, mini-expeditions in hot pursuit, and beefed up presence on the border, along with Carranza's belated crackdown settled the situation.

§

Fred took some quiet time to go to Medina dam or along the Salado River in the late afternoons with other officers to fish, relax, and soak in as much breeze off the lake as possible. Frequently he took Freddie and Barbara along. Eda and Fred with his aides motored to New Braunsfels for a cooling swim party at Landa Park, and stayed for supper, returning late in the evening. Weather in south Texas was extremely hot and humid and taking a heavy toll on Eda and little Elizabeth. They discussed taking little Betsy to a more favorable climate—California. Fred needed his family close although he was gone far too often.

Eda prepared to return to San Francisco for the summer because of the effects of the heat on the baby. Fred informed Scott in a personal note that Betsy has been "giving us a terrible fright by a violent attack of summer complaint" and that he would send his whole family to San Francisco as soon as the baby was able to travel. "I look forward with dread to another long summer in this hot place all alone." The trip was delayed.

Pershing's troops were consolidating but still caught up in occasional hostile incidents. Horses had been subsisting on prairie grass without more nourishing fodder. Pershing's aide, Lieutenant George Patton, set out in an automobile with armed escorts to purchase feed for horses. As he approached a possible source near Rubio he was fired on from a ranch house. In the fire fight that ensued, three Villistas were killed, two by Patton with his pistol. He strapped the bodies to the hood of his automobile like big game, and returned to headquarters with his trophies for identification. One turned out to be Julio Cardenas, one of Villa's top generals. Newspaper reporters at Colonia Dublan made it a big story, much to the satisfaction and future prospects of George Patton.

§

A serious incident nearly brought the countries back to the brink of war. Pershing got reports of ten thousand Mexican troops concentrating near Ahumada, eighty miles from his forward headquarters. He sent a troop of the 10th Cavalry, Buffalo Soldiers, under Captain Charles Boyd, to reconnoiter. Pershing personally briefed Boyd his mission was to gather information only, not fight. He warned to avoid surprise, shun a fight, but if attacked use judgment. He stressed avoiding Mexican troops, and sent similar orders to Captain Lewis Morey, commanding another troop of the 10th Cavalry. The two troops linked up ten miles east of Carrizal. The combined force was understrength with eighty men and three officers between them. Boyd was senior so assumed overall command. He intended to ride straight through Carrizal, the most direct route to Ahumada. Morey disagreed, fearing a bad outcome in the town, and tried to convince him otherwise. Boyd proceeded directly.

As they approached the town, several hundred Mexican soldiers blocked their route. Boyd put troopers in defensive posture and sent Lemuel Spillsbury, an American guide, to request permission to pass. Spillsbury returned with General Felix Gomez, who reiterated orders to turn back. Spillsbury again urged Boyd go around, but Boyd ordered the troopers to walk straight through the town in two columns, horses on halters.

They walked only a hundred yards before Mexicans opened fire. Mexican cavalry struck their rear and horses scattered. Outnumbered, buffalo soldiers broke and scattered in small groups. All officers but Morey were dead, ten soldiers killed and twenty-three captured—more than half the small force. Carrizal was an unmitigated disaster, but the Mexicans were satisfied and didn't pursue survivors. Most made their way back to Colonia Dublan after several days' on foot. Pershing was out of communication with the cavalry but hadn't expected trouble. His concern heightened as he pieced together information from straggling survivors.

Mexican newspapers hailed the encounter at Carrizal as a great victory for the *federales*. Funston got word of it in San Antonio through Mexican newspapers before Pershing found out. He fired a scathing telegram to Pershing about the disaster, and especially his lack of communications, reiterating instructions about prompt reporting. Scorching diplomatic ultimatums broke out between capitals and anti-American demonstrations flared in Mexican cities. Scott warned Funston to prepare for all-out war.

Washington warned Funston's large army along the border to prepare to seize all international bridges, occupy border towns, push Mexican *federales* out, and reinforce Pershing with another ten thousand troops. He ordered Pershing to consolidate at Colonia Dublan and notified General George Bell to prepare to push a reinforcing column toward Pershing. Funston was also directed to consider another contingency plan—a naval feint threatening Vera Cruz and Tampico to draw Mexican forces toward the coast to facilitate his large-scale attack to seize and hold northern Mexico. This would be intended to force a diplomatic settlement.

War seemed imminent. Pershing pieced bits of information combined with Captain Morey's report and understood the incident at Carrizal was a military disaster but misreading it had almost led to war. Pershing's follow-up report with a more accurate accounting of Boyd's errors put invasion preparations on hold. Wilson found a proposal more to his liking—a joint Mexican-American peace commission. American prisoners captured at Carrizal were released by the Mexicans at El Paso as an act of good faith and negotiations began anew. Meetings of the joint commission accomplished nothing but diffused the crisis and avoided war.

With the invasion on hold, Pershing's troops pulled in their claws. The regular soldier's life, even in Colonia Dublan, took on a routine rhythm through the remainder of 1916 and into 1917. Washington turned more attention to Europe, but developments along the border would have a significant bearing on how the United States would eventually fight the Great World War.

Pancho Villa emerged again when he recovered from his leg wound, gathering a few hundred followers for a final campaign. First, he attacked a small garrison at Satevo, routing the *federales*. Then he entered Chihuahua City, although several thousand Mexican troops were stationed there. Villa freed hundreds of prisoners and persuaded a thousand Mexican soldiers to join him. For twenty-four hours he ruled the town, captured all the artillery and sixteen vehicles loaded with ammunition and small arms. He used his booty to conduct other raids within Mexico. Pershing notified Funston that Villa seemed to have regained complete control of the Mexican state. Funston recommended to Washington to implement the plan to have Pershing and Bell take Chihuahua City. But, Wilson was in a wait-and-see mode, hoping for the joint commission to find a way out. Funston, Pershing, and Bell had to wait it out, too.

Villa was emboldened and attacked the federal garrison in Chihuahua City again. But this time, Mexicans were prepared and waged five days of urban warfare before Villa took control. Juarez was expected to be the next target and General Bell grew anxious. Funston lobbied Washington to crush Villa once and for all. Again, Wilson refused. But by the end of 1916, *federales* regained control of Chihuahua City and Villa's influence began withering.

§

During this crisis, practically everything the army did was cleared with Funston. He communicated regularly with the adjutant general between mid-1915 and early 1916, critiquing proposals to improve the national military establishment. This was aimed at building a vast army for the war in Europe. Funston's comments were drawn from his vast experience with all the combat arms and services in battle and in training officers and men.

Meanwhile, tensions at the border were high and calls from Arizonans to arm citizens were deflected by the army as that could spiral out of control. General Scott advised Funston he was telling Arizonans he had no arms to give and no legal authority to do it. But, he actually bounced the decision to Funston, informing him that he would "simply send them down to you to do what you think is right."

Two Kansas infantry regiments were transferred there to be incorporated into the newly formed 12th Division. They were the first large body of troops to be moved by motor march instead of on foot or by rail. The move required one hundred thirty-two vehicles over two days to transport them one hundred eighty miles. Troops sat on planks spanning the sideboards as trucks bounced hard on rutted roads and they used blanket rolls as seat cushions. Funston was on hand for their arrival in San Antonio, pleased to meet regiments holding the lineage of his old 20th

Kansas. But he allowed no rest and put them on a road march from San Antonio to Austin and back on foot. They were allowed only one canteen of water per day on the march, all part of their training and toughening up.

In 1914, the fighting strength of the U.S. Army was just under three thousand officers and fifty-one thousand enlisted, almost half in overseas stations. The National Defense Act of 1916 was stimulated by preparation for possible involvement in World War I. Secretary of War Garrison recommended in 1915 that the standing army be increased to 141,843 officers and men. This would be supplemented by four hundred thousand more reserves. He also recommended support to the states for militias. Wilson took the idea to Congress and two bills were developed and debated. The National Defense Act of 1916 resulted.

A more realistic defense policy was promising and the vast army responding to the emergency on the southern border provided a means to validate it. Trouble with Mexico made implementation of the National Defense Act of 1916 more than just a planning exercise. The General Staff needed to activate the larger forces, General Funston would have to receive the troops, organize, supply, and train them for action, field test new equipment, all the while implementing crisis management on the border as the new army organization was still emerging. That put Frederick Funston where he wanted to be—at the center of the action.

The United States Army benefited from border trouble by shaking out problems and innovations in many categories, especially supply and transportation. At the beginning of the crisis the entire quartermaster corps had only one hundred eighty-five officers with some of those overseas. Complex demands for procuring, storing, transporting, distributing, and repairing fell to this small corps. This led to confusion, delays, and forced Pershing's expedition to rely primarily on local procurements. Denial of Mexican rail lines complicated long range resupply, forcing reliance on horses, pack mules, and trucks.

Along with supply, modernization of transportation was essential to move troops and supplies. The army developed motor vehicles as a means of military transport since the first army truck was purchased in 1906. When Funston and Pershing organized the expedition into Mexico in 1916, there were still only fifty-six automobiles and one hundred five trucks in the inventory, only sixteen in the Southern Department. When Funston advised the War Department that mules and horses were inadequate to support Pershing, five hundred eighty-eight vehicles were purchased that year. These were shipped to the border, including fifty-seven tankers for water and fuel, ten shop trucks, six wreckers, seventy-five automobiles, sixty-one motorcycles, eight tractors for road repairs and miscellaneous related equipment. But trucks arrived in every conceivable state of readiness, some not even assembled. In the beginning there were no garages—assembly and repairs done in the open. The Jeffrey Truck Company provided mechanics and the Locomotive Company a supervisor. Civilian drivers and mechanics assisted soldiers and taught the military the ins-and-outs of automation, sometimes even driving and repairing vehicles deep inside Mexico. By mid-1916, Funston had a motor transport division with ten companies of twenty-seven one-ton-capacity trucks and six companies with twenty-eight three-ton-capacity trucks. Twelve companies operated along the border and lines of communications supporting Pershing.

Before the end of the crisis, regimental and post dispensaries were established and large hospitals set up in Brownsville, San Antonio, and El Paso in Texas and in Douglas, Arizona. The nation's first hospital train operated with cars designed by the Pullman Corporation in Chicago. The ten-car medical train could care for seventy-six bed-ridden patients and one hundred twenty ambulatory. It included a kitchen car, one for medical staff living quarters, one for operating and recovery, seven for treatment and patient recovery. The staff of three medical officers, twenty-five corpsmen, and seven nurses treated wounded or sick soldiers along the broad front.

Due to horrible roads in Mexico, army engineers trained on-the-job in maintenance and construction to support the load of continuous truck traffic. Wheels of heavily loaded supply convoys cut deep ruts in the dust and sank into mud when it rained. Engineers started with virtually no experience in this work but in a year and a half were capable of difficult road improvement tasks that lay ahead in the muddy ruts of France.

The punitive expedition found the aeroplanes provided were unable to perform reconnaissance effectively and were not efficient as conveyers of messages and orders. They were already old and needed replacing, and the mission proved better and more capable planes were needed. Aviator training also needed to be revamped and increased.

The War Department used Funston's field army to field test new equipment and emerging concepts and organizations, and Funston was tireless in that. In 1916, thirteen types of motor trucks from eight manufacturers were tested under field conditions resulting in a standardized model by 1917. Rolling field kitchens were tested to furnish hot soup and other items to troops on the move, resulting in a basis of issue of one kitchen per company, troop, or battery in 1917. Emergency rations were given the taste test by soldiers in the field, and passed. Operations in Mexico proved the regulation army shoe inadequate and too light to hold under difficult conditions. Because of this learning experience, those doughboys that deployed to France wore more satisfactory foot-wear, and had better equipment and medical care than they would have otherwise.

Border operations and the long-range expedition modernized the Signal Corps. By the end of 1916, the corps had six hundred seventy-seven miles of buzzer and telegraph lines along the border, six hundred forty-two miles of telephone lines, and nineteen radio stations. Lines were strung to Pershing's advanced command post at Colonia Dublan and connections within his command. Appropriations for new equipment allowed the corps to negotiate with telegraph and telephone companies for prototypes, and with manufacturers and educational institutions for training. Signal supplies went forward to meet needs and modernized at the same time.

New equipment, tactics, and techniques were field tested and proven, and officers and soldiers gained valuable experience. Exercise of an expansive mobilization drill eliminated many unforeseen problems in organizations while preparing the country for massive mobilization. Mobilization demonstrated deficiencies in strategic cross-country transportation, especially trains, and the need for supply depots carefully located and decentralized. The General Staff developed ways to prioritize units and procure transportation assets to move them efficiently coast-to-coast and between cities and borders, much like paper exercises run at Fort Leavenworth schools ten years before.

Along the sprawling Mexican border and deep inside the country, units patrolled, drilled, and completed organizations and re-organizations while learning about new equipment and camp life on the front lines. Additional camps, depots, and hospitals sprang up all over the southwest, centralized for training and supporting a modern army while replacing or retrofitting remote camps and outposts of the Indian wars. Concentrating troops along the border and in camps such as Colonia Dublan afforded commanders like Funston, Pershing, and others of divisions, brigades, and regiments opportunities for large unit deployments in real time. The differences between working out solutions on paper at service schools and realities of the field were vivid. As troops began arriving, Funston put in motion rigorous training for all regular army and National Guard troops on the border, and Pershing did the same inside Mexico. Emphasis was on moving, shooting, and communicating at brigade and division level, along with understanding better the principles of war.

Funston supervised and supported Pershing's punitive expedition while maintaining security along the entire length of the border from the Gulf of Mexico to California. Pershing got the headlines, but Funston pioneered a future pattern of high level military command and mobilization as one hundred fifty thousand National Guardsmen were federalized. He modeled leadership and mentoring to several subordinates who would prove critical leaders in the future, including General "Black Jack" Pershing, Captain Douglas MacArthur, Lieutenants George Patton and Dwight Eisenhower, and many brigade and division commanders.

Since the occupation of Vera Cruz and duty along the southern border, Funston had worked tirelessly with little time to rest. He had become overweight at one hundred twenty pounds on his small frame, his reddish-brown hair and beard flecked with grey. But he remained a firebrand; only the wrinkles around twinkling eyes divulged the truth that a boy still lived inside that well-worn and badly abused body. In his office at Fort Sam Houston, he sat erect at his desk, piled high with papers awaiting decisions. When he was excited or angry, he rose from behind the stacks of work and seemed larger, fiery enough to command the armies of the world. Due to the heavy work load, Funston restricted access of reporters to scheduled conferences and denied subordinate officers at his headquarters permission to talk to the "vultures." But L.V.B Rucker, an International News Service correspondent who circled Southern Division for a story, said of him "no man in public life is better liked by newspaper men than General Funston. They have learned to trust, as well as like, the general."

"Commanding a compact, trained army of this size would not be so difficult," Funston said on one of his inspection trips. "But commanding these troops from forty or more states, of trying to combine them into an effective fighting force, of training 'untrained' men, of equipping 'unequipped' men, of piecing units into regiments and brigades and divisions right under the shadow of trouble, is a tremendous job, more so because it must be done in haste and because we are dealing with inexperience among one hundred thousand of these troops."

"Every week I have to do the same work over and over. As units come to the border, and they are withdrawn, everything has to be rearranged again, and this rearrangement is difficult because of the lack of adequate railroad facilities for the handling of large forces on the border." When he was asked questions about government policies from Washington, Funston replied, "My business is to fight and not to talk. The officials and the politicians do the talking, and when they get through with that and give us orders to fight, we'll fight."

§

On October, 1916, a Saturday, Funston accompanied Mr. Tillingharst, a golf course architect, to look over the new golf course for Fort Sam Houston. That was Captain Ball's last day as aide and he was replaced by Captain Fitzhugh Lee, son of the Civil War general and American counsel who hustled Funston out of Cuba.

In early January 1917, Funston left San Antonio in a special car on the Southern Pacific railroad, traveling with his staff to visit border posts west of San Antonio. He made stops in El Paso, Douglas, Yuma, and Tucson. In addition to the inspection tour, he was accompanying Eda and the children going home to Oakland, where they would spend some time with Otto Blankart, as the elderly professor was still recovering from having a hip and shoulder fractured when hit by an automobile. "Moving," said Eda "is the hardest duty of an army man's wife. She has to be ready to shift her household from one place to another in perhaps a few days' time. This means that furniture must be sold, some stored away, some shipped to the new home, other kinds selected, trunks packed, and the children outfitted, different kinds of clothing bought and what not. When I was living in San Antonio, Texas, I had the double problem of keeping one home ready in California and another open on the border. And the income of an army man is not so big that this is a simple matter." Then quickly added, "But I wouldn't have changed a single day of my life for anything."

On January 14th, on the return trip, Funston made the journey south from Columbus, New Mexico, to five miles north of Colona Dublan, where he was met by Pershing and his staff. They passed together through an honor guard of infantry and cavalry to Pershing's headquarters, where Funston had dinner with Pershing and staff. Next day, he reviewed the troops before motoring with Pershing further south to visit the most southerly outposts. Shortly after Funston returned to San Antonio, Pershing got orders to begin redeployment out of Mexico.

Men cheered news of going home. None were sorry to be leaving Mexico but they were proud of what they had done despite reporters and historians calling the expedition a "wild goose chase" or a "famous fumble." They knew their assigned mission had been accomplished—to disrupt Villa's band—and he would surely have been captured or killed except for Carranza's interference. A corner was turned on national security and valuable field experience prepared the army for a wider war.

Pershing began his return march with the 24th Infantry leading, followed by 10,690 men, 9,307 horses, 2,030 Mexican refugees, and 197 Mormons. They also brought over twenty Villista prisoners, and 523 Chinese who had taken refuge with Americans. They assembled at Palomas and marched across the border to Columbus on the morning of February 5th. Prisoners were turned over to the New Mexico civil authorities for civil trial but the Chinese posed a problem. It was unlawful to bring them undocumented into the United States. Funston ordered Pershing to send them to his headquarters until he had consent from the Bureau of Immigration to remain. They were employed as cooks and craftsmen.

When the United States declared war on Germany in April 1917, the means and methods of expanding to forty-three divisions to help defeat Germany were in place. While Fred Funston preferred to run down Pancho Villa, as he had Aguinaldo, the nation needed him in a larger role. He was instrumental in commanding a Field Army and preparing General "Black Jack" Pershing for that role. Although Pershing had garnered the headlines leading the punitive expedition, Funston remained America's most valuable general.

TWENTY TWO

Major General Frederick Funston could feel the inexorable pull toward another war in early 1917, this one on the continent of Europe. General Sherman had famously declared "war is hell" and Funston would agree, yet he always marched to the sound of guns and sought trouble wherever it was found. Tensions reached a peak during the late winter of 1917. The army had been in a long-running conflict along the Mexican border and Funston had dispatched an expedition to stop the infamous and bloodthirsty bandit, Pancho Villa. A theater army was mobilized under his command to hold the fragile line along the line in the sand while a major conflict was unfolding in Europe and allies and enemies seemed intent to drag the United States into it despite President Woodrow Wilson's attempts to avoid it. Funston anticipated he would soon be called on again to command, perhaps the American Expeditionary Forces in France.

From his headquarters at Fort Sam Houston, Texas, Funston read news reports about the war, checked cables from Washington, and monitored the progress of Pershing's expedition as the troopers returned home. On February 3rd, 1917, the president severed diplomatic relations with Germany due to unrestrained submarine warfare against allied shipping. On February 5th, Funston privately sought out his physician with complaints about increasing abdomen and chest pains. On February 7th, Pershing reported all his troopers had safely returned to Columbus, New Mexico. Funston's life-long friend, Charles Gleed, the man who had bid him farewell going to Cuba and met him at the docks upon his return, had said of him: "The study of heroism is a task pursued with never-failing interest and enthusiasm. And when a hero is really found, the world is astonished that it has overlooked the man it sought and waited for him to be unveiled by achievement."

War had not been declared, and no official announcement had been made about mobilizing the forces, or who would command American troops. However, Funston was the most experienced field commander in the army and his next duty assignment was anticipated. His sources in Washington had assured him that it was all but decided by President Wilson, Secretary of War Baker, and Chief of Staff Hugh Scott. He would again lead troops who clamored to fight beside "Fighting Fred." This time there would be a vast multitude of them going over there, to the war to end all wars. War was hell—also a daring adventure.

It was late afternoon on February 19th, 1917, when he left his headquarters at Fort Sam Houston. He had just signed the last order returning home the mobilized National Guard units and a telegram to the War Department with his regular report. He rode in his 1915 Cadillac sedan, U.S. No. 11661, type 53, which had been issued new on September 20, 1915. It was well used along the border all during the Mexican campaign by the time he rode to his quarters on the beautiful post.

He poured a Gin Rickey to settle his stomach, agitated by life in the field on a diet unimaginable to most people. His persistent indigestion had returned, a burning that rose high in his chest. The gin would help. He considered Eda, waiting with the children and her injured father in Oakland. A man like this was more at ease in wartime where the danger is greatest, but he missed his family. Eda had stayed close through the fighting in the Philippines, during the trauma of San Francisco's earthquake and fire, this time beside him on the overheated border, all for better or worse. But as this emergency ended, the next was not yet public and he was stranded again in the doldrums between wars. As a fifty-one year-old Major General, he held the highest rank in the army, although still the youngest despite having been passed over twelve times for promotion. He was the army's most combat experienced general, and felt the pains of his many old wounds. That Cuban Mauser round that had pierced his chest and both lungs twenty years before had passed close to his heart, and had been especially painful of late.

Funston's cousin from Emporia, Miss Maude Minrow, was spending the winter in San Antonio with friends. They had spoken on the telephone, agreeing to have dinner later in the week. He was not so interested in the meal, but looked forward to catching up with news of family and friends from Kansas. He told her about his recent enjoyable hunting trip at the ranch of Major Miller, also mayor of Corpus Christi. Captain and Mrs. Fitzhugh Lee had accompanied him on the weekend excursion, hunting on

Saturday and resting on Sunday. He was in good spirits and looked ahead to dinner with his cousin.

He changed into a civilian suit and waited for his driver to pick him up for dinner with friends at a favorite restaurant in San Antonio's luxurious Saint Anthony Hotel. He had worked tirelessly for the past four years and was ready for rest. His only relaxation had been occasional hunting trips, dinners with friends, brief relaxation with family, or fishing with the children. He'd regularly managed only four hours sleep during the crisis. He tried to relax, sipped his gin, considered how tired he felt, how much he missed Eda, and what the future held for him and the army he loved. His short beard was well groomed, shoes shined, creases of his pants as straight as iron rails, but that uneasy feeling that something had been missed stalked him. As he thought again of Eda and their three surviving children, he felt a pang in his chest at the remembrance of young Arthur. Charles Gleed had written, "He likes a low seat in a quiet corner, with an audience of juvenile listeners, to whom he can tell the most wonderful stories in the most wonderful way." He had enjoyed telling his stories to young Arthur, the cruise of the *Dauntless*, long hikes through the wildernesses. He needed time with his family. They'd play together in Alameda County, walk in Golden Gate Park, and Eda would play her violin for him. Nothing was more gratifying than poetry, music, Eda and his children.

His driver and aide, Captain Fitzhugh Lee, arrived and was waiting in the automobile in front of his quarters. He remembered fondly young Lee's father, Confederate General Fitzhugh Lee, who had almost shot him before he spirited him out of Cuba. But it was time to go. Funston enjoyed evenings with friends, but knew he would eat little as he had been battling that confounded indigestion for weeks. Although he had seen his doctor, he had "fought it out alone."

When he reached the hotel with Captain Lee he was greeted by many Texas friends, including Major Miller. It seemed everyone in San Antonio knew the short general on sight. Soldiers and Texans alike had taken to calling him the "little guy." Mexicans called him *chicito diablo*—the "little devil." When a correspondent asked a Texas Ranger captain if Funston was like the small Napoleon, he said, "France never had no general like 'our little man.' ... When they send him after Villa, they'd better send a chaplain and an undertaker." When trouble sprang anywhere in the border region the response was, "send it up to the little man."

When he sat for dinner, Miller ordered a heavy meal for his big Texas appetite. Funston ordered a light one, saying he was on a "straw diet." He fiddled with the food, eating little. During dinner, conversation returned to trouble with Mexico and more disturbing news from France. It was difficult to discuss current events while keeping mum about his expected role. After dinner, Funston stood slowly, feeling the many wounds from having been so seriously sick, shot, and smashed. His body was racked by an assortment of diseases, but nothing could keep him down for long, certainly not a little chest pain.

They strolled into the lobby and were standing talking when little Inez Silverberg, visiting from Des Moines with her parents, came in. Funston stopped to play with her for a few minutes until she ran off to her mother. He was drawn by the sounds of lyrical strings drifting from the grand ballroom. He found a chair to listen to lilting strands of the Blue Danube Waltz, a selection very appropriate for his current mood and probable role as commander of the great American army in Europe. "How beautiful it is," he said to Major Miller.

Suddenly his head sagged back against the chair, his crossed leg dropped to the floor. He groaned slightly. Miller at first thought he was relaxing with the music, then realized something was wrong. He rushed to the desk and summoned an army doctor. His pulse was very slight as three doctors rushed to his side. Captain Lee stood helpless, tears in his eyes, but there was nothing anyone could do. "The heart that had done the work of a hundred years in the life of an ordinary man refused to work longer...."

Fighting Fred Funston had fallen hard, dropped not by the action of any enemy who had tried so hard to kill him, but by a fighting heart worn out far too soon. He had always expected to die a soldier's death on a far-flung battlefield, not listening to the peaceful sounds of music he loved ... and so far, far away from his beloved Eda.

§

In Washington, D.C., Major Douglas MacArthur had night watch for the General Staff at the War Department that night. The General Staff was on alert for more trouble from Mexico or serious aggression by the Germans. His friend, Lieutenant Colonel Peyton March, had corresponding duty in the Adjutant General's office. When the first call came, MacArthur was stunned. While waiting for the confirming telegram he remembered his daring adventures in Vera Cruz while Funston was commanding that expedition, his time under him at Fort Leavenworth, his father's unquestioned admiration for the small general.

Secretary of War Newton Baker was hosting a formal dinner for President and Mrs. Wilson and left word not to be disturbed except for something of critical importance. Just before 2200 hours, Peyton March handed MacArthur the official wire from Colonel Malvern-Hill Barnum, Adjutant General at the Department of the South, official notification that General Funston had died. MacArthur and March agreed the secretary should be informed immediately as this clearly met the test of critical importance— the possible commander of the American field army was down before the first shot was fired. With paper in his hand, MacArthur dreaded disturbing the private party with such news but he was the duty officer and it was his duty to deliver the announcement.

When MacArthur reached Secretary Baker's home, the butler refused to admit him. The dining room opened onto the entrance hall exposing a joyful party filled with lights and laughter, the tinkle of glasses, soft music and happy conversation. MacArthur, never shy, pushed past the butler and attracted the attention of Secretary Baker to report privately what had occurred. But President Wilson saw him first and called out, "Come in, Major, and tell all of us the news. There are no secrets here." Everyone in the room heard the president speak and someone started clapping hands at the anticipation of news from Europe. MacArthur clicked his heels and saluted. "Sir, I regret to report that General Funston has just died!" The room fell instantly silent. MacArthur later remembered, "Had the voice of doom spoken, the result could not have been different. The silence seemed like that of death itself. You could hear your own breathing. Then, I never saw such a scattering of guests in my life. It was a stampede."

The President and Secretary of War adjourned to an adjacent room alone with MacArthur. Their first action was to dictate a sincere message of sympathy to Eda Funston. Then President Wilson asked Secretary Baker, "What now, Newton, who will take the army over?" The Secretary paused a moment then asked MacArthur, "Whom do you think the army would choose, Major?" MacArthur tactfully replied, "I cannot, of course, speak for the army, but for myself the choice would unquestionably be General Pershing." The President starred a moment, and then said quietly, "It would be a good choice."

With one beat of the heart, America was deprived of one of its greatest heroes, an adventurer, soldier, husband and father, and loyal citizen. At the time of his death, Frederick Funston was the best known soldier in the country. But with the United States' entry into World War I in only one month, the great warrior would soon be forgotten. However, his life of adventure and courage, his impact on the army he loved, all of it should long be remembered.

§

Major General Franklin Bell, Arthur MacArthur's chief intelligence officer in the Philippines, friend and admirer of Funston, now commander of the Pacific Division, broke the sad news to Eda Funston at The Presidio, where she waited in temporary quarters with the children for her beloved husband's return. Eda's sister, Mrs. William O. Cullen—Liz—was with her when the distressing news arrived. Eda fell prostrate to the floor in her grief. She was now alone with their thirteen year old Fred junior, eight year old Barbara, and three year old Betsy, as they faced the future without the shining light of their lives. She pulled herself together like a soldier and directed Fred's body be returned to her in San Francisco, not to Arlington. There he would be interred on February 24th, 1917, at the National Cemetery at The Presidio. She wanted her husband laid to rest beside their first-born son, Arthur MacArthur Funston, and always close to her.

Fred had dedicated the account of his two wars in Cuba and the Philippines to young Arthur: "the little boy who in happy days gone by often sat on my knees and, open-eyed and wondering, listened to the story of the cruise of the *Dauntless* and to accounts of midnight rides in the Philippines; but who now sleeps forever ... under the shadow of the flag that his childish heart so loved...."

§

Fred's cousin, Maude Minrow, waited at his quarters at Fort Sam Houston—her phone call with him were the last words any of his family would have. "Tuesday morning Captain Lee sent a car for me and I was there when they brought him home. Flowers kept coming and were perfectly beautiful. He was in full dress uniform, the sash across the front, with white gloves, the major general's sword in the casket, which was entirely covered by a large American flag. He looked as if he could speak. The expression around the eyes as if he had just told a joke and finished laughing." The service was short and simple before he was taken to the Alamo. "He has surely won the Texas people."

§

The nation long held Frederick Funston in awe as a national hero. People across the land were grief stricken as were his widow and surviving children. But before he could go home there were duties to be attended, final salutes to be bestowed. The only religious services in Texas were at his official quarters on Fort Sam Houston. Chaplain Barton Perry read the regular army funeral rites, followed by a rendition of "Lead Kindly Light." A military caisson bore his body from Fort Sam Houston into the center of San Antonio. The procession formed at the commanding general's quarters in the order of police, mounted orderlies, 19th Infantry band, 37th Infantry, 7th Field Artillery, and Alabama Cavalry. The coffin was carried on a caisson followed by his horse, pall bearers, and officers of his staff. Brigadier General Henry Green accompanied the body. Men from the 19th Infantry formed a V-shaped honor guard at the entrance of the old stucco shrine—the Alamo. The coffin was carried inside by six non-commissioned officers. Ten thousand people streamed through the portals of the Alamo to pay their final respects. Funston's popularity with San Antonio's citizens extended to all classes, evidenced by abundant floral offerings. Costly flower arrangements were displayed side-by-side with simple tributes from humble ranchers and workers who stood with heads uncovered, hats in hand.

Fred Funston lay in state at the most sacred shrine in Texas—the first person honored such. This, the ultimate expression of gratitude and respect for his actions in securing Texas and the other southwestern states, as Davy Crockett and Jim Bowie had done before him—now an honored defender of Texas, Arizona and New Mexico. General Pershing, the acting department commander, ordered all flags at army posts within the Department of the South be flown at half-staff until General Funston body passed from his command area.

His mother, Ann, was ill before this news, confined to bed at the home of her daughter, Mrs. Frank Eckdall, Ella, in Emporia, Kansas. She was unable to go to Texas. The Kansas legislature requested an honorary viewing at the State House in Topeka and Eda approved, but the army couldn't work out details in such short order, and disapproved. A special funeral car—the Texas, used by him between border outposts and for the Scott-Obregon meetings—behind a Southern Pacific locomotive departed San Antonio at 2030 hours. Captain Lee and six privates with heavy hearts accompanied his body from San Antonio to the California coast at San Francisco. At El Paso, Major General Pershing met the train at Union Depot with his staff and soldiers to pay final respects with a salute fired by the 5th Artillery. Pershing stood with head bared while the train slowly passed and the colors dipped low. The 22nd Infantry formed double files along both sides of the tracks, the 23rd Infantry band played a funeral dirge, and the 8th Cavalry presented sabers as thousands of citizens stood quietly by, shedding tears. Orderlies entered the Texas and covered the coffin with fresh wreaths from the city of El Paso and the Daughters of the Confederacy. They were met all along the route by military and civilian mourners. On the brink of a larger war, Americans already missed their man of action, the man always marching to the front.

At last, California's golden hills lay ahead where Eda waited. He had declared martial law in San Francisco, dynamited half the city to save the other, and created order when there was none. There were no laws to justify his actions, none except the laws of humanity. And by his actions he captured the hearts of the people of that city, too. Funston would lie quietly in state in San Francisco's rebuilt City Hall rotunda for two days. He was the first person to be honored with such a tribute there. He would finally rest at The Presidio, across the bay from Eda's hometown of Oakland, the city where he had convinced her to marry him only days before he took his regiment to war; and she went with him.

Drizzling rain spattered dress uniforms of army officers and four companies of coastal artillery from Fort Scott as they stood at attention, under arms, while the flower covered coffin was moved from the train through the city. The march of the funeral cortege was headed by a corps of police going to City Hall. All traffic over the two-mile route was blocked while Californians crowded in the rain, remembering the soldier who won their hearts. Veterans of the Civil War and the Philippines wept when Mayor Rolph said, "My fellow citizens, Major General Funston is dead, his mortal remains rest in that casket in the care of the people of San Francisco, who loved him so well. The casket will not be opened. It is the wish of Mrs. Funston that we remember him as he was in the active service of his country." Thirty-two corporals stood vigil all night.

The next day, another procession moved the casket under escort from City Hall to the funeral services at the First Presbyterian Church in Oakland, the Blankart's church. Services were led by the Reverend William Kirk Guthrie. The governor of California and the incoming mayor of San Francisco attended with select friends and family. Fred's mother, Ann Funston, had risen from her sick bed in Kansas to stand with Eda in California. Before the services, Eda Funston had the casket opened for a final, but private, look into the face of her dear husband, Fred.

At noon on February 24th, Major General Frederick Funston was buried in the San Francisco National Cemetery at The Presidio in full dress uniform, on a hill overlooking the bay. Escorts included two regiments of coastal artillery. Major General Franklin Bell and his staff, a company of bluejackets, companies of the United Spanish War Veterans, Loyal Legion, Veterans of Foreign Wars, Grand Army of the Republic, army and navy veterans, and other military and semi-military organizations followed. Judges, city officials, churchmen, and thousands of citizens trudged in the rain, following the procession to the end. Captain Fitzhugh Lee, the general's aide, stood bareheaded beside the grave with close family.

Tributes were read in a storm, the sun only flashing in sync with the final thirteen-gun artillery salute. Secretary of War Newton Baker, Major Generals Leonard Wood, Tasker Bliss, and Hugh Scott, members of Congress and countless others joined those sending homage. President Wilson expressed his sympathy in a telegram to Eda Funston: "I feel confident that I am expressing the feeling of the whole country when I say that we have lost in him an officer of unusual gallantry, capacity, and loyal devotion to the interests of the country." Secretary Baker: "General Funston's death is a loss to the Army and a loss to the country.... His conduct has been that of a soldier, and he has exemplified the high tradition of the American army by his quick, intelligent, and effective action.... His loss to the country is very great." General Scott: "General Funston's unassuming ways endeared him to all with whom he was associated, and his military efficiency earned the confidence of the War Department... Personally, I feel the loss of a great friend."

Flags and banners were massed nearby, the scene encircled by soldiers and sailors. Three volleys of rifle fire, an artillery salute, signaled the end of the man but not the legion. The last sound over Frederick Funston's body was music played by a single bugler—taps. The entire city fell silent for two full minutes—the only sound, falling rain.

§

Lake Merced military reservation, San Francisco's coastal defenses, was renamed Fort Funston in his honor, while the training camp built in 1917 next to Fort Riley in his home state of Kansas was named Camp Funston, a war ship was named for him. Funston's beloved Eda, and his daughter, son, and grandson, who served in the United States Air Force, were later interred beside him. Yet the official obituary in the Army and Navy Journal opened with an insinuation that his inclusion into the general officer ranks didn't receive a cordial welcome. Senior officers had been bypassed by an officer with little military preparation. The editor explained that the "modest, considerate and generous-hearted gentleman" on several occasions "held back to allow his juniors to pass over his head. At the time of his death he was number five on the list of seniority and the youngest major general on active duty."

Funston's many exploits were played out during a vanishing era of romantic adventurism, individual courage and achievement. As a soldier, he was unorthodox, a genuine maverick of an entirely different brand than the hand-stamped West Pointers and those brought up within the traditional old-army longevity system. He had cut a unique path from a mercenary in Cuba to the highest regarded general in the army. When Funston died, the mold was broken but others would be called to fill his empty boots. His old college friend, the publisher William Allen White, called him "one of the most colorful figures in the American army from the day of Washington on down." Funston's friend, Charles Scott said, "the heart that had so often beaten the battle charge for his willing feet... the heart upon whose altars the fires of loyalty to flag and country had burned unceasingly was still, and the dauntless spirit of the greatest and best loved military leader the United States has produced since the Civil War had taken its flight."

§

When he died in San Antonio while listening to the music he loved, it is likely Funston's last conscious thoughts were of Eda and the children. Had his life flashed before his eyes in a split second, he would have had no regrets for a life well lived, only regrets of leaving the "loves of his life." Hiding from Indians as a child growing up in the wilds of the Kansas plains, helping his father, "Foghorn Funston," with the facts to support his political campaigns, standoffs with drunken cowboys and being run out of town as a newspaper reporter, all would have been shoved into the background. He'd overlook contrasts of desolate Death Valley and snowy Yukon where weather, wild Indians, and Eskimos coalesced with nature to mark his presence, trying unsuccessfully to kill him even then. To Cuba on the *Dauntless* as a filibuster with an insurgent army fighting for freedom, forming an infantry regiment from scratch and shaping it in his image to fight in the Philippines were only dim images from the past. Chasing down the guerilla leader, Aguinaldo, award of the Medal of Honor, and saving the city of San Francisco from nature and lawlessness were all in the past. Funston always lived in the present. In his last days he had served as military governor of Vera Cruz, controlled the hunt for the bandit Pancho Villa, and shaped and tested the largest field army the country could assemble. He had married the love of his life and lost his first born son.... Through it all he never shirked controversy. But all of those images, too, faded from view. His was a life well lived, not for the glory that befell him, but for a deep and compelling quest for adventure. It was a thirst he could not quench, and it ended all too soon.

Frederick Funston had sprung from the shadows onto the dramatic stage of life and never once flinched. Giant characters and extraordinary events always surrounded the diminutive young man while the re-united states shaped a new American century. Funston stared unafraid into its manifest destiny, seized it, thrived on it. The same land that germinated this prized seed of America produced others of the same brand, men and women who hacked out the totem of the American story with their bare hands.

Funston's life story is an epic among those daring adventurers. During his life the Wild West still coexisted within a nation struggling for civilization. When Frederick Funston was born in 1865, the landscape was overrun with railroads and wagon trails all reaching out into the unknown. He was unafraid to go anywhere, try anything. America and Frederick Funston looked beyond that wide horizon. When he died in 1917, Funston and America were standing together at the door to larger adventures, greater challenges. And beside him had been the beautiful and talented Eda Blankhart, who loved him and backed him up with all her heart.

In the end, his slight frame cast a very long shadow across the annals of American courage, adventure, and achievement and over the storied lineage and honor of the U. S. Army while shaping doctrine for the future and testing a modern army fit to fight in the great European war. He was a favorite son of Kansas, Texas, and California, and hero to a nation.

William Allen White remembered his old friend in his memoirs. "And Funston and I, in … matters of extracurricular interests, hunted, ran together like sheep-killing dogs. We held our friendship until death severed it thirty years after we met. As I look at it, classroom pictures blur in my memory of the university. Fraternity meetings are clear…. I cannot remember him in a uniform: as a soldier he was offstage in my life. As a young fellow he had been always falling in love. … And it saddened me so that even today as I write across more than a quarter of a century I cannot recall it (his death) without a shadow of the sorrow that I felt."

Funston's long-time friend, Charles Gleed, had written in *Romance and Reality in a Single Life* in 1899, that his friend had "…never seen himself as a heroic figure in gay military attire, doing heroic things or wearing the decorations of victory. … He has not dreamed of greatness. All he has ever longed for has been hard work enough to keep him busy. … No man loves life more truly than he, and his love for it increases the more he faces death and danger."

But perhaps the higher honor of a soldier than that from his friends is recognition by a former enemy. Emilio Aguinaldo lived until February 6th, 1964. After a long look back at his own colorful experiences, he wrote in 1957 of Funston in *A Second Look at America*, forty years after Funston's death. In the chapter titled, "Funston and I," he described the tactics

Funston had employed in capturing him as "ungentlemanly," "unsportsmanlike," and "not exactly cricket." He complained about being fooled by the forgeries, disguises, and his hospitality abused—essentially parroting Mark Twain. But Aguinaldo conceded that none of that "could change the fact that he was captured." However, he also admitted that he "developed an indefinable admiration for Funston." And he described him as "a husky, almost muscle-bound man; he was literally as hard as nails. But I felt, too, that he had a big heart.... He had fierce courage. He was resourceful to the extreme. And at the height of his personal triumph, he was simple, matter-of-fact, and even humble."

§

Debate on the Army bill in the United States House of Representatives was interrupted by tributes to the memory of General Funston, "Fighting Fred," a half dozen times. Congressman Slayton of Texas told the House that "the frontier had confidence in Funston. It felt secure while he was on guard." The Senate passed a bill granting a pension of $100 a month to his widow, Eda Funston. And far from Washington, "Dynamite Johnny" O'Brien was officially honored on his eightieth birthday by the Republic of Cuba.

§

Eda and their children had followed as his military career led him overseas and across the country. After her husband's death and funeral at The Presidio, Eda lived only a few hundred feet from where he was buried at The Presidio until 1921, when the army moved all widows off the post. She remained nearby for the rest of her life and stayed active in military, social, and political circles. She was especially committed to providing for disabled World War I veterans when they returned from The Great War. She also provided advice freely to widows, sweethearts, mothers, and sisters of servicemen. But she could not have avoided wondering about the experiences she would have shared with her husband in France, or all they might have done afterwards.

Funston died without a will, but his meager estate and insurance policy totaling only $40,000 went to Eda and the children. Her survivor pension not enough to support her children, Eda sold several pieces to the Newspaper Enterprise Association and to the *Delineator*, a woman's fashion magazine—patriotic pieces in the midst of World War I. In one she described her visit with their good family friend, General Franklin Bell, preparing troops for deployment from Camp Upton. In her first *Delineator* piece, she was introduced as someone "who knows every side of army life—its delightful social advantages; its opportunities for travel and for meeting people who are making world's history, and also its dark side—its privations, danger, separation—and yet she has never been sorry she married a soldier." She wrote to mothers, "There are tears in the heart for the mother who sends her son to the firing-line, but her devotion to America should be stronger than sorrow for her personal loss." And about the sons, "a year or two in the army is the best possible preparation for the rest of his life."

When evicted from The Presidio, Eda lived for a time with her daughters in the Sea View area nearby, visiting Frederick's and Arthur's gravesides often. She accepted a job working on lost accounts for businesses, "by tact and personal charm, re-establishing cordial relations" between customers and business. She also worked with the California League of Women Voters to encourage women to go the polls as a patriotic duty. And she continued to use her musical and acting talents to raise money to support veterans. On June 7th, 1932, at the young age of fifty-five, Eda also suffered a fatal heart attack and died at Letterman Hospital where she had given so much service.

Through all the pain and passion, they were one and the same.

The End

Notes on Sources

This study is intended to make it readable and believable, unburdened from the format of a Ph.D. dissertation or academic exercise. I trust this approach empowers the story, because it is almost too fantastic to be true anyway. Yet it is. I hope the reader will admire Frederick Funston and Eda Blankhart as much as I do.

If you enjoyed reading about Frederick and Eda Funston in *Pain and Passion: The Lives and Times of Frederick Funston and Eda Blankhart,* you might want to read Eda's story as told by the author in *My Life with a Soldier: Eda's Story,* or selected research from the bibliography.

Limited Bibliography

Books

- Aguinaldo, Emilio. True Version of the Philippine Revolution. (Reprint) LeVergne, TN: DodoPress, 2009.
- Aguinaldo, Emilio. A Second Look at America. New York: Robert Speller & Sons, Publishers, Inc. 1957.
- Ambrose, Stephen E. Eisenhower: Soldier, General of the Army, President-Elect, 1890-1952 (Volume One). New York: Simon and Schuster, 1983.
- Bain, David Haward. Sitting in Darkness: Americans in the Philippines. Boston: Houghton Mifflin Company, 1984.
- Beaver, Daniel, R. Newton D. Baker and the American War Effort, 1917-1919. Lincoln: University of Nebraska Press, 1966.
- Blake-Alverson, Margaret. Sixty Years of California Song. San Francisco: Sunset Publishing House, 1913.
- Blount, James H. The American Occupation of the Philippines: 1898-1912. New York: G.P. Putnam's Sons (The Knickerbocker Press), 1912.
- Boot, Max. The Savage Wars of Peace: Small Wars and the Rise of American Power. New York: Basic Books, 2002.
- Brereton, T.R. Educating the U.S. Army: Arthur L. Wagner and Reform, 1875-1905. Lincoln: University of Nebraska Press, 2000.
- Clendenen, Clarence C. Blood on the Border: The United States Army and the Mexican Irregulars. Toronto: The Macmillan Company, 1969.
- Connelley, William E. A Standard History of Kansas and Kansans. Topeka: Lewis Publishing Company, 1918, transcribed, 1997.
- Cotner, Thomas E., Editor, and Carlos E. Castaneda, Co-editor. Essays in Mexican History. Chapter XIV, Donnell, Guy R. "The United States Military Government at Veracruz, Mexico." Austin: The Institute of Latin American Studies, University of Texas, 1958.
- Cray, Ed. General of the Army George C. Marshall: Soldier and Statesman. New York: W.W. Norton & Company, 1990.
- Crouch, Thomas W. A Leader of Volunteers: Frederick Funston and the 20th Kansas in the Philippines, 1898-1899. Lawrence: Coronado Press, 1984.

- Crouch, Thomas W. A Yankee Guerrillero: Frederick Funston and the Cuban Insurrection, 1896-1897. Memphis: Memphis University Press, 1975.
- Degler, Carl N. Out of Our Past: The Forces that Shaped Modern America. New York: Harper & Brothers, Publishers, 1959.
- Duncan, Wallace L. and Charles F. Scott, History of Allen and Woodson Counties, Kansas. Iola: Iola Registers, Printers, and Binders, 1901.
- Eisenhower, John S.D. Intervention!: The United States and the Mexican Revolution, 1913-1917. New York: W.W. Norton & Company, 1993.
- Elliott, Charles Burke, The Philippines: To the End of the Commission Government. Bobbs-Merrill Company, Inc., 1917. (Republished by Greenwood Press, New York, 1968).
- Faust, Karl Irving. Campaigning in the Philippines. New York: Arno Press & The New York Times, 1970. (Reprint) (Original title published in San Francisco in 1899 by The Hicks-Judd Company).
- Funston, Frederick. Memories of Two Wars: Cuban and Philippine Experiences. Originally by C. Scribner's Sons: New York, 1911. (Republished by Bison Books with introduction by Thomas Bruscino, Lincoln: University of Nebraska Press, 2009.)
- Gates, John Morgan. Schoolbooks and Krags: The United States Army in the Philippines, 1898-1902. Westport, CN: Greenwood Press, 1973.
- Halstead, Murat. Aguinaldo and his Captor: The Life Mysteries of Emilio Aguinaldo and Adventures and Achievements of General Funston. Cincinnati: The Halstead Publishing Company, 1901.
- Hinshaw, David. The Story of William Allen White. New York: G.P. Putnam's Sons, 1945.
- Jessup, Philip C. Elihu Root. Volumes I & II. New York: Dodd, Mead & Company, 1938.
- Johnson, Walter, Editor. Selected Letters of William Allen White, 1899-1943. New York: Henry Holt and Company, 1947.
- Karnow, Stanley. In Our Image: America's Empire in the Philippines. New York: Ballantine Books, 1989.
- King, James L., editor. History of Shawnee County, Kansas, and Representative Citizens. Chicago: Richmond & Arnold, 1905.
- Kurzman, Dan. Disaster! The Great San Francisco Earthquake and Fire of 1906. Waterville, Maine: G.K. Hall & Co. (Large print edition) 2001.

- Langley, Lester D. The Banana Wars: United States Intervention in the Caribbean, 1898-1934. Lexington: The University Press of Kentucky, 1983, revised 1985.
- Lee, Fitzhugh. Cuba's Struggle Against Spain. New York: The America Historical Press, 1899.
- Link, Arthur S. Wilson: Confusions and Crises, 1915-1916. Princeton, NJ: Princeton University Press, 1964.
- Linn, Brian McAllister. The Philippine War: 1899-1902. Lawrence: The University of Kansas Press, 2000.
- Linn, Brian McAllister. The U.S. Army and Counterinsurgency in the Philippine War, 1899-1902. Chapel Hill: The University of North Carolina Press, 1989.
- Lodge, Henry Cabot, Editor. Selections From the Correspondence of Theodore Roosevelt and Henry Cabot Lodge, 1884-1918, Volume I and II. New York: Charles Scribner's Sons, 1925.
- MacArthur, General of the Army Douglas. Reminiscences. New York: McGraw-Hill Book Company, 1964.
- Mason, Herbert Molloy, Jr. The Great Pursuit. New York: Random House, 1970.
- Miller, Stuart Creighton. Benevolent Assimilation: The American Conquest of the Philippines, 1899-1903. Westford, MA: Murray Printing Co. 1982.
- Millett, Frank D. Expedition to the Philippines. New York and London: Harper & Brothers Publishers, 1899.
- Morison, Elting E., Editor. The Letters of Theodore Roosevelt, Volume II and III. Cambridge, MA: Harvard University Press, 1951.
- Nenninger, Timothy K. The Leavenworth Schools and the Old Army: Education, Professionalism, and the Officer Corps of the United States Army, 1881-1918. Westport, CN: Greenwood Press, 1978.
- O'Conner, Raymond G. American Defense Policy in Perspective: From Colonial Times to the Present. New York: John Wiley and Sons, 1965.
- Odom, William O. After the Trenches: The Transformation of the U.S. Army, 1918-1939. College Station, Texas: Texas A&M University Press, 1999.
- Palmer, Frederick. With My Own Eyes, A Personal Story of Battle Years. Indianapolis: The Bobbs-Merrill Company, 1932.
- Pier, Arthur S. American Apostles to the Philippines. Boston: The Beacon Press, 1950.

- Quirk, Robert E. An Affair of Honor: Woodrow Wilson and the Occupation of Vera Cruz. New York: McGraw-Hill Book Company, 1964.
- Sarkesian, Sam C. America's Forgotten Wars: The Counterrevolutionary Past and Lessons for the Future. Westport: Greenwood Press, 1984.
- Scott, Hugh Lenox. Some Memories of a Soldier. The Century Company: New York, 1928.
- Sexton, William Thaddeus. Soldiers in the Sun. Freeport, NY: Books for Libraries Press, 1971.
- Smith, Dennis. San Francisco is Burning: The Untold Story of the 1906 Earthquake and Fires. New York: Viking Penguin Group, 2005.
- Smythe, Donald. Guerrilla Warrior: The Early Life of John J. Pershing. New York: Charles Scribner's Sons, 1973.
- Taylor, Richard. Homeward Bound: American Veterans Return from War. Westport, CT: Greenwood Publishing Group, 2007.
- Thomas, Gordon and Max Morgan Witts. The San Francisco Earthquake. New York: Stein and Day Publishers, 1971.
- Thomas, Lowell. Old Gimlet Eye: The Adventures of Smedley D. Butler. New York: Farrar & Rinehart Publishers, 1933.
- Tompkins, Colonel Frank. Chasing Villa. (Originally published by Military Service Publishing Company, Harrisburg, PA, 1934) Silver City, New Mexico: High-Lonesome Books, 1996.
- U.S. Army Field Manual (FM 3-24) and U.S. Marine Corps Warfighting Publication (3-33.5), Counterinsurgency Field Manual. Foreword by General David H. Petraeus and Lieutenant Colonel John A. Nagl, introduced by Sarah Sewall. Chicago: University of Chicago Press, 2007.
- Wagner, Arthur L. Organization and Tactics. New York, London, Leipzig, Paris: B. Westerman and Co., 1895.
- Weigley, Russell F. The American Way of War. Bloomington: Indiana University Press, 1977.
- Weigley, Russell F. History of the United States Army. Bloomington: Indiana University Press, 1984.
- Weir, William. Soldiers in the Shadows. Franklin Lakes, NJ: New Page Books, 2002.
- White, William Allen. The Autobiography of William Allen White. New York: The MacMillan Company, 1946.
- Winchester, Simon. A Crack in the Edge of the World: America and the Great California Earthquake of 1906. New York: Harper Collins Publishers, 2005.

- Young, Louis Stanley and Henry Davenport Northrop. Life and Heroic Deeds of Admiral Dewey. Philadelphia: World Bible House, 1899.
- Young, Kenneth Ray. The General's General: The Life and Times of Arthur MacArthur. Boulder, Colorado: Westview Press, 1994.

Newspapers

Baltimore Sun
Buckeye of Troy, Ohio
California Evening News
Colorado Springs Gazette-Telegraph
Columbus Georgia Ledger-Enquirer
Emporia Gazette
Fort Worth Star-Telegram
Grand Forks North Dakota Herald
Grand Rapids Michigan Press
Idaho Statesman
Iola Register
Kansas City Star
Kansas City Times
Lexington Herald
Morning Olympian
New York Evening World
New York Times
Omaha World Herald
Pawtucket Times
Portland Oregonian
Pueblo Colorado Chieftain
San Antonio Daily Herald
San Francisco Chronicle
San Francisco Examiner
Salt Lake Telegram
San Jose Mercury News
Sedan Lance
Topeka Capital
Tucson Daily Citizen
Tulsa World
Wilkes-Barre Times
Williamsburg Star
Wyoming State Tribune-Cheyenne State Leader

Periodicals

American Heritage Magazine
- Zornow, William F. "Funston Captured Aguinaldo," February 1958.
Army
- Patterson, Richard M. "A Genius for Timing: Funston." May 1975, pp. 41-46.
- Barker, Colonel Stockbridge H. "Funston's Folly," February 1964, pp. 73-80.
Army and Navy Journal
- "Death of Gen. Frederick Funston." February 24, 1917, p. 818.

- "General Funston's Report." July 20, 1901, p 1133.
- "Latest from Manila," May 6, 1899.

Century Illustrated Monthly Magazine, The
- Fenn, Emory W. "Ten Months with Cuban Insurgents." Vol. 52, Issue 2. June 1898. Pp. 302-307.

Collier's Weekly
- Palmer, Frederick, "The Campaign in Luzon," date unknown.

Cosmopolitan
- Funston, Eda Blankart. "A Soldier's Wife in the Philippines," May 1900.
- Funston, Frederick. "How the Army Worked to Save San Francisco," Vol. XLI, No. 3, July 1906.
- Gleed, Charles S. "Romance and Reality in a Single Life: General Frederick Funston," July 1899.

Delineator, The.
- "Eda B. Funston, Widow of Fighting Fred Funston, Will Advise Soldiers' Mothers, Wives, Sisters, and Sweethearts for the Delineator," January 1918, pp. 2.

Diplomacy in Action.
- U.S. Department of State. "Punitive Expedition in Mexico, 1916-1917," p.1.

The Evening World
- Eda Funston. "What is Done for the American Boys...." Oct 18, 1917

Everybody's Magazine
- Aguinaldo, Emilio. "The Story of My Capture: An Account of Gen. Funston's Exploit by the Captured Filipino Leader Himself," Vol. V. No. 24, August 1901.
- Funston, Frederick, "The Capture of Emilio Aguinaldo," September 1901, Vol. V, No 25. Pp 259-272; and continued October, 1901, pp. 471-478.

Fortnightly Review, The
- Lee, Fitzhugh. "Cuba and Her struggle for Freedom," Vol. LXIII, p. 855-866.

Harper's Weekly
- Funston, Frederick, "Across the Great Divide in Midwinter," (December 22, 1900).
- Funston, Frederick, "Along Alaska's Eastern Boundary." (Feb 1, 1896).
- Funston, Frederick. "Desmayo: The Cuban Balaklava," 42 (March 5, 1898): 225-226.

- Bass, John F. "The Philippine Revolt—The Campaign in the North," (July 1, 1899): 648-649.
- White, William A. "General Frederick Funston," Vol. 43 (May 20, 1899): 496.
- White, William A. "Frederick Funston's Alaska Trip," (date unknown): 492
- Martin, E.S., "This Busy World." (July 15, 1899): 689.

Infantry Journal
- Brown, Colonel W.C. "Incidents in Aguinaldo's Capture." (June 1925): p. 627-632.
- Howland, Colonel Charles, R. "The Philippine Insurrection of 1899: A Study," April 1927, pp. 395-406.

Journal of the Historical Society of the Georgia National Guard
- Griffith, Joe. "In Pursuit of Pancho Villa 1916-1917," date unknown. pp. 1-7.

Kansas Historical Quarterly
- Crouch, Thomas W. "Frederick Funston of Kansas: His Formative Years, 1865-1891," Summer, 1974.
- Eckdall, Frank F. "Fighting Fred Funston of Kansas." Speech at the annual meeting, published in the *Kansas Historical Quarterly*. Spring 1956, p. 79-86.
- Wagoner, Todd L. "Fighting Aguinaldo's Insurgents in the Philippines." May 1951. Pp. 145-173.

Military Heritage
- Swift, Shippen. "Soldiers," June 2001, Pp. 10-17.

Military Review
- Bruscino, Thomas A, Jr. Ph.D. "A Troubled Past: The Army and Security on the Mexican Border, 1915-1917," July-August 2008, Pp. 31-44.
- Burdett, Thomas, F. "Mobilizations of 1911 and 1913," July 1974. Pp 65-74.
- Forster, Lieutenant Colonel Merlin H. "US Intervention in Mexico: The 1914 Occupation of Veracruz," August 1977, Pp. 88-96.
- Ginsburg, Robert N. Colonel, U.S.A.F. "Damn the Insurrectos!" January 1964, Pp. 59-70.
- Sawyer, Major Robert K. "Viva Villa!" August 1961, Pp. 60-75.
- Trussell, Colonel John B.B., Jr. "Frederick Funston: The Man Destiny Just Missed," June, 1973.

National Geographic Magazine

- August 1905, p 405.
National Guardsman, The
- Joseph G. O'Keefe. "The Fabulous Funston." April 1953. pp 2-4 & 29
Nebraska History, A Quarterly Magazine
- Johnson, J.R., "The Saga of the First Nebraska in the Philippines," June 1949, pp. 139- 162.
Newspaper Enterprise Association
- Eda Funston. "Mrs. Funston writes a series about the New Army." Sep. 27, 1917.
North American Review
- Twain, Mark. "A Defense of General Funston." No. 174, May 1902
- Anderson, Brigadier General Thomas, M. "Our Rule in the Philippines," Vol. 170, Issue 519, February 1900, pp. 272-284.
Oregon Historical Quarterly
- Thompson, H.C. "Oregon Volunteer Reminiscences of the War with Spain." September, 1948. Pp. 192-204.
Periodical
- Strobridge, William F. "Funston Remembered" Periodical (Summer 1976, No. 28, Vol. VIII, No.2): pp. 28-30.
Prologue
- Langley, Lester. "Fighting Fred Funston and the Rebellion in Cuba," Spring 1986, Vol. 18, No. 1. Pp. 7-23.
- Livingston, Rebecca. "When an American City was Destroyed: The U.S. Military as First Responders to the San Francisco Earthquake a Century Ago." Spring 2006, Vol. 38, No. 1.
- Yockelson, Mitchell. "The United States Armed Forces and the Mexican Punitive Expedition: Part I," Fall 1997, Vol. 29, No. 3. Pp. 1-5.
- Yockelson, Mitchell. "The United States Armed Forces and the Mexican Punitive Expedition: Part II." Winter 1997, Vol. 29, No. 4. Pp. 1-7.
Retired Officer Magazine, The
- Scholin, Allan R. "Fighting Fred Funston," (March 1982): pp. 26-31.
Review of Reviews
- Canfield, J.H. "Funston: A Kansas Product," Vol XXIII, pp. 571-579.
St. Nicholas Magazine
-Funston, Frederick, "Storm Bound Above the Clouds." July 1891, pp. 657-663.
Scribner's Magazine

- Funston, Frederick. "Cascorra: The First Cuban Siege," (October, 1910): 390-401.
- Funston, Frederick. "To Cuba as a Filibuster," 48 (September 1910): 314-318. ?
- Funston, Frederick. "A Defeat and a Victory," (October 1910): p. 735.
- Funston, Frederick. "Fall of Guaimaro," 48 (November 1910): p. 759.
- Funston, Frederick. "Over the Chilkoot Pass to the Yukon," (November 1896.)
- Funston, Frederick. "The Capture of Emilio Aguinaldo," Vol. L, July-Dec, 1911, pp. 522-538.
- Funston, Frederick. "Caloocan and its Trenches," Vol. L, July-Dec, 1911, pp. 60-75
- Funston, Frederick. "Up the Railroad to Malolos," Vol. L, July-Dec, 1911, pp. 165-283
- Funston, Frederick. "From Malolos to San Fernando," Vol. L, July-Dec, 1911, pp. 284-297

The World's Work
- "Brigadier-General Funston." May 1901, pp 696-698.

Veterans of Foreign Wars Magazine
- Leyden, John. "Daring Capture in the Philippines: A turning point in the war." March 1, 2001.
- Kohl, Richard K. "Bamboo Vets Fought in Philippines." February 1999.
- Anonymous. "Jayhawker Regiment Shows Mettle in Philippines." February 1999.

Academic Studies, Dissertations, Thesis

-Crouch, Thomas W. "The Making of a Soldier: The Career of Frederick Funston, 1865-1902," Ph. D. Dissertation. The University of Texas, 1969 (Copyright 1971, University Microfilms, Ann Arbor, Michigan).
-Cyrulik, Major John. M. "A Strategic Examination of the Punitive Expedition into Mexico, 1916-1917," Thesis for Master of Military Art and Science, Fort Leavenworth, KS, 2003.
-Davis, Major Floyd J. "Soldiers Amidst the Rubble: The United States Army and the San Francisco Earthquake of 1906," Thesis for Master of Military Art and Science, Fort Leavenworth, KS, 1980.

-Dorsey, Charles, J. Major, U.S. Army. "The Punitive Expedition into Mexico, 1916: Political-Military Insights," Thesis for Master of Military Art and Science, Fort Leavenworth, Kansas, 1997.
-Early, Gerald H. Major, U.S. Army. "The United States Army in the Philippine Insurrection: 1899-1902," Thesis for Master of Military Art and Science, Fort Leavenworth, Kansas, 1975.
-McMonagle, Major Richard C. "The Small Wars Manual and Military Operations other than War," thesis for Master of Military Art and Science, Fort Leavenworth, Kansas, 1996. Pp. 27-29.
-Seelinger, Matthew J. "A Desperate Undertaking: Funston Captures Aguinaldo," The Army Historical Foundation.

Collections, Depositories, Museums

-Author's Collection
-Field Service Regulations, United States Army, 1905.
-United States Army Heritage and Education Center, U.S. Army Military History Institute. Carlyle, Pennsylvania.
-Report of Brigadier General Frederick Funston, United States Army, on the Department of Luzon Field Inspection, 1912. Pershing, Major General
-John J. "Punitive Expedition," Colonia Dublan, Mexico, October 10, 1918.
-Frederick Funston Boyhood Home & Museum, Iola, KS
-Funston, Frederick. "Over the Chilkoot Pass to the Yukon."
-"Funston is Lion." Williamsburg Star, March 21, 1902.
-Sears, William H. Letter to Mr. Richard J. Oulahan, New York Times, explaining how Frederick Funston was selected Colonel of the 20th Kansas Volunteer Regiment, and other stories about Funston, February 27, 1917.
-Taft, Secretary of War. Telegram to Funston, April 19, 1906.
-Kansas State Historical Society, Topeka, KS
-Frederick Funston papers, 1895-1915 (microfilm). MS 75-MS 77. Job order 102.
-Young, 1st Lieutenant Dave, Kansas Air National Guard. "Maj. Gen. Frederick Funston: Kansas National Guard's Greatest Soldier." Plains Guardian, October 1997.
http://skyways.lib.ks.us/kansas/museums/funston/ksgreat.html
-Roosevelt, Vice President Theodore. Letter to Frederick Funston urging him to stay in the military, Washington, D.C., August 20, 1901.

-Roosevelt, Vice President Theodore. Letter of congratulations to Frederick Funston, Oyster Bay, N.Y., March 30, 1901.
-Funston, Honorable Edward H. in the House of Representatives, May 14, 1888, Washington, D.C. (Congressional Record)
-Fort Riley Museum and Museum of the Kansas National Guard
-Fort Leavenworth Museum and Combined Arms Center, Combined Arms Research Library, Center for Army Lessons Learned.
"Annual Report of the Commandant" The Army Service Schools, Fort Leavenworth, KS. Year ending August 31, 1909.
"Annual Report of the Commandant" The Army Service Schools, Fort Leavenworth, KS. Year ending August 31, 1911.
-Partin, Dr. John W. "A Brief History of Fort Leavenworth, 1827-1983" Combat Studies Institute, U.S. Army Command and General Staff College, Fort Leavenworth, KS, 1983.
-Raine, Linnea P. "The Philippine Insurrection, November 1899-July 1902." Historical Evaluation and Research Organization, Washington, D.C. Volume III, 1 February, 1966. Pp77-115.
-Fort Sam Houston Museum.
-California Military Museum.
-Denger, Mark J. "Major General Frederick Funston, U.S.V." Californians and the Military, The California Military Museum, http://militarymuseum.org/Funston.html.
-The City of San Francisco Museum, San Francisco, CA (The Virtual Museum of the City of San Francisco)
-Coleman, Le Vert, Captain. Letter to The Adjutant of the Presidio of San Francisco, California included in Major General Greely's final report. May 2nd, 1906.
-Unpublished article by Mr. Lafler intended for *The Argonaut*. "Lafler's Attack on General Funston;" and Jerome H. Hart's rejection letter, dated July 24th, 1906.
-Humphreys, William P. Major and Judge Advocate, letter and report of inquiry dated April 28th, 1906.
-Letter by Captain Orrin R. Wolfe of the 22nd Infantry dated May 24th, 1906.
-Excerpts from hearings by the inspector general questioning Captain Wolfe, dated February 2, 1907; Letter from Pacific Division to Garbini Brothers and Company denying claim.

-Relief Work in San Francisco, California, excerpted from the History of the Medical Department, U.S. Army, 1906.
-Secretary of War Taft telegram to General Funston, April 21, 1906, and Mayor E.E. Schmitz, reply on April 22, 1906.
-Telegram from Secretary of War to Commanding General, Pacific Division, April 25, and responses from Governor George C. Pardee, Governor of California on April 27th, 1906.
-Metcalf, Victor H., Secretary of Labor and Commerce, personal representative of President Roosevelt in San Francisco, Letter to the President, describing the situation as of April 26th, 1906.
-Order Governing Conduct of Civilians, General Orders Number 12. Headquarters Pacific Division, Fort Mason, California, April 22, 1906.
-Dougherty, John, Letter to Theodore Roosevelt, San Francisco, October 3, 1906.
-Frederick N. Funston's Service Record compiled in 1903 by the Adjutant General's Office.
-Funston, Frederick. telegram to Secretary of War, 30 August 1915.
General Order Number 1 on destruction of liquor, by order of Colonel Morris.
-Letter from Major General Greely, June 25, 1906; two letters on the subject of liquor actions and
claims by Brigadier General Funston dated, June 13, 1907 and July 16, 1906.
-Letter by Colonel Morris, July 3d, 1907.
-War Department Judge Advocate General letter of September 5, 1907.
-Lieutenant General Arthur MacArthur letter of October 19, 1906.
-National Archives, Washington, D.C.
-The Library of Congress, Washington, D.C.
-Wadsworth, James W., Jr., The Autobiography of James W. Wadsworth, Jr., The James W. Wadsworth, Jr. Papers, "Diaries, Autobiographies," Box 15, Mss. Division.
-Taft, William Howard. Philippine Commission, "William Howard Taft Papers," Series 4A, 1-537, Box 681, Mss. Division.
-Taft, William Howard. Philippine Commission, "Letter Book, Series 8, April 17, 1900 – October 12, 1903, Mss. Division.
-MacArthur Memorial Museum, Norfolk, Virginia.
-Yale Law School (Avalon Project)

-General Order Number 100: The Lieber Code, "Instructions for the Government of Armies of the United States in the Field," Prepared by Francis Lieber for President Lincoln, 24 April, 1863. Yale Law School, The Avalon Project.

Audio-Visual Media

-Miller, Daniel A. and Daniel B. Polin, writers and producers. Crucible of Empire: The Spanish American War. South Carolina ETV and PBS: The Great Projects Film Company, 1999.
-Winchester, Simon. Seeking 1906. PBS Home Video: KQED and Luna Park Productions, 2006.

Made in the USA
Charleston, SC
19 December 2015